Petit Palais
Guide

PARIS musées

Since becoming Mayor in 2001 I have been working to give Parisians better access to the artistic treasures of their city. An agenda that includes free entry to the permanent collections and an active policy of heritage restoration has brought a marked rise in public interest and attendance figures.

The renovation of the Petit Palais, the City of Paris fine arts museum, was begun some time ago. The triumphant return of this landmark – a 19th-century architectural jewel and a symbol of the glory of Paris – represents a real success and a great source of satisfaction for the many different teams involved in the project. The people of Paris are being offered a work of art in its own right, set between the Seine and the Champs Elysées.

With its original appearance restored, the Petit Palais has recovered all its interplay of light and transparency, and all the visual fluidity that sets the exhibits off to their best advantage. New exhibition spaces, improved visitor services, better educational facilities and greater receptivity to the outside world reflect an ambitious set of goals: to generate emotion and curiosity, awaken a sense of discovery and wonder, and challenge the intellect.

Visitors to the refurbished Petit Palais can now rediscover the fabulous riches of its collection: an artistic panorama extending from Antiquity to the 20th century and including objcts d'art, paintings, sculpture, engravings, drawings and icons. These are works that embody the experience of beauty and pay homage to man's creative intelligence.

One thing is certain: this splendid monument, a tribute to the modernity of the Paris of 1900, has found its rightful place in the city of the 21st century.

BERTRAND DELANOË
Mayor of Paris

Contents

Contributors

Maryline Assante di Panzillo
Françoise Barbe
Marie-Christine Boucher
Isabelle Collet
José de Los Llanos
Patrick Lemasson
Dominique Morel
Paulette Pelletier-Hornby
Amélie Simier

Preface

As part of the preparations for the Universal Exhibition in Paris in 1900, it was decided to create a new thoroughfare between the Palais de l'Elysée and the Hôtel des Invalides. The outcome was a new bridge over the Seine - Pont Alexandre III - and Avenue Nicolas II, now Avenue Churchill. Flanking the new avenue would be exhibition centres that could continue to be used when Exhibition was over: one for state events and the other for cultural activities organised by the City of Paris.
In the competition for the new municipal building, the judges opted unanimously for the proposal made by architect Charles Girault. On the banks of the Seine and among the trees of the Champs-Elysées, Girault created, in the form of the Petit Palais, the last great success of the Eclectic movement, a skilful mix of the Louvre colonnade, the arched porch and the dome of the Invalides, and the hall of mirrors at Versailles. At the same time he achieved real modernity in terms of ease of internal traffic, an abundant use of natural light and the daring of the windows giving onto the Champs-Elysées.
With a trapezoidal floor plan, the Petit Palais is set around a semicircular interior garden bordered with a sensitively handled Doric peristyle. The central entrance rotunda, the corner pavilions at each end of the imposing galleries of the main facade, and the two monumental staircases of the rear facade are all topped with domes that are a feature of the Paris skyline. The principal facade comprises two Ionic colonnades, one each side of the raised central porch. Like the balconies and the railings of the sweeping staircases - also designed by Girault - the main gate is a masterpiece in iron. The distinction of the facade is superbly rounded off by a profusion of sculpted ornamentation.

Designed as a showcase for art masterpieces, the Petit Palais was home, during the 1900 Universal Exhibition, to an impressive "Retrospective of French Art". It was natural, then, that on 11 December 1902 it should be opened as a museum, with the title of *Palais des Beaux-Arts de la Ville de Paris* ("Fine Art Museum of the City of Paris"). Its function was to present to the public the City's collection of painting and sculpture acquired since 1870 by commission or purchase either at the annual Salons or directly from the artists themselves. This collection from the late 19th and early 20th centuries remains one of the two major aspects of the Petit Palais' present holdings.
The universal appeal of the building's architecture quickly led to an influx of donations and bequests. In 1904 came the Hoentschel bequest of two hundred sculptures and ceramic pieces by Jean-Joseph-Marie Carriès, complemented in 1967 by Jean Soustiel's gift of some twenty fragments of the same artist's *Porte monumentale*; in 1905 the Henner and Ziem bequests; in 1906-09 eight

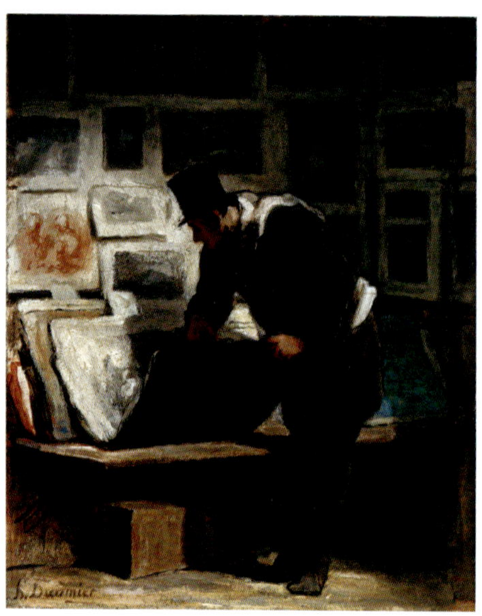

HONORÉ DAUMIER (1808-1879) The Print Lover
c. 1860-1870, oil on canvas
Eugène Jacquette Bequest, 1899 - Inv. PPP00039

Courbets donated by the painter's sister Juliet; in 1916 the Zoubaloff donation of paintings and drawings by Redon and Harpignies, sculptures by Barye, Maillol and Rodin, and objets d'art by Husson and Cros; in 1937 and 1945 the Ambroise Vollard bequest of paintings by Cézanne and Renoir, ceramics by André Metthey, and engravings by Bonnard, Vuillard and Denis; in 1938 works by Carpeaux donated by the sculptor's daughter; in 1979 fifty Brokman paintings, donated by his son; and in 1998 two hundred drawings and sculptures by Paul Landowski, donated by his family.
The number of masterpieces was further boosted by an energetic acquisitions policy that brought even broader coverage of the 19th century in France, with purchases including the contents of Dalou's studio in 1905; the contents of Falguière's studio in 1907; Corot's *Marietta* in 1934; Courbet's *Sleep* in 1953; Delacroix's *Combat of the Giaour and the Pasha* in 1963; Géricault's *Italian Landscape* in 1970; Gustave Doré's *Valley of Tears* in 1985; and Boilly's *Portrait of Athénaïs d'Albenas* in 1999.
In addition to the paintings and sculptures, a substantial collection of drawings and prints was built up during the museum's first few years. This field is currently the focus of intense buying activity: purchases include drawings by Bracquemond, Cros, Redon and others, and engravings by artists including Corot, Daubigny, Jongkind, Manet, Bracquemond. A photography collection devoted to the Petit Palais itself, the Universal Exhibition of 1900 and the Paris of the time is also being created.

The extensive holding of objets d'art from the same period is due to the transfer, in 1979, of the City of Paris collection of modern industrial art, begun at the Palais Galliera in 1895. Notable items are glazed stoneware pieces by Chaplet, Dalpayrat and Dammouse, glassware by Gallé, Daum and Decorchemont, and enamels by Point and Feuillâtre. These pieces are accompanied by the Husson goldsmithed works and jewellery donated by Zoubaloff in 1916, the Fouquet jewellery acquired by the City of Paris in 1937, and the Guimard dining room suite from the artist's former town house.

Ongoing acquisition means this remarkable collection is continuing to grow, examples being the 2003 purchase of an enamel by Grandhomme after Gustave Moreau and, in 2004, Rodin's *Vase of the Titans*.

Among recent donations and bequests in the objets d'art field are two remarkable sets of jewellery drawings: 4500 drawings by Charles Jacqueau, Louis Cartier's main collaborator; and almost 800 by Georges Deraisme, engraver for René Lalique and François Coty's collaborator. Further purchases including Lalique and Boucheron items fill out this collection.

All in all, the Petit Palais holdings offer visitors a comprehensive overview of trends in the plastic arts – painting, sculpture, objets d'art, drawing and printmaking – in France between 1880 and 1914: Academic Art – Laurens, Cormon, Bouguereau; Naturalism, the heir to Courbet and Daumier's Realism – Dalou, Roll, Lhermitte, Pelez; monumental art – Besnard, Carrière, Baudouin; Impressionism – Monet, Pissarro, Sisley, Rodin; Symbolism, following in the steps of Gustave Moreau and Puvis de Chavannes – Carriès, Redon, Lévy-Dhurmer; Art Nouveau – Guimard, Lalique, Gallé, Daum; the Nabis – Bonnard, Vuillard, Denis; and the aesthetic breakaways heralding or accompanying Fauvism and Cubism – Gauguin, Cézanne, Bourdelle, Maillol, Jacqueau.

Looking back further into the past, the lover of France's 19th century can find Neoclassicism (Gros), the Troubadour style (Ingres, Granet), Romanticism (Géricault, Delacroix, Chassériau) and the unclassifiable Carpeaux.

ÉDOUARD VUILLARD (1868-1940) The Tuileries Gardens
1896, colour lithograph
Acquired with income accruing from the Dutuit bequest, 2001 - Inv. GDUT10818

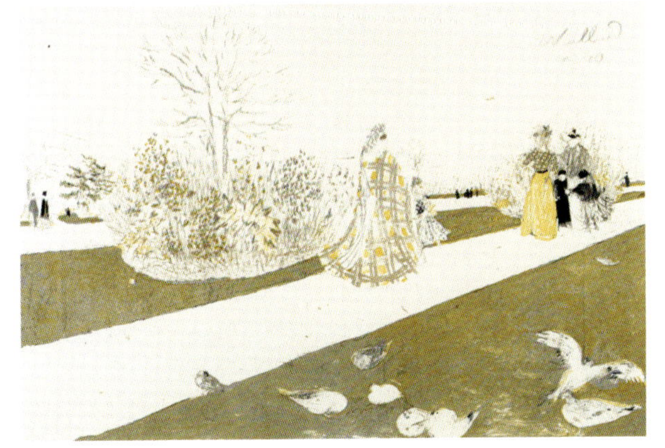

To the collection established around 1900 the Petit Palais was able to add, in 1902, the bequest of ancient art made to the City of Paris by the Dutuit brothers, Auguste and Eugène. This second segment of the museum's holdings highlights the passion that developed during the 19th century for all earlier periods of Western

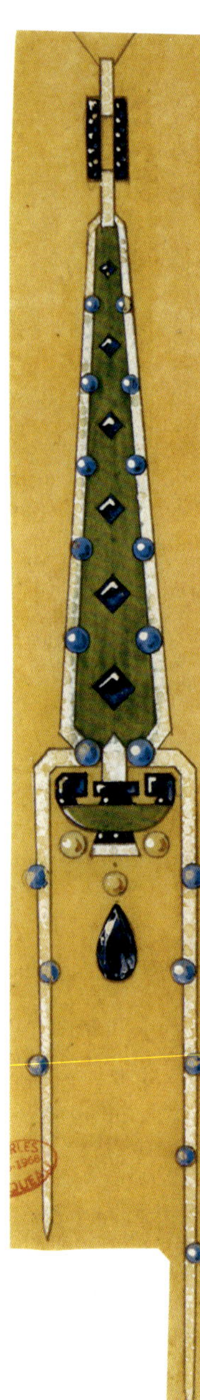

CHARLES JACQUEAU (1885-1968)
Pendant
1913, pencil, ink, gouache on transparent vellum
Jacqueau Donation, 1998
Inv. PPJAC01678

art and the art of the rest of the world. Thus in addition to Greek and Roman works rediscovered in the 15th and 16th centuries, it comprises medieval and Renaissance objets d'art, 17th-century Dutch and Flemish paintings and drawings, manuscripts from the 15th to the 18th century, and 12,000 engravings including complete sets of Rembrandt, Dürer and Callot, together with Islamic, Chinese and Japanese items. Their quest for excellence led the Dutuit brothers systematically to collect only the most precious works of the highest quality.

Since then, the collection of ancient art has been regularly enriched using income from Paris rental property bequeathed by the Dutuits, and by fresh donations. In 1930, for example, the generosity of Edward and Julia Tuck brought new material in the form of items illustrating all the sophistication and preciosity of the decorative art of the 18th century. With donations and bequests continuing to flow in, 1998 brought a splendid addition in the form of icons, mainly Greek and Russian of the 15th - 18th century, donated by Roger Cabal. This gift made the Petit Palais the owner of France's largest public collection of icons.

The Petit Palais is intended neither as an all-embracing museum nor as a continuous, chronological account of Western culture. The presentation of the collection is based on quite a different principle: that of evocative association.

The comparisons begin with the various artistic techniques, period by period. Each era, according to its way of thinking, system of values, aesthetic preferences, technical choices, habits and customs, produces works of art reflecting the range of methods available to it. And so, to help visitors towards a fuller aesthetic and intellectual appreciation of the forces underlying the high points of Western civilisation, paintings, sculptures and objets d'art are shown side by side. The interplay between exhibits as complementary as they are different gives each room its own special ambience, and visitors are helped to find their bearings via the relevant chronological and geographical information. The auditorium complements this "polyphonic" approach with presentations of literature, music and dance.

Also in the spotlight are the multiple aesthetic currents of the period around 1900. Their variety is notably embodied in the external appearance of building itself, the culmination of all that was best in architectural Eclecticism. Then, in the gallery running along the facade - reminiscent of the hall of mirrors at Versailles - splendid Art Nouveau pieces are on display in vitrines. Next, in the enormous interior gallery, with its original scale and zenithal lighting restored, the visitor can make the acquaintance of the big realist and naturalist paintings and sculptures that were all the rage at the time. In addition, recently recreated doorways give access to the 18th-century treasures of the Tuck gallery, an eloquent reminder of the taste of the wealthy collectors of 1900 for the artistic refinement of the Louis XV and Louis XIV periods.

Looking onto the garden of the Champs-Elysées are two rooms devoted to the revolutionary developments in landscape painting in the second half of the 19th century and the emergence of the modern movement before the First World War. The Petit Palais' Cubist and Fauve collections having been used to found the City of Paris Musée d'Art Moderne, the aesthetic upheavals in the painting and sculpture of the decade preceding the War cannot be featured; by contrast various gifts - the Jacqueau donation is vital in this respect - and a policy of ongoing acquisition mean that the graphic and

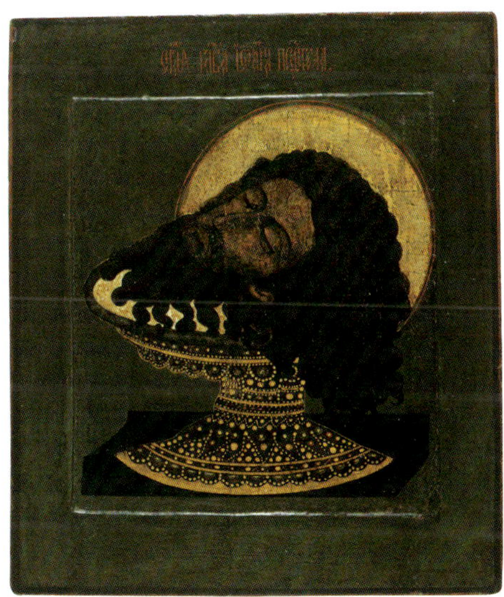

SCHOOL OF MOSCOW
Head of St John the Baptist on a Dish
Late 16th century, tempera on wood
Roger Cabal Bequest, 1998 - Inv. PPP04908

decorative arts of the period are thoroughly covered. On the ground floor rooms dedicated to such major artists as Carpeaux, Dalou, Guimard, Carriès, Vuillard and the crucial Symbolist movement add a further dimension to the visitor's discovery of the enormous artistic variety of the years 1870-1910. The same comparative approach has been applied to ancient art. The rooms devoted to Rome, Greece and the Renaissance are next-door to each other, an arrangement that gives the visitor a comprehensive idea of the links in terms of technique, iconography and worldview. Not far away the spotlight is on the aesthetico-theological contrast between Western Christianity - notably painting and sculpture from the late Middle Ages - and its Oriental counterpart, mainly represented by Cretovenetian, Greek and Russian icons. They in turn are adjacent to works in the Troubadour and Romantic styles, marking the return of Catholicism in post-Revolutionary France, and Symbolist works pointing up the diversity of spiritual quests under way in the years around 1900.

Lastly, there are reminders of the 19th century's all-embracing curiosity, with the resultant passion for every aspect of the artistic history of the West and of other civilisations all over the world. The Troubadour and Romantic works, for example, are situated not far from the medieval and Renaissance art they largely drew on for technique and content. Eastern objets d'art are at the entrance to the room devoted to the Nabis and Japonism, and close to Carriès' ceramics. Dutch painting rubs shoulders with the Troubadour pictures it influenced in so many ways. And the paintings in the Historicism Room tell us how artists of the 1880s saw prehistory, the Middle Ages and the Renaissance.

GILLES CHAZAL
Conservateur général du Patrimoine
Director of the Petit Palais
Musée des Beaux-Arts de la Ville de Paris

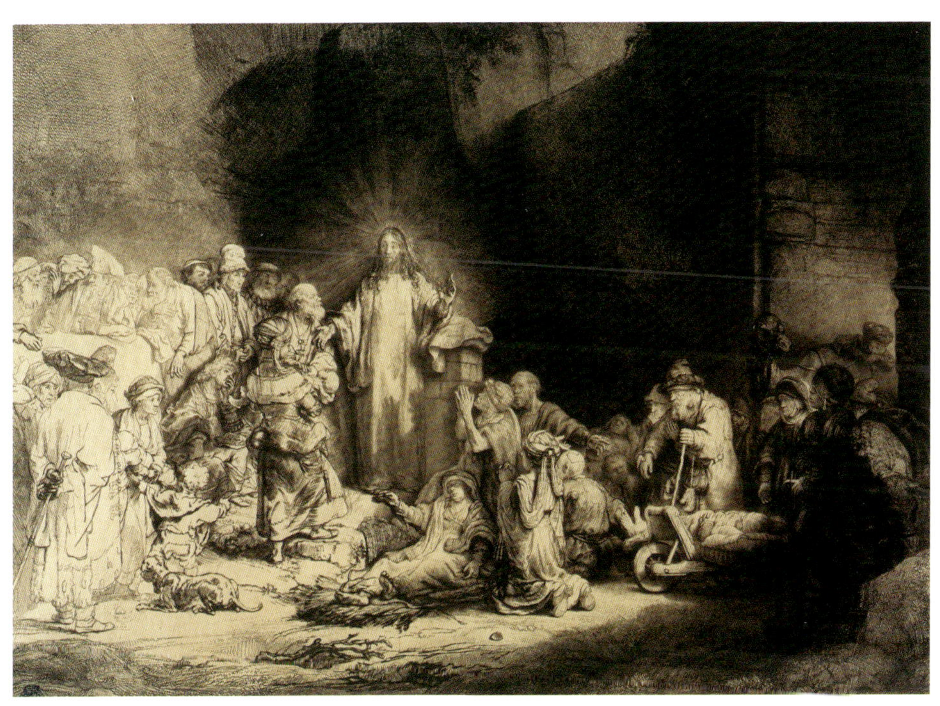

REMBRAND VAN RIJN (1606-1669) The Hundred Guilder Print (Bartsch 74)
Completed c. 1649, first state of two, etching with drypoint and burin on papier japon - Dutuit Legacy, 1902 - Inv. GDUT07743

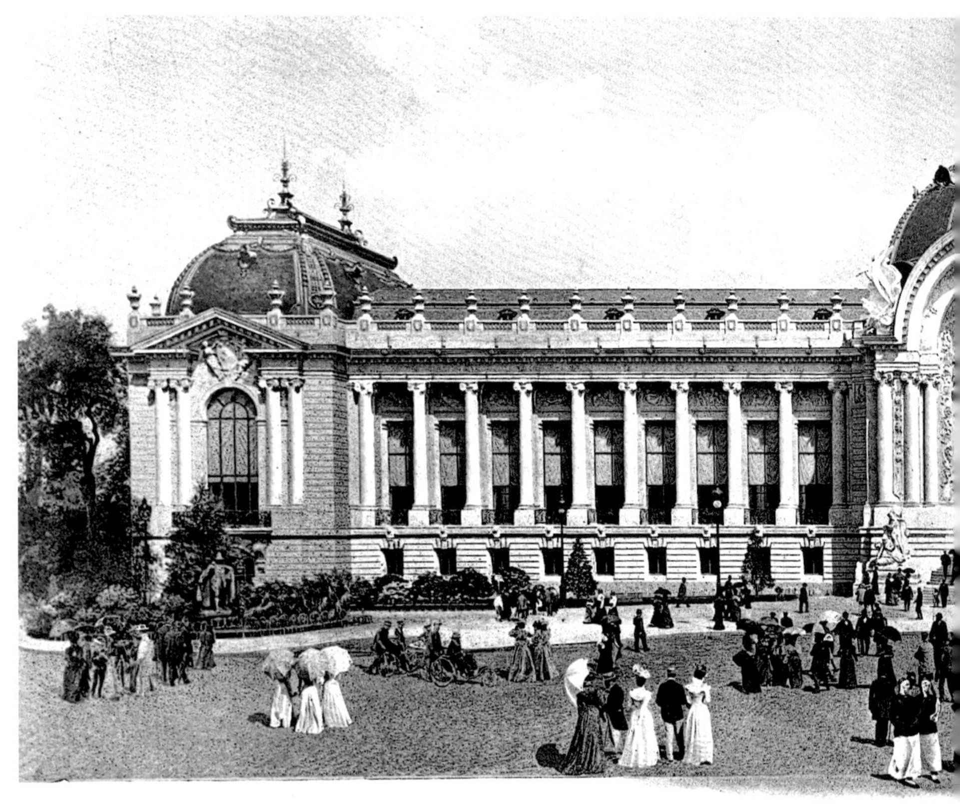

Sculpted decoration at the Petit Palais

The Petit Palais' main facade, like the rear facade and the interior courtyard, are marked by a profusion of carving that includes sculpture in the round at the foot of the steps, low reliefs between the columns, and high reliefs above the porch. The building as a whole is embellished with ornamental carvings of flowers, fruit, *putti* and lion's heads in a display of exuberance characteristic of the building's Neo-Rococo style and of the energetic preferences of its architect: as the project advanced Charles Girault gave sculpture an increasingly important role, even succeeding, in 1907, in getting the go-ahead for the sixteen plaster busts that bring the finishing touch to the decoration of the large galleries.
The unmistakable unity of the sculpted decoration is attributable to the precision of Girault's drawings and his insistence that the many sculptors – mostly established artists accustomed to working closely with architects – meet his requirements as exactly as possible. For the bravura pieces he chose famous figures: Injalbert for *The City of Paris Protecting the Arts*, above the steps; and Saint-Marceaux for *Painting* and *Sculpture*, two allegories set above the entrance, that surprise the visitor with their oblique and elongated cannon.

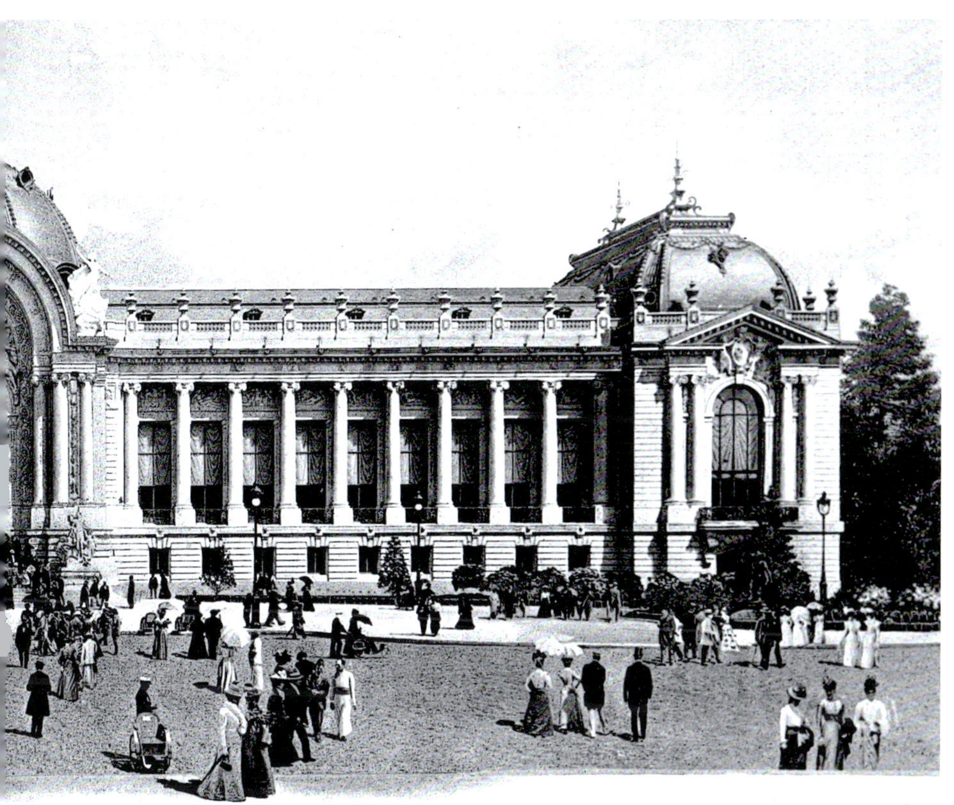

The Petit Palais – The Panorama
Universal Exhibition, new series no. 8, photograph Neurdein Brothers - Inv. PPL00105

The visual repertoire, by contrast, is relatively banal: glorification of the City of Paris, the future tenant; the Arts, as the building's prime rationale; and those same Arts as – naturally – eternal. The ornamentation makes considerable use of allegory, a timelessly noble idiom most appropriate to the works inside.
The profuseness of the decoration emphasises the role of the French state and the City of Paris as the building's instigators. In the course of the works Girault put greater stress on colour, adding two gilt zinc *Fame* statues by Peynot. This boldly innovative use of zinc, a malleable material used for roof decoration, was entrusted to the founder Foretay. Today we are still struck by the contrast between the outside of the building, for which Girault made play with harmonies of colour and stone, and the interior courtyard where mosaic pools and ground surfaces, marble facings, painted vaults and gilt statuary vie for the visitor's attention.

Painted decoration at the Petit Palais

True to the building's palatial spirit, a painted decor has been provided for the vaults of the visitors' entrance and the second floor, the 15-meter high north and south galleries, the peristyle running along the interior garden and the east cupola of the Dutuit staircase. The siting of the paintings was stipulated by Girault, who limited them to the ceiling panels, the walls being kept free for the displaying of the art collection. As was customary, the choice of the six artists - each invited to create an original work - lay with the City of Paris: the first commission was issued in 1903, the year after the museum opened, and the programme was ended in 1925.

Preference was given to established artists with real experience in decoration on a monumental scale. Paris was the unifying theme, but Eclecticism was the most notable feature in terms of both style and content. For the four ceiling panels in the vestibule Besnard offered a free interpretation of the scientific theories of transformism in gravely sweeping illustrations of *The Christian Mystique, Pagan Beauty, Matter* and *Thought*. In the north gallery Cormon, champion of Historicism, decided to focus on the past with a recounting of the history of Paris from its beginnings up until the Revolution. In the south gallery Roll celebrated the *Triumph of the Republic*. Factory chimneys symbolising the modern city rise among the monuments of Paris. It is interesting to note the contrast between Cormon's clarity and sweep and Roll's bright, edgy colours.

In the south pavilion, the sensual lightness of Georges Picard's homage to Woman reminds us of the turn of the century taste for Rocaille grace. In the north pavilion Humbert chose, as a symbol of the city's intellectual life, a contemporary figure reading in a public garden: rising between the trees, allegories of Peace and Liberty watch over him. On the vaults of the peristyle, Baudouin goes back to the historical origins of the French Republic with a fresco of the months of the Revolutionary calendar. Denis is the only one to home in on the building's function as a museum, juxtaposing the great figures of French art from the Middle Ages through to a modernism embodied by Cézanne, Rodin and Gauguin.

A veritable artistic Babel, the surge of decoration of public buildings begun by the 3rd Republic found one of its ultimate expressions in the heights of the Petit Palais. The recent restoration campaign has brought back a brightness and luminosity that had gradually been lost over the years, leaving us free to appreciate its scope and astonishing eclecticism.

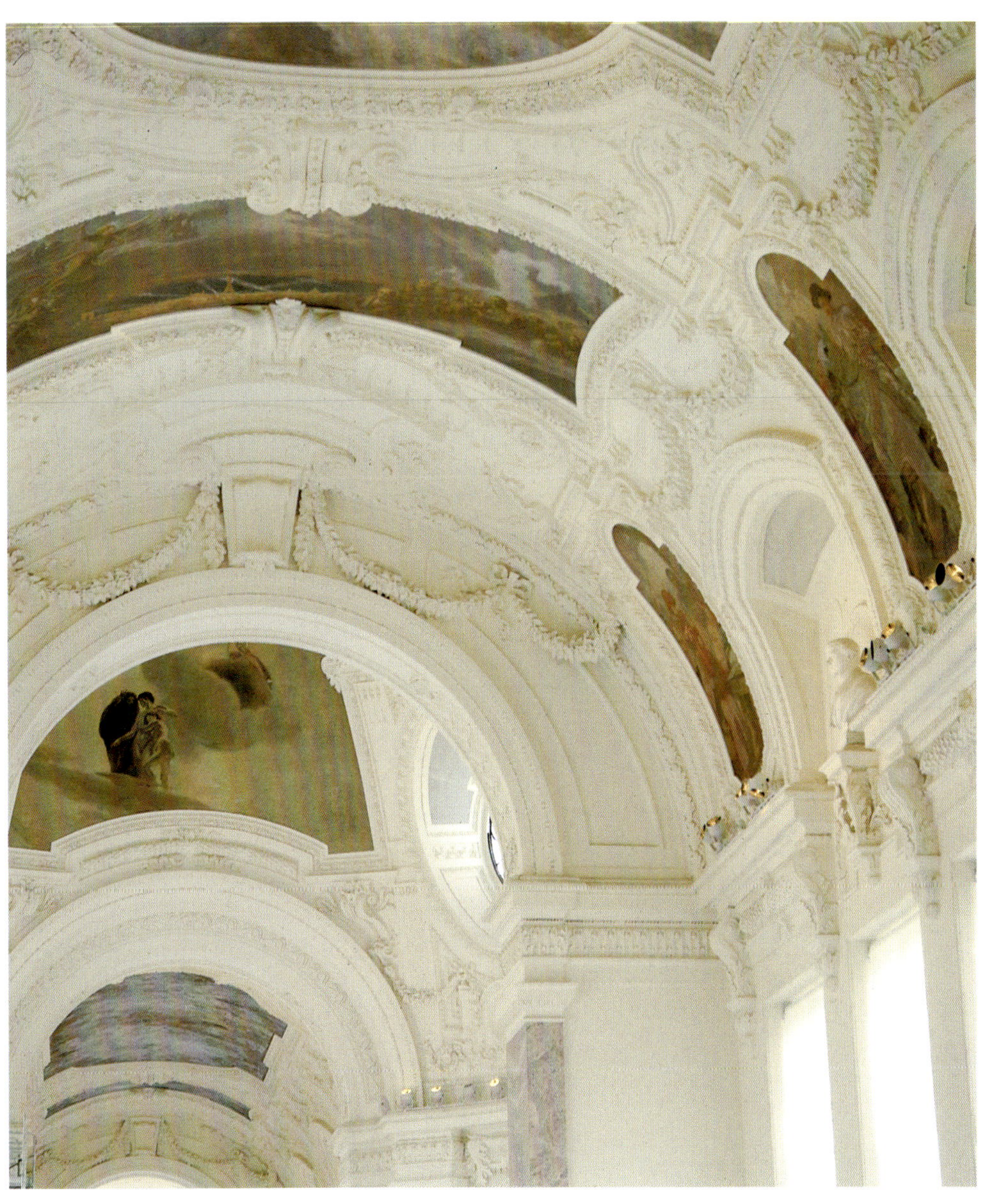

View of the great galleries and the vestibule

Garden level

Rooms 1-13

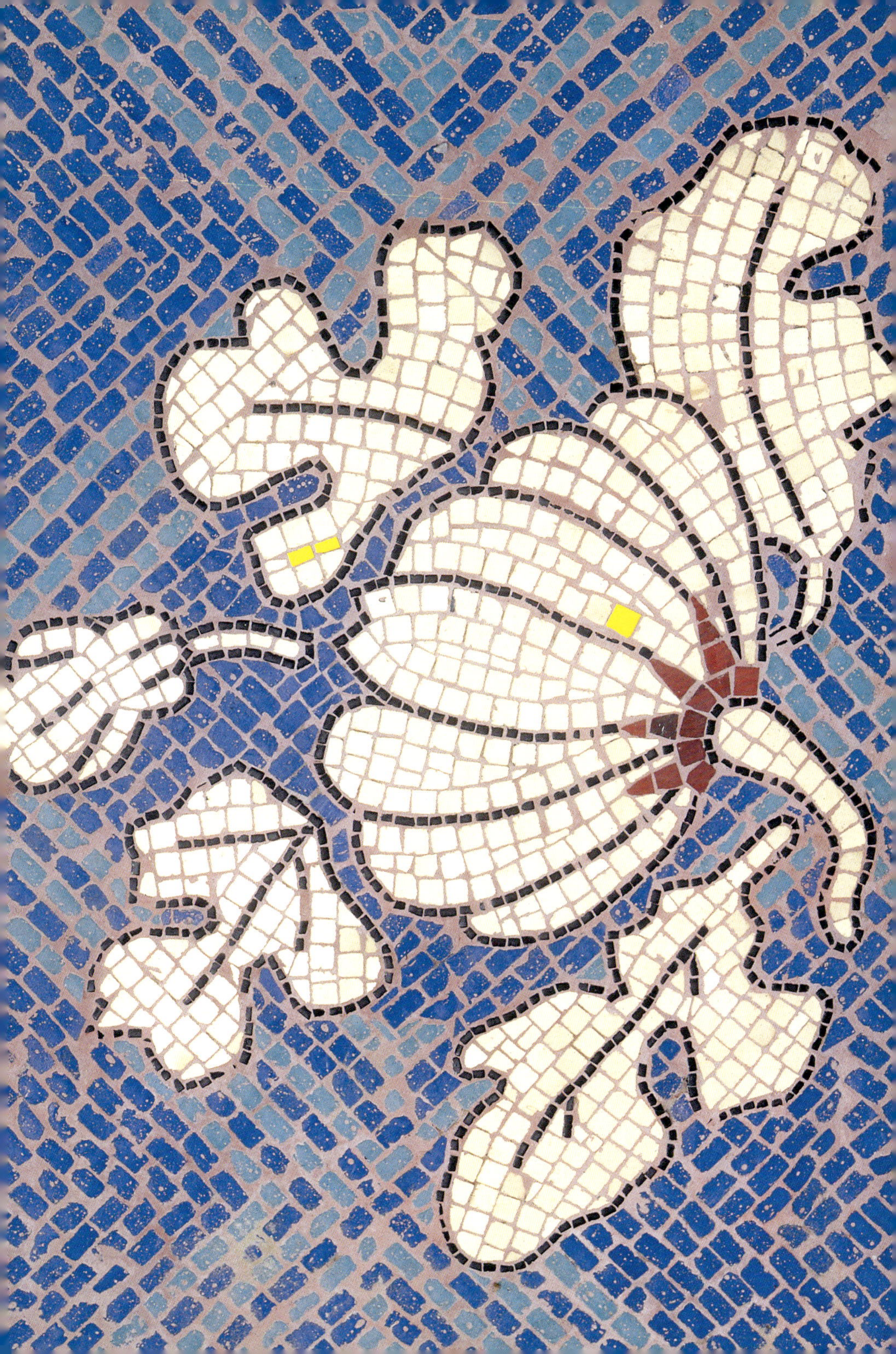

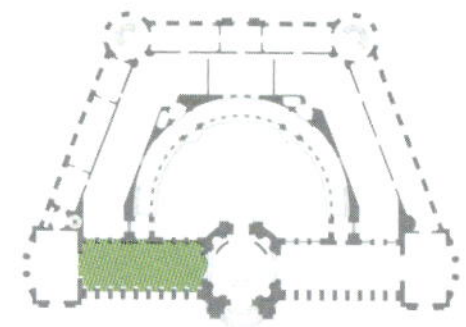

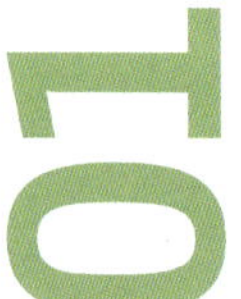

New life for the crafts

The crafts underwent a period of spectacular development around 1900. Reacting against industrialisation and the cult of the machine, craftspeople set out to show that "art is just as present in the shape of an everyday object as in oil painting and statuary" (Carabin, vitrine, Room 18), while major creators appeared in all fields of the "industrial arts": ceramics, glassware, enamelware, metalworking and the precious arts. They put their talents on show both at the Universal Exhibitions and at the annual Salons, which little by little opened their doors to the objet d'art: the Société Nationale des Beaux-Arts did so in 1891 and the Société des Artistes Français in 1895. Art Nouveau blossomed between 1895 and 1904 and exponents like Grasset and Guimard - see the Guimard townhouse's dining room suite in Room 20 - were advocates of a "total art": their goal was a modern decor whose objects were not simple trinkets, but part of an artistic, decorative whole.

1 | **ARMAND POINT (1861-1932)** Peacock Casket

1899, wood, chased gilt bronze, enamel, lapis lazuli, cabochons - Purchased 1899 - Inv. OGAL00075

The painter and interior decorator Armand Point was a great admirer of the English Pre-Raphaelites, with whom he shared a taste for the Italian Renaissance in general and Botticelli in particular. In 1896 he founded, on the outskirts of the Forest of Fontainebleau, the craft community Haute-Claire, named after the sword so heroically wielded by Olivier in the *Chanson de Roland*. In its extreme sophistication the casket is reminiscent of the medieval goldsmithing masterpieces from Limousin. In paleochristian art the repeated peacock motif symbolises immortality.

2 | **ÉMILE GALLÉ (1846-1904)** Ladyslipper Vase

1898, blown layered crystal, carved wooden base - Purchased 1898 - Inv. OGAL00070

This splendid vase with its Ladyslipper orchid motif was shown at the Salon de la Société Nationale des Beaux-Arts in 1898 and at once acquired by the City of Paris. This is one of the first examples of the glass marquetry technique invented by Emile Gallé, which involved the inlaying of fragments in the molten glass. The Maeterlinck quotation is from *The Treasure of the Humble*, published in 1896. Here a dense network of mysterious correspondences is woven between the poetic world of the Belgian Symbolist writer and Gallé's art in glass.

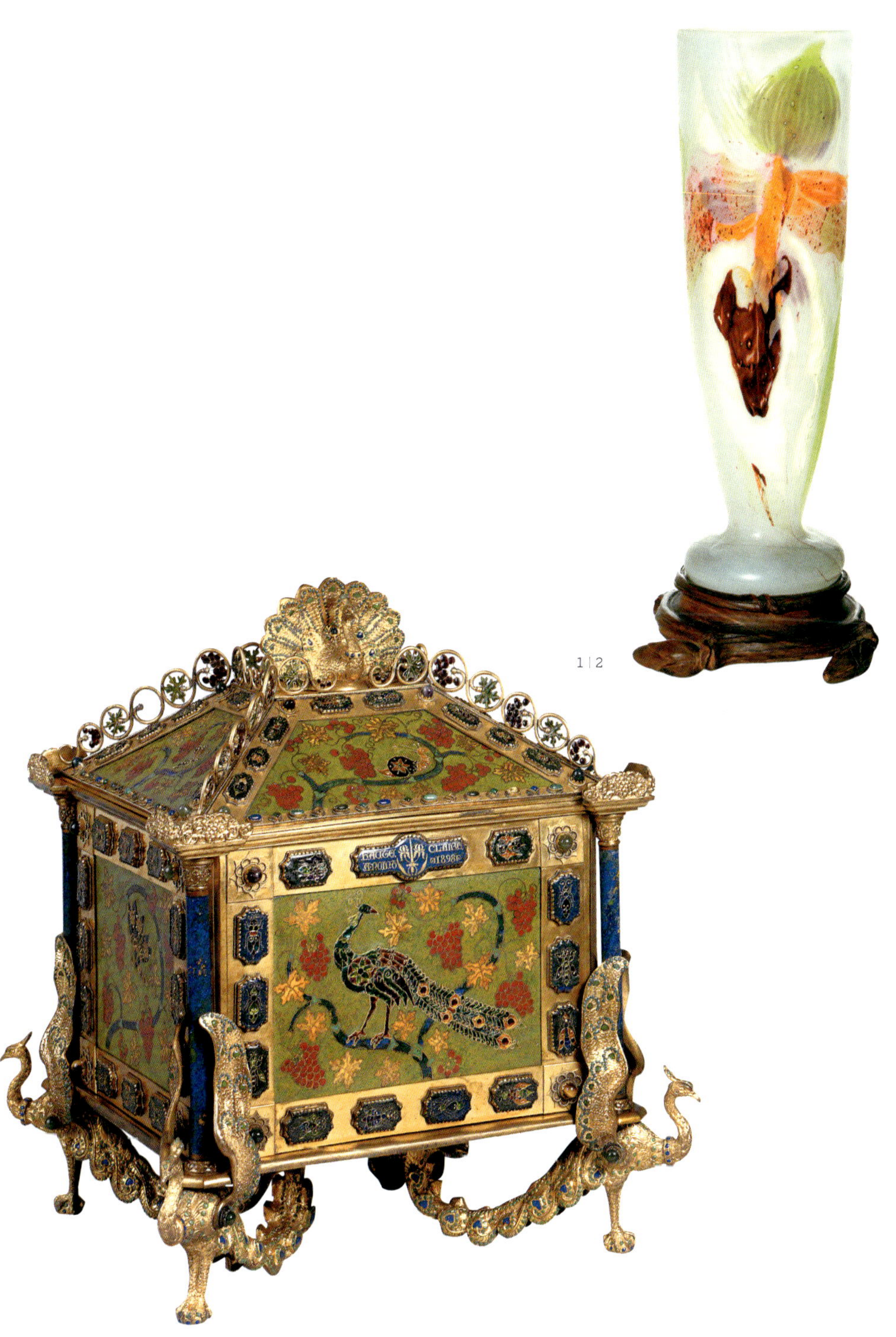

1 | 2

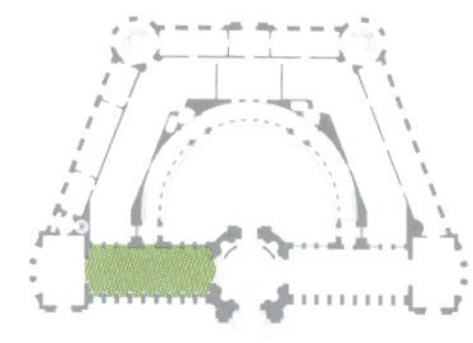

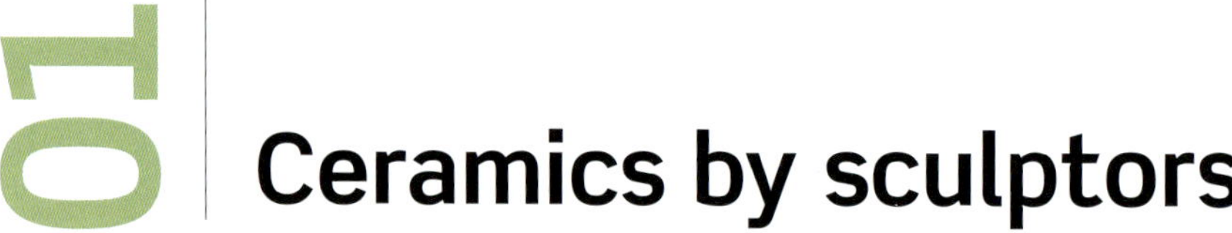

01 Ceramics by sculptors

The late 19th century saw an entire generation of artists become passionately involved in polychrome sculpture. Industrial and craft ceramics provided them with both a means of expression and a broader audience.

1 | **CAMILLE ALAPHILIPPE (1874 -after 1934)** Woman with an Ape

1908, Stoneware and bronze - Purchased 1908 - Inv. PPS00893

A stay at the French Academy's Villa Médicis in Rome in 1901 triggered Camille Alaphilippe's interest in the formal and decorative potential of ceramics, and in 1814 he became director of Alexandre Bigot's pottery at Mer, in western central France, a concern mainly producing architectural ceramics.
Bought at the Salon des Artistes Français in 1908, *Woman with an Ape* offers the weird image of a mysteriously hieratic woman with a primate on a leash: pet, prisoner or worshipper? The work is a daring assemblage of gilt bronze - the woman's head and hands - and glazed ceramic plaques mounted on a wood and iron frame and held together with crushed brick mortar. Coloured plaster is used for the joins. The result is a kind of gigantic objet d'art whose eye-catching contours and shimmering colours tend to obscure the enormous technical skill of an artist now too little known.

2 | **THE CHOISY-LE-ROI POTTERY - AUGUSTE RODIN (1840-1917), ALBERT CARRIER-BELLEUSE (1824-1887)** Vase of the Titans

Earthenware - Purchased 2004 - Inv. ODUT01914

In 1864 Rodin met Carrier-Belleuse, a leading Second Empire sculptor and interior designer, and worked extensively for the latter in his studio. *Vase of the Titans* was in all likelihood made after 1876 and a trip to Italy that had left its mark on Rodin. Signed "Carrier-Belleuse" on its base and decorated with images of Atlas, the piece is characteristic of Rodin, an admirer of Michelangelo. The support also bears the stamp of the Choisy-le-Roi pottery near Paris. Throughout his career Rodin took an interest in ceramics and in 1879-82 he worked in association with the Manufacture de Sèvres, for which he created a number of decorative figures and a host of porcelain vases. Later he had several of his sculptures interpreted by leading ceramicists: Jeanneney, for example, was commissioned to make a stoneware reproduction of his *Head of Balzac* and one of the figures from the *Bourgeois of Calais*.

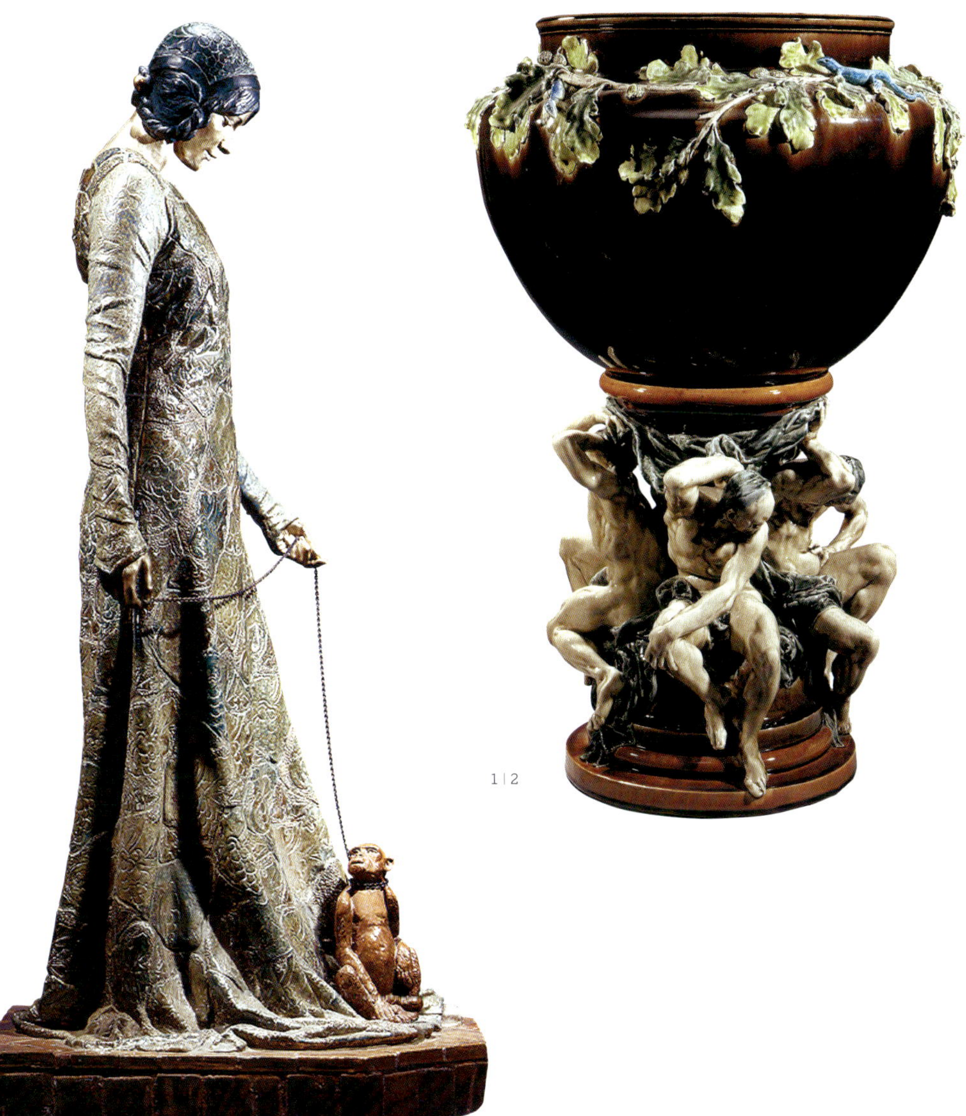
1 | 2

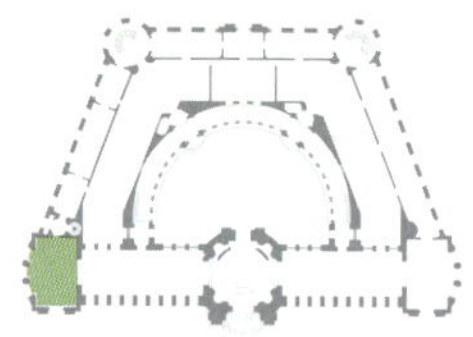

02 The walls of the Republic

The building of the city halls for Paris' twenty municipalities was rounded off with an elaborate programme of decoration. Beginning in 1872 the Service des Beaux-Arts, an offshoot of the Travaux de Paris department – headed until 1892 by Adolphe Alphand (see portrait in Room 3) was in charge of organising these extensive works. With the 19th century drawing to a close the dominant taste was the Eclecticism favoured by the Academy, which provided many of the jury members. The goal of these commissions was civic as well as ornamental: the Republic's official buildings required a dignity that would affirm the nation's founding values in the eyes of all. In the city halls the main staircase, wedding hall and reception room were each given an appropriate painted decor, with themes including marriage, the family, work, universal suffrage and defence of the homeland.

EUGÈNE CARRIÈRE (1849-1906) The Ages of Life: Young Mothers

1900, oil on canvas - Commissioned from the artist in 1897 - Inv. PPP00415

When the city hall of the 12th Arrondissement was being extended in 1897, Carrière was commissioned to decorate the wedding hall. This was his second – and last – major decoration project, the first having been at the Paris City Hall. His work is a highly personal aspect of the Realist current that was steadily gaining ground in monumental painting.

His repertoire draws on daily life and his experience as the father of a family, but his aim in focusing on their symbolic and spiritual dimension was, he wrote, "to bring a new look to immortal truths". Rather than the social role of marriage, then, he emphasises the gift of life and its underpinning of the family down through the generations. The bond between his figures finds expression in the fluidity of movement conveyed by the curve of his line.

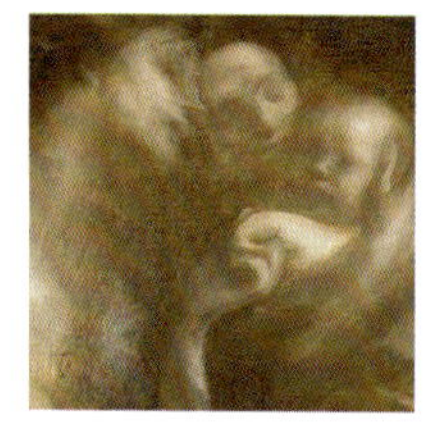

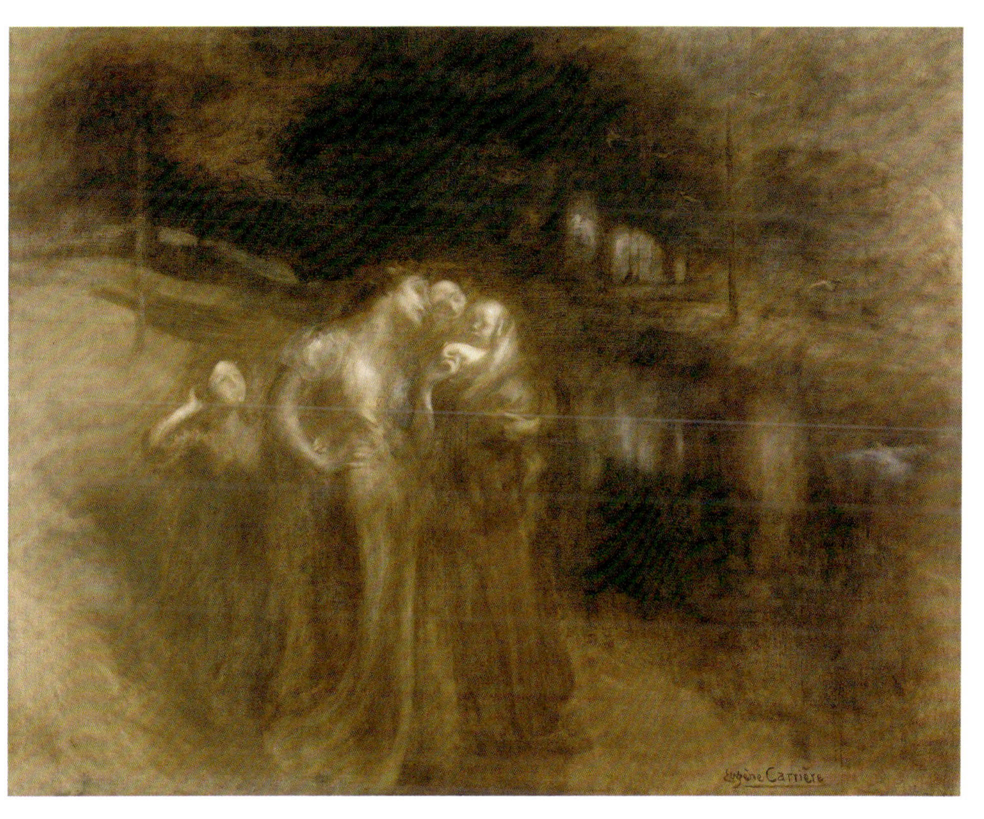
Eugène Carrière

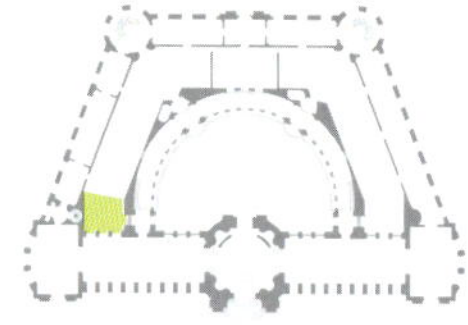

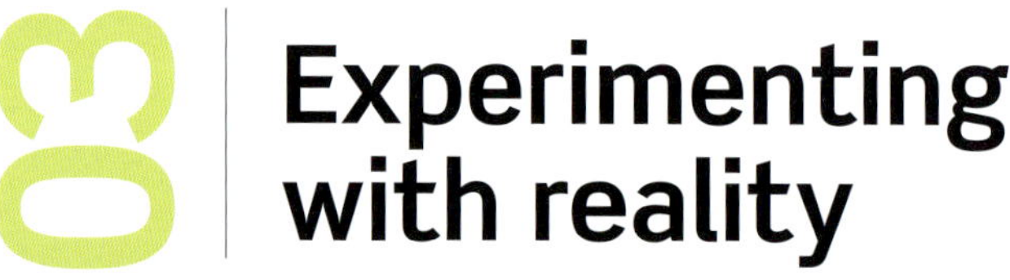

03 Experimenting with reality

The extraordinary rise of industry and urbanisation in the 19th century brought growing aspirations towards social progress and democracy. The arts, like the social sciences, reacted to these changes by attempting to show people in their real settings, and so homed in on the underlying mechanisms of modern society. More than just an art movement, Naturalism echoed and amplified this major shift, with painters and sculptors following the novels of Emile Zola in meticulously accurate - if sometimes rather plodding - descriptions of peasants, workers, the bourgeoisie and the destitute.

With no misgivings about having recourse to photography, the advocates of Naturalism sought to describe while holding fast to the narrative principles of history painting, and were totally at home in a use of mise en scène that did not shrink from the large format. The City of Paris' social policy led to purchases at the Salon which even now remain one of the features of the Petit Palais collection.

1 | **ALFRED ROLL (1846-1919)** Portrait of Adolphe Alphand

1888, oil on canvas - Purchased 1892 - Inv. PPP00112

This painting is Roll's tribute to one of the driving forces behind the transformation of the capital in the 19th century. Naturalistic in spirit, the portrait shows Alphand at work on the site of the Universal Exhibition of 1889, one of the major projects of a long and active career. The dome of the Invalides can be descried in the background; soon it would be accompanied by Gustave Eiffel's famous tower, completed in March 1889. More effective than the still hesitant photography of the time, Roll's canvas is a lively rendering of this severe-looking, sharp-eyed engineer of seventy-one.

2 | **LOUIS CARRIER-BELLEUSE (1848-1913)**
Flour Carriers: Paris scene
1885, oil on canvas
Acquired with income accruing from the Dutuit bequest, 1985 - Inv. PDUT01445

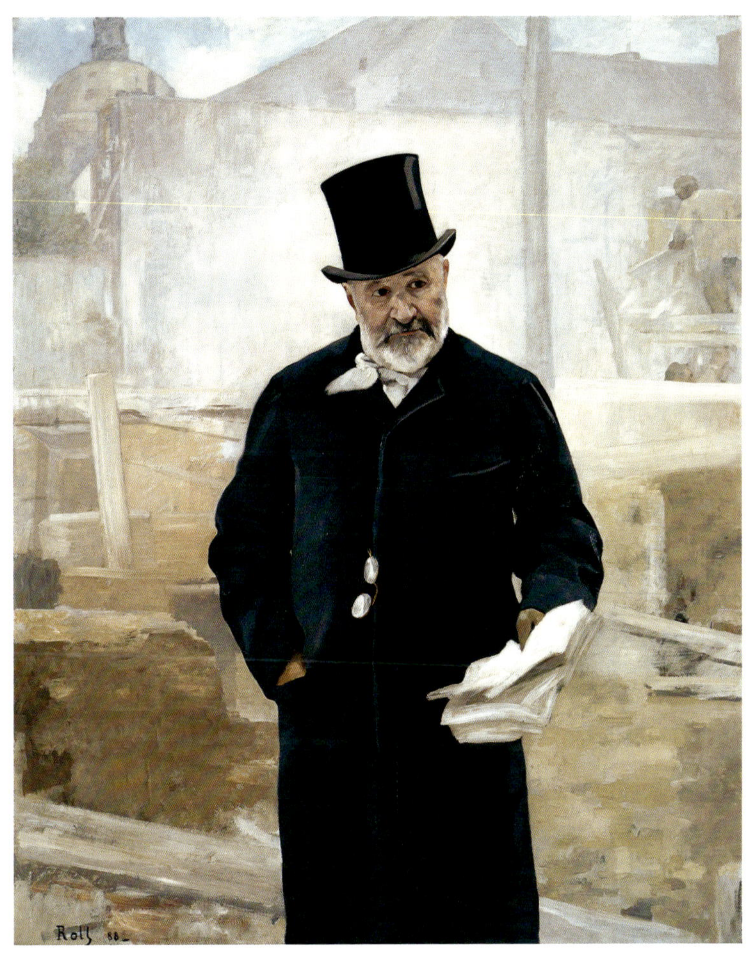

1

2

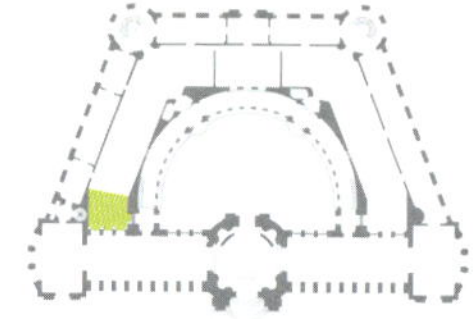

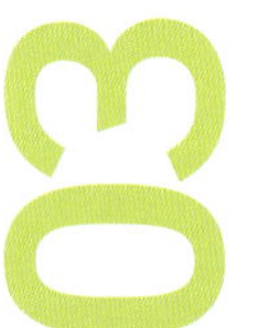

The Parisienne

The fascination Paris - the city of light - held for the rest of the world in the late 19th century led to the crystallisation of a type: the Parisienne. This was the name given by the Naturalist novel and the arts to a range of pretty women: the elegant bourgeoise, the striking society figure and the frivolous young working-class creature.
Thus it was that the sculptor Chatrousse gave the title of *A Parisienne* to the graceful plaster figure he showed at the Salon in 1876 and bequeathed to the City of Paris in 1896. With her simple dress and bunch of lilacs she represents the new breed of working woman then generating such colourful terms as *trottin*, from the verb "to trot": a *trottin* was a girl apprentice who made deliveries for her dressmaker employer.

1 | **CHARLES AUGUSTE ÉMILE DURANT,** known as **CAROLUS-DURAN (1837-1917)**
Portrait of Mrs Edgar Stern
1889, oil on canvas - Gift of Gérard Stern, 1978 - Inv. PPP03619

Painter par excellence of the Parisienne, Carolus-Duran approached the elegant woman of the time with the frankness of a Courbet and the sweep of a Velázquez. A stunning, calculatedly daring colourist, he brought new life and a fresh truthfulness to the commissioned portrait. In this no-frills portrait of Marguerite Fould, wife of the banker Edgar Stern, the vivid red of the evening gown sets off perfectly all the sparkle of the twenty-three year old subject.
Unlike his friend Manet, whom he met in 1855 at the Académie Suisse in Paris, Carolus-Duran was quick to find fame and fortune, travelling as far afield as New York, where he painted portraits for many of the city's leading families.

2 | **CHARLES-ALEXANDRE GIRON (1850-1914)**
Woman Wearing Gloves, also known as The Parisienne
1883, oil on canvas
Gift of Simone Giron-de Pourtalès, 1960 - Inv. PPP03587

3 | **ÉMILE FRANÇOIS CHATROUSSE (1829-1896)**
A Parisienne
1876, patinated plaster
Gift of the artist, 1896 - Inv. PPS03400

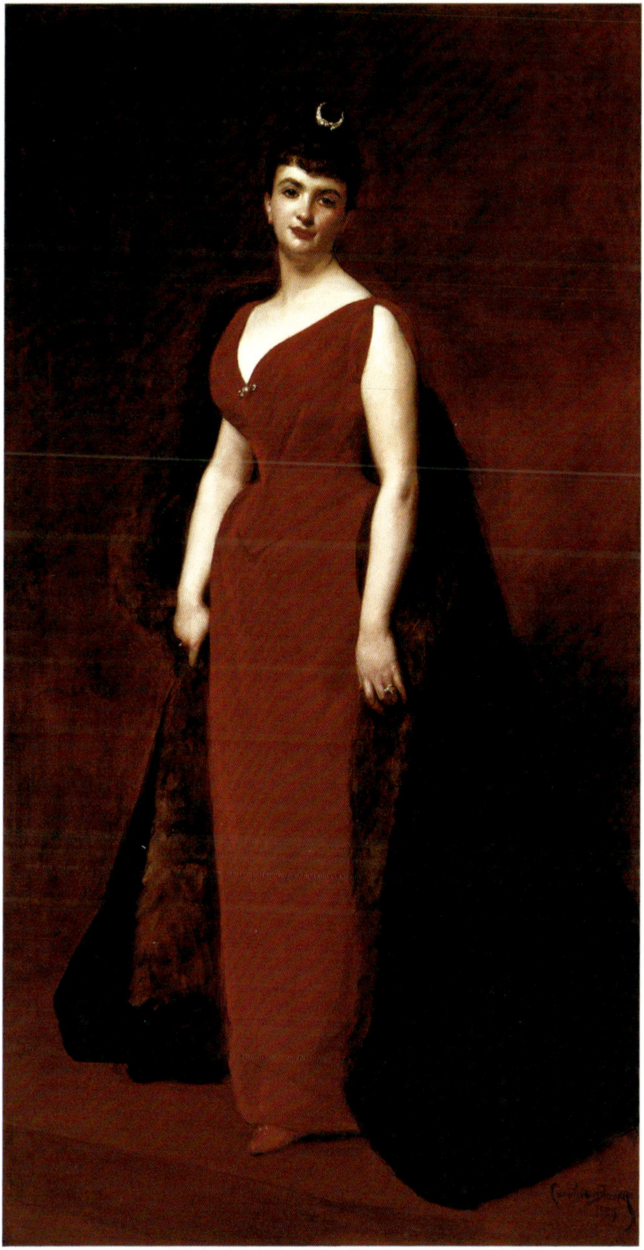

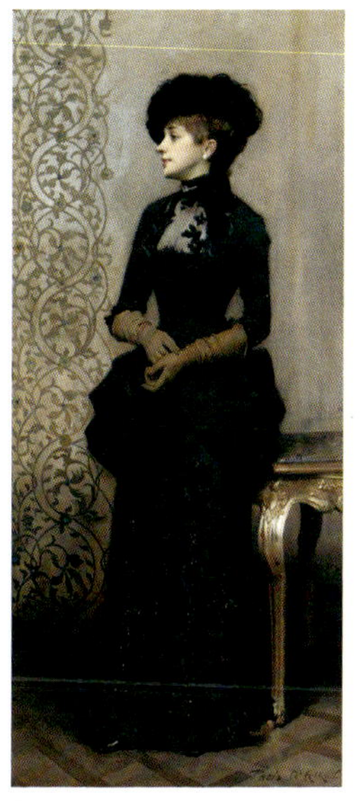

2

3

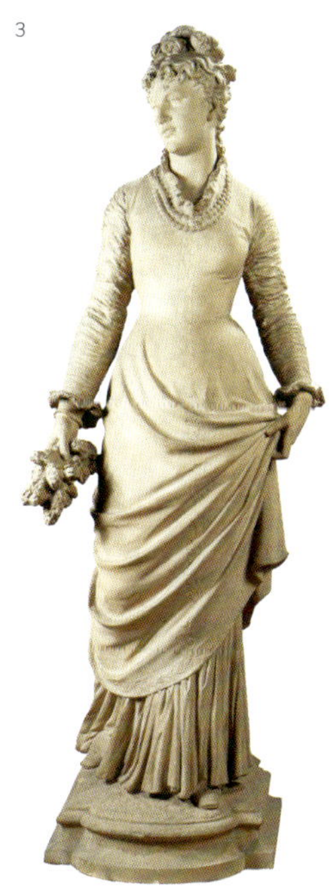

1

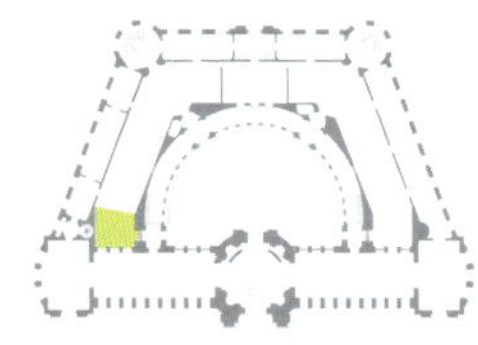

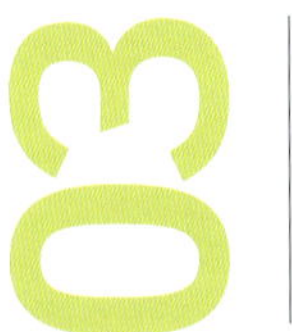

Grimaces and Misery

FERDINAND EMMANUEL PELEZ DE CORDOVA, known as **FERNAND PELEZ (1848-1913)**
Grimaces and Misery (Circus Performers)
1888, oil on canvas - Purchased 1914 - Inv. PPP00594

Trained in the great classical tradition at the École des Beaux-Arts in Paris, Pelez abandoned historical subject matter once and for all in 1880 to focus on the humble and the wretched. Named "the painter of pity" by art critic Joséphin Péladan, he pilloried the social evils of the Paris he lived in on the Butte Montmartre.

Coming upon his spectacular *Grimaces and Misery* at the Salon des Artistes Français in 1888, the critic André Michel was struck by its emblematic quality: "Today we are devoting as many paintings to physical, social and moral suffering as Veronese did to the festivities in Venice." The same year saw Seurat's *Circus Sideshow* (New York: Metropolitan Museum of Art) at the Salon des Indépendants, but while the subject is very similar, the pointillist style is at the other extreme from Pelez's direct confrontation with his figures. There is no ambiguity of intent here as the artist lays bare the joyless celebration Rimbaud's *Illuminations* described as "the most violent paradise of the enraged grimace" ("Parade", 1886): the fatigue of the young acrobats, the endlessly repeated routines of the white-faced clown, the resigned indifference of the musicians, the grubby backdrop... Arranging his performers left to right from the youngest to the oldest, in a way reminiscent of the standard image of the *Ages of Life*, the painter brings a symbolic dimension to his realistic rendering.

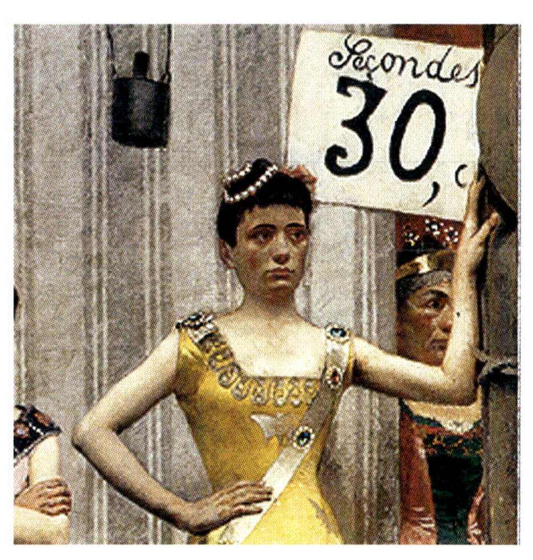
Secondes
30,

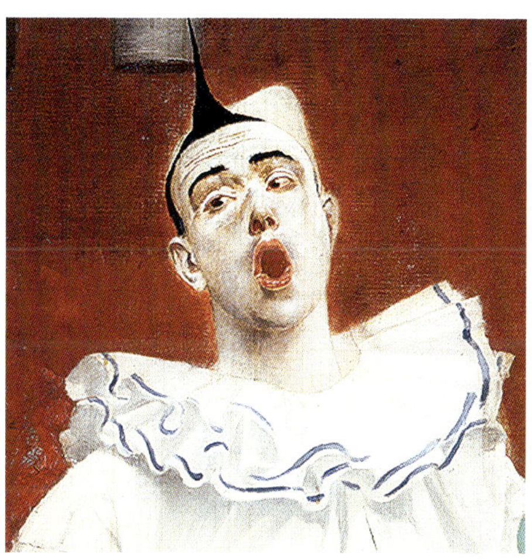

Grimaces and Misery (Circus Performers)

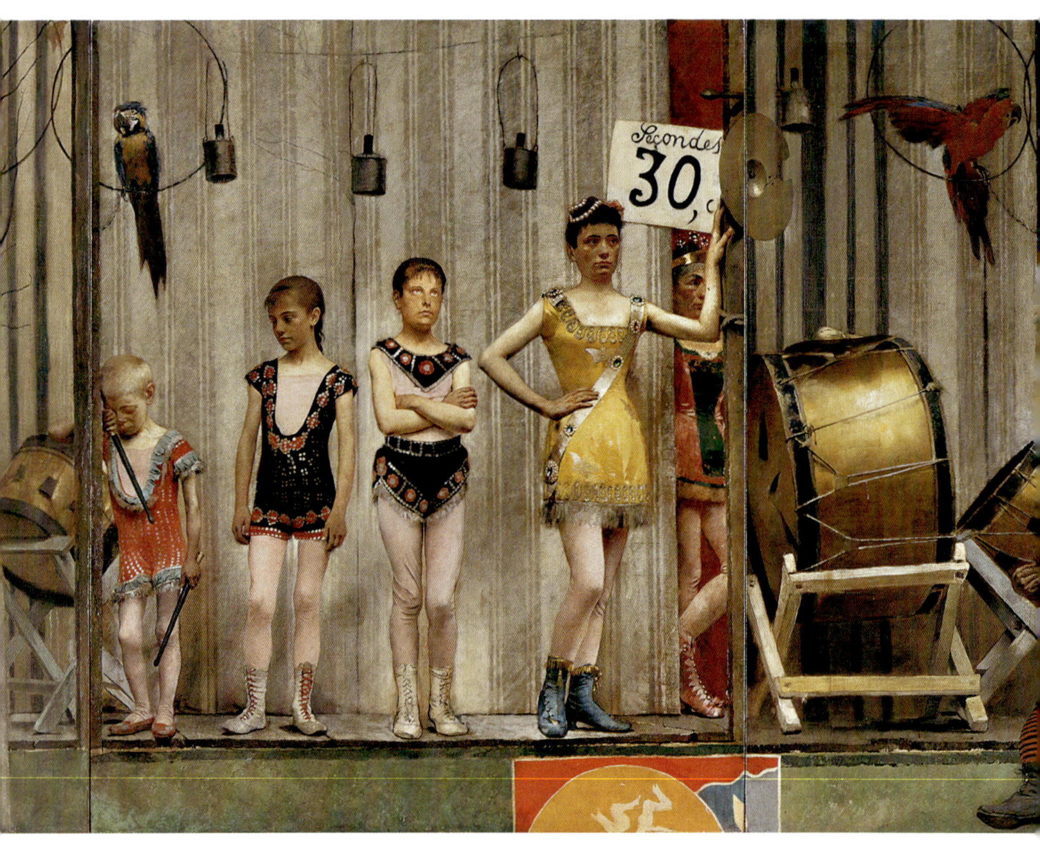

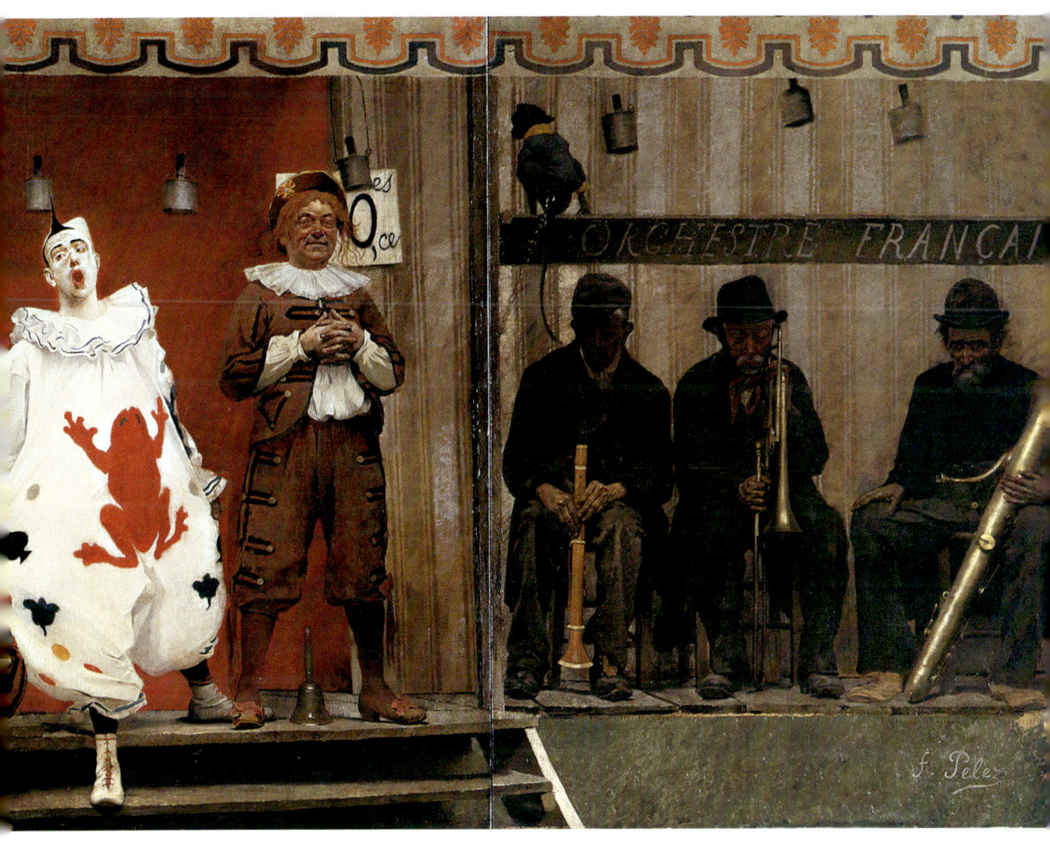
ORCHESTRE FRANÇAI
F. Pelez

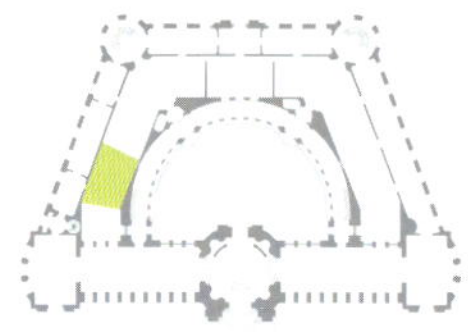

04 Painting true

Realism set out to offer the closest possible representation of everyday life, an aesthetic stance that crystallised around the work of Courbet just after the 1848 revolution.
Born in 1819 into a well-off Franche-Comté farming family, Courbet remained faithful to his rural roots as a source of inspiration. The 1849 Salon marked his maturity as an artist: in the favourable context of the Second Republic his *After Dinner at Ornans* (Lille, Musée des Beaux-Arts) - an everyday domestic scene he set out to raise to the dignity of history painting - received a gold medal. Shown in 1851, *A Burial at Ornans* (Paris, Musée d'Orsay) triggered both the interest of the public and artistic controversy. Equally ambitious, *Firemen Going to a Fire* was cut short by Louis-Napoléon Bonaparte's coup d'état in December 1851; it would appear to contain an underlying political message of hostility to the new emperor.
A friend of Proudhon, whose portrait he painted posthumously, Courbet described himself as a republican since birth and in 1870 joined the Paris Commune uprising. Arrested when Paris was retaken by Loyalist troops, he spent his time in prison painting still lives of flowers and fruit permeated with his sensual love of nature. Falling ill, he left prison to go into exile, spending the last years of his life in Switzerland. His originality stands out most clearly in the female nude. Sexual desire and voluptuousness are embodied in women with bodies whose living flesh is in total contrast with the diaphanous nymphs of Salon painting. In his ongoing struggle against academicism and in favour of modernity of subject and treatment, Courbet was a founding father for the following generation of artists. The Petit Palais is home to one of the major collections of Courbet: the first acquisition dates from 1881 and has since been complemented by donations from the painter's sister Juliette and art lover Théodore Duret.

GUSTAVE COURBET (1819-1877) Young Ladies on the Banks of the Seine (Summer)
1857, oil on canvas - Gift of Étienne Baudry through Juliette Courbet, 1906 - Inv. PPP00377

The Young Ladies are two city-dwellers who have come to cool off at the water's edge. The modernity of the subject is enhanced by the frankness of the facial expressions and the naturalness of the poses. Yet despite its realism, the work is more evocative than narrative. Champfleury, the bard of Social Realism, saw the ambiguous seductiveness of these semi-nude Parisiennes surrendering to the languor of summer as proof of the Second Empire's moral laxness.
Its subject matter and the broad strokes used to achieve the lighting effects make this a forerunner of the Impressionist celebration of the banks of the Seine a generation later.

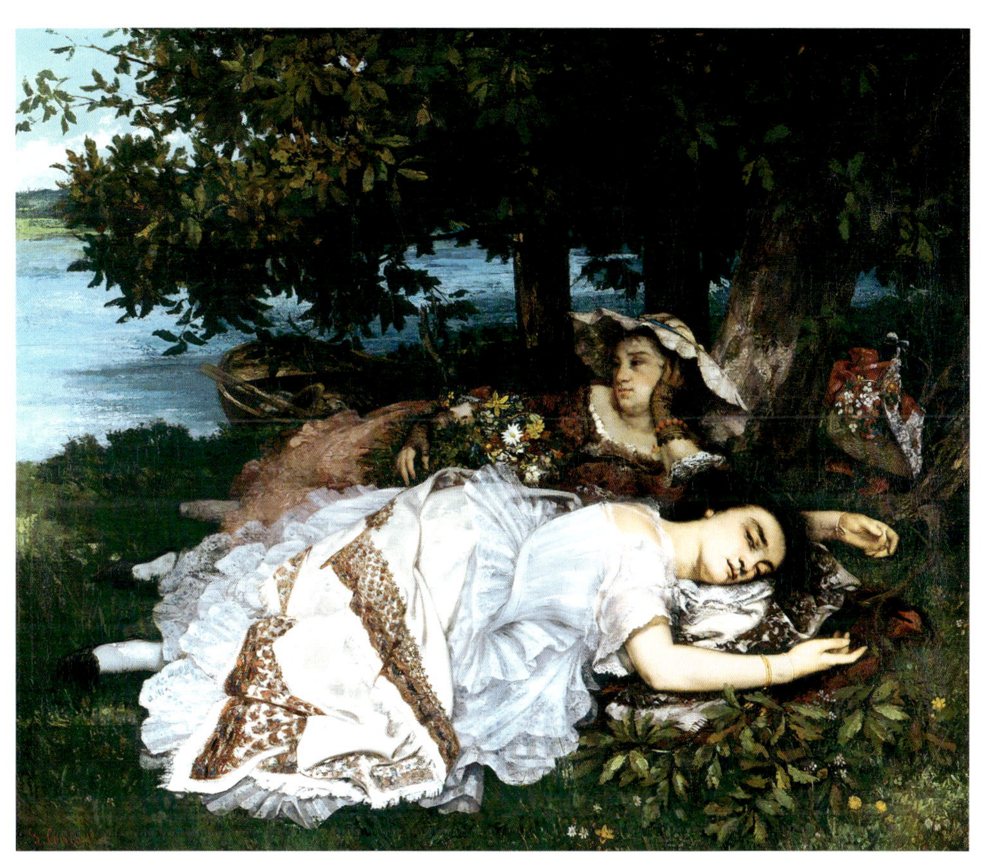

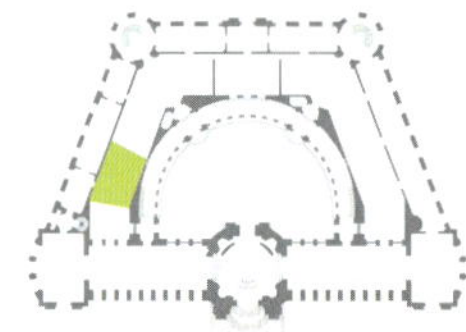

04 | Painting true

1 | **GUSTAVE COURBET (1819-1877)** Firemen Going to a Fire

1851, oil on canvas - Gift of Juliette Courbet, 1882 - Inv. PPP00737

In 1846 Courbet went to Holland, where the museums provided him with a decisive lesson in painting. His memories of the trip seem to have influenced *Firemen Going to a Fire*, whose format and composition are reminiscent of Rembrandt's *Night Watch*, which he had seen in the Rijksmuseum in Amsterdam.

The picture shows firemen setting out along a Paris street at night. A man in working clothes has given the alarm and the passers-by are making way for the fire engine.

Courbet painted this large canvas - the only urban scene in his entire oeuvre - in a real firehouse and he asked the firemen to enact a torchlight departure for a fire.

The coup d'état of 2 December 1851 led to an uprising by the staff of the Poissy firehouse that definitively halted this ambitious, complex project after a year's work. The unfinished canvas was rediscovered in Courbet's studio after his death.

2 | **GUSTAVE COURBET (1819-1877)** Sleep

1866, oil on canvas - Purchased 1953 - Inv. PPP03130

When living in Paris the Turkish diplomat Khalil-Bey built up a collection focusing on contemporary painters. In 1865 he became the owner of Ingres' last masterpiece *The Turkish Bath* (Paris, Musée du Louvre) and was interested in Courbet as a painter of the sensually feminine.

The collector commissioned this work, in which Courbet's highly original composition transposes the world of the harem into the closed ambience of a flagrantly luxurious bedroom. Drawing his subject matter from the licentious prints of the 18th century and literary descriptions of lesbian love, he offers a portrayal of two sleeping women. All element of thought or feeling has been eliminated from their intertwined bodies. As Manet had done in his *Olympia* (1863, Paris, Musée d'Orsay), Courbet contrasts two female types by playing on skin tone and hairstyle. Recalling the masterpieces he had copied in the Louvre, he sets out here to vie with Titian and Rubens, great masters of the female nude.

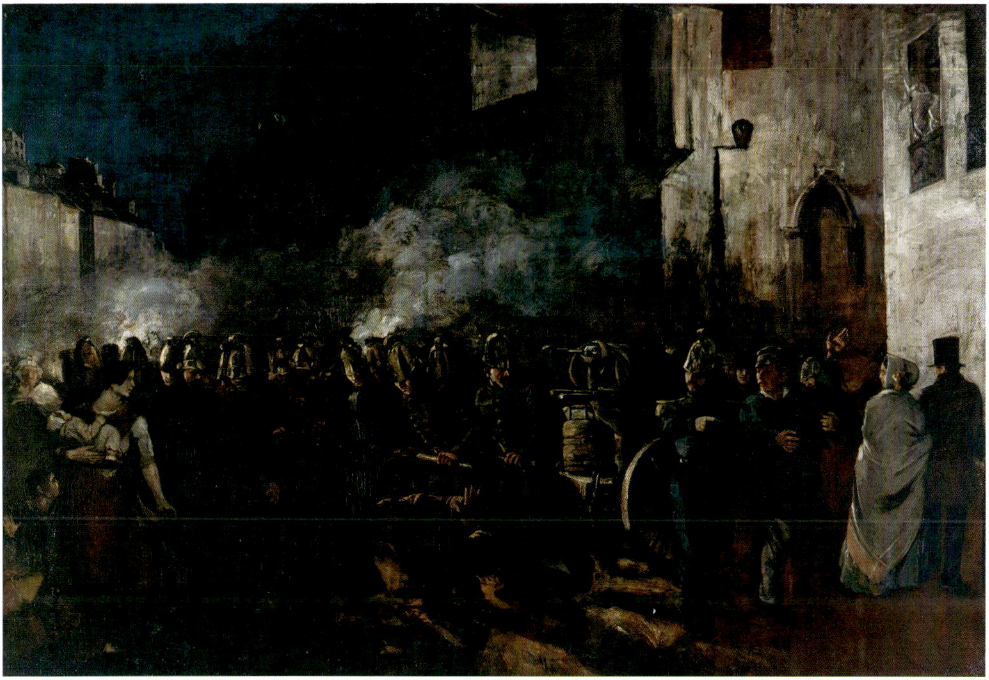

1

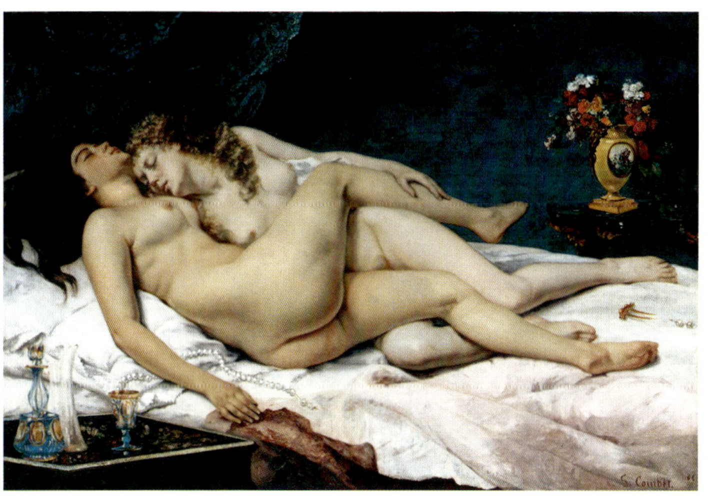

2

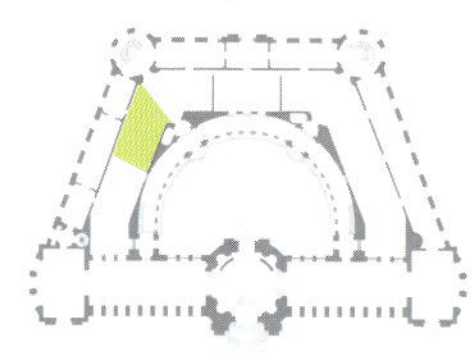

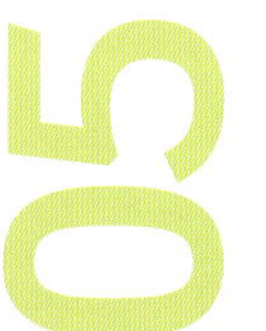

Art for the Republic

In the 19th century a substantial proportion of artists made their living from state purchases and commissions, with successive regimes seeking legitimacy through art programmes on a generous scale: by portraying the high points of the nation's history, painters and sculptors glorified the powers that be as the heirs to the national tradition. Thus a painter like Philippoteaux, who had worked extensively for the Museum of French History founded by King Louis-Philippe at Versailles, produced on his own initiative a version of an episode from the very recent 1848 revolution, hoping it would be bought by the new Republic.

From the beginning of the Third Republic both the State and the City of Paris used artists to proclaim their Republican values. The artists whose works were acquired or commissioned for the squares and city halls of Paris also had to surrender all relevant sketches and models. A leading figure in this context was Aimé-Jules Dalou, a gifted producer of sculptures for the city.

1 | **AIMÉ-JULES DALOU (1838-1902)** The Triumph of the Republic

1879, patinated plaster - Commission, 1880 - Inv. PPS00075

Ten years before the centenary of the French Revolution, the City of Paris launched a competition for a monument to the glory of the Republic. Dalou failed to win, but the city fathers were so impressed by his proposal that they commissioned a bronze casting for what is now the Place de la Nation. *The Triumph of the Republic* was officially unveiled in 1899.

A fervent republican, Dalou gave his piece the élan of humanity bound for a new golden age: the Republic is set triumphantly on the chariot of the Nation, drawn by lions with Liberty holding the reins. The chariot is flanked by Work in the form of a blacksmith and Justice, while Peace distributes the fruits of abundance. The swirling movement of the composition and the exuberant realism of the figures revolutionised the sculptural conventions of the time.

2 | **FÉLIX PHILIPPOTEAUX (1815-1884)**

Alphonse de Lamartine Rejecting the Red Flag of the Socialists, 25 February 1848

1848, oil on canvas

Acquired with income accruing from the Dutuit bequest, 1986 - Inv. PDUT01468

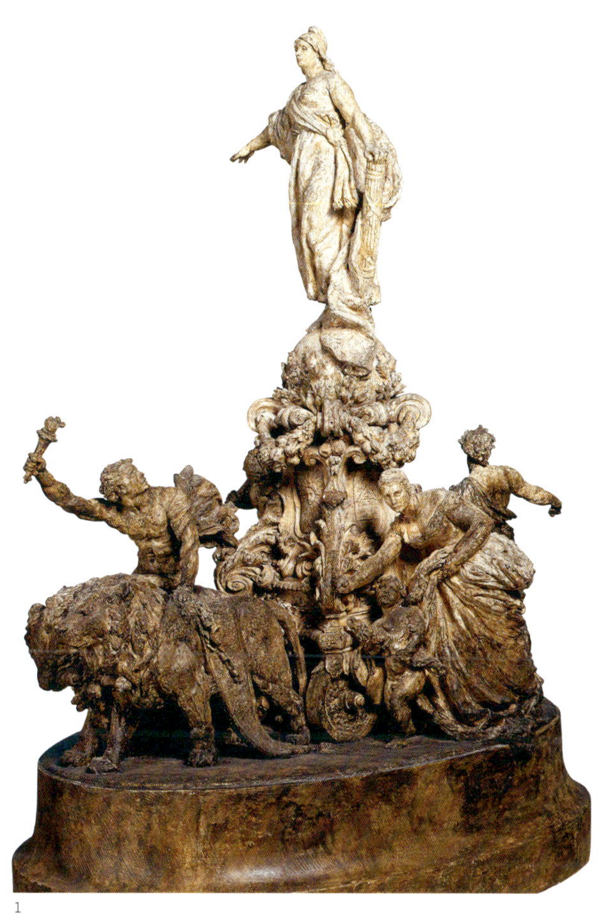

1

2

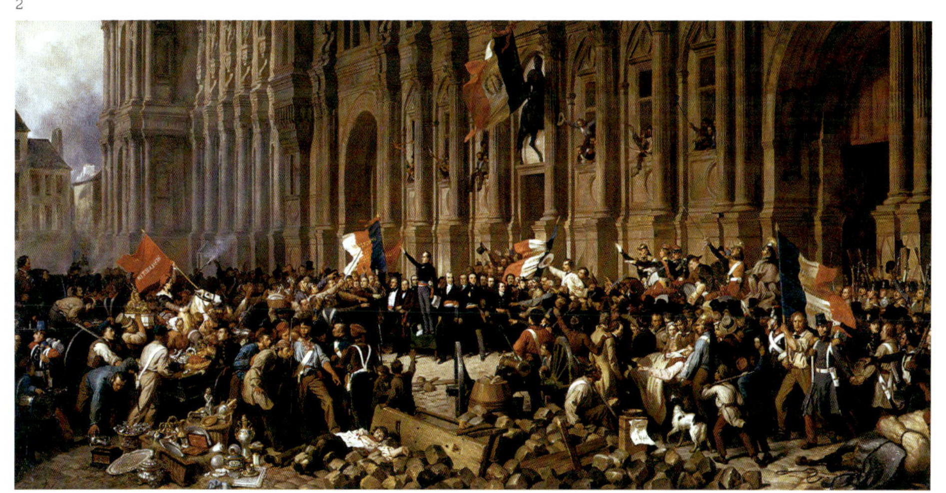

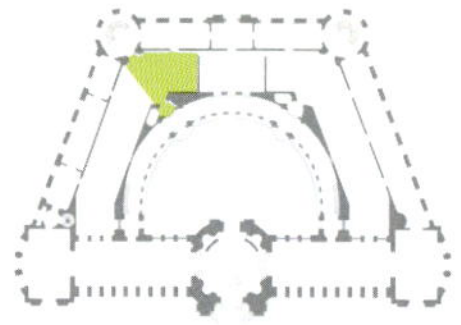

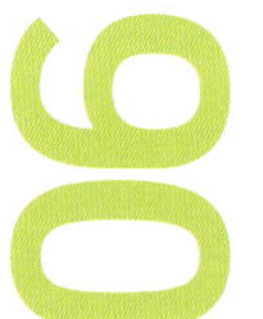

Christian subjects

In the period between the violently anti-Catholic persecutions of such phases of the French Revolution as the Terror, and the law of 1905 separating Church and State, the Church's official status varied constantly: the Concordat under the Empire (1802-1814), union with the throne under the Restoration (1814-1830), coexistence under the July Monarchy (1830-1848), favoured status under the Second Empire (1852-1870) and sidelining under the Third Republic (1875-1940).
Artists' relationships with Catholicism, Catholic circles and Catholic subject matter during this period were equally diverse, but contrary to the received wisdom, works of art on Christian themes were abundant throughout the 19th century. Among the contributing factors were the artists' religious convictions, the considerable number of commissions, a continuing taste for history and personal quests for a meaning somewhere beyond the visible.

GUSTAVE DORÉ (1832-1883) The Valley of Tears

1883, oil on canvas - Acquired with income accruing from the Dutuit bequest, 1984 - Inv. PDUT01437

The host of commissions generated by the July Monarchy and the Second Empire mostly benefited artists with little taste for innovation, yet at the same time more inventive figures were taking a personal approach to Christianity. Born into a traditional Catholic family, the deeply tortured Gustave Doré seems to have sought solace in religion and his fascination with Christ. This permeated the paintings in the Doré Gallery in London. This example was commissioned by Fairless and Beetforth in 1867 after the enormous success of his *Illustrated Bible* in England.
During the twenty-four years of its existence, the Doré Gallery, with its twenty canvases, received some two and a half million visitors. In 1892 most of the pictures were sent to the United States for a travelling exhibition lasting until 1898 and then disappeared into oblivion. Rediscovered in a Manhattan warehouse in 1947, they were dispersed at auction. Since 1985 three of them have been part of the Petit Palais collection, including the last of the series: *The Valley of Tears* of 1883. Like the other works from the Doré Gallery, this one adds to the Romantic sensibility and heralds the questing of the Symbolists (Room 18).

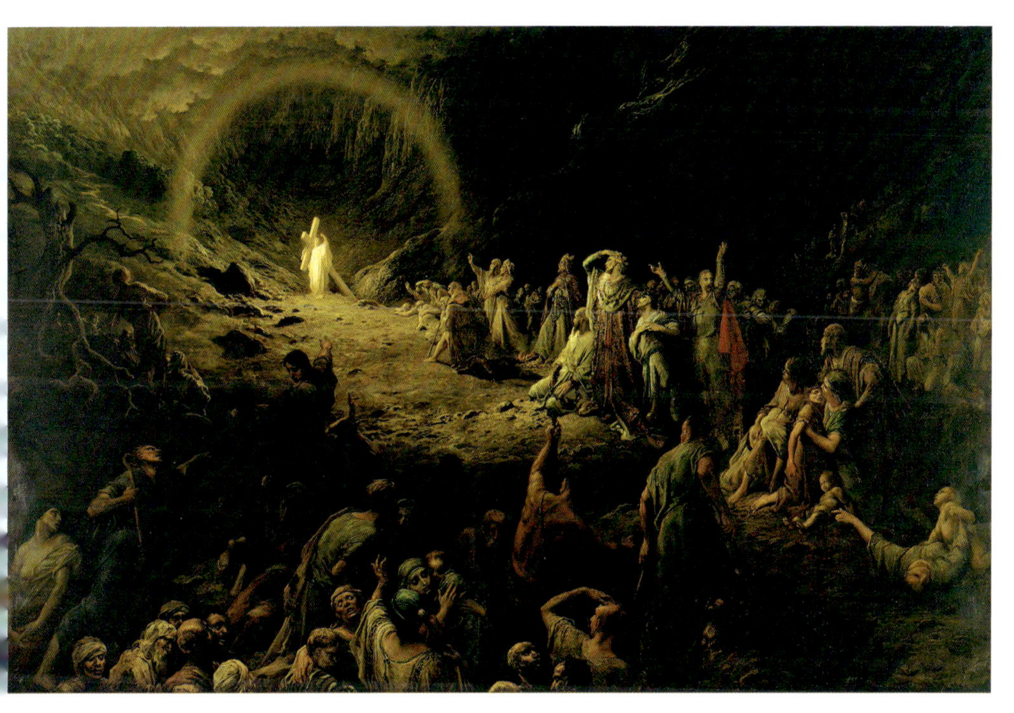

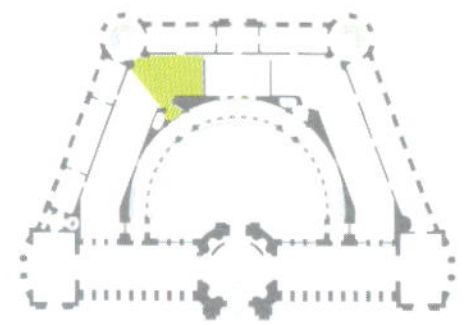

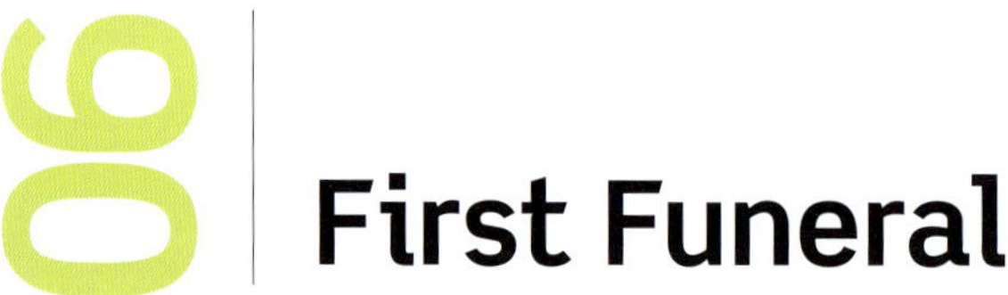

06 First Funeral

LOUIS ERNEST BARRIAS (1841-1905) First Funeral

Marble, 1883 - Commission, 1878 - Inv. PPS00007

This Biblically inspired group shows Adam and Eve bearing their son Abel, victim of the jealousy of his brother Cain. Winner of a medal of honour at the Salon of 1878, the plaster model was considered at the time "the highest manifestation of the feelings sculpture can express".

Barrias' scene of mourning is set in an imaginary prehistory suggested by a stone tool, with Adam's fiercely Gaulish countenance a further allusion to the ancestral past. This fantasised framework was probably based on the archaeological, historical and palaeontological notions of the period. The artist devoted a number of sketches to the theme, some of these belonging to the Petit Palais.

At the same time Barrias owes a considerable formal debt to Michelangelo and Bernini, and the bodies of Eve and Abel recall Renaissance versions of classical models. The figures are grouped in a stepped pyramidal composition that plays on the relationship between the three bodies. This is a kind of prehistoric Pietà, a brilliant union of the Neo-Classical, the Romantic and the Realist.

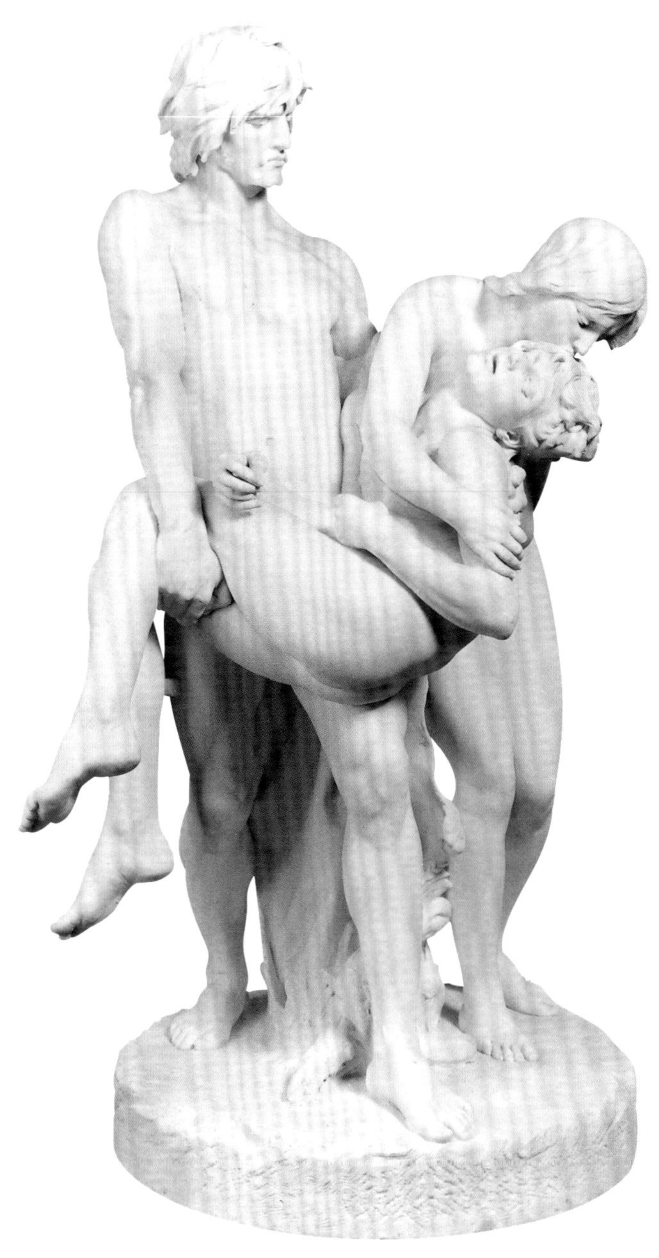

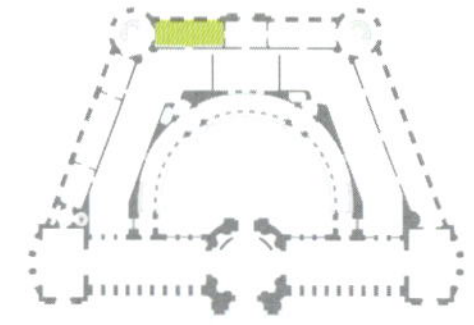

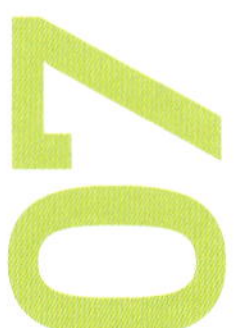

Painting in the open air

Landscape was a central concern for 19th-century painters. Increased ease of transport, the Romantic-inspired quest for a more authentic contact with nature and experiments with greater truth to the subject - these were factors conducive to the blossoming of a genre that was cutting free of the rules.
At the same period in England the increasingly popular watercolour technique allowed for direct, rapid transcription of fleeting scenes and light effects.
In 1865 Monet, bent on preserving the spontaneity of studies from the life, abandoned the travelling artist's standard quick sketch approach and actually set about producing finished canvases outdoors.
Notwithstanding, even among the Impressionists - Sisley, Pissarro, Cassatt and their forerunners Jongkind and Boudin - alternation between outdoor and studio work remained both a choice and a necessity.

1 | **CLAUDE MONET (1840-1926)** Sunset on the Seine at Lavacourt (Winter)
1880, oil on canvas - Gift of Edward Brandus, 1906 - Inv. PPP00439

Not far from Paris, Lavacourt was a village on the left bank of the Seine opposite Vétheuil, where Monet set up house in September 1878. After the river iced over during the particularly harsh winter of 1879-80, Monet captured the gradual thaw in some twenty paintings dating from the early months of the new year.
Disregarding the village itself, he concentrated in this work on capturing the atmosphere between water and sky just as the sun was setting. The combination of a new emphasis on the moment and a lively use of saturated colours makes this large painting an Impressionist masterpiece.

2 | **ERNEST RENOUX (1863-1932)**
Studies of Paris landscapes. Oil on wood.
Outdoor painting equipment.
Anne-Marie Renoux Donation, 2002
Inv. PPP04942 , PPP04943, PPP04944, PPO03681

3 | **FÉLIX ZIEM (1821-1911)**
Gust of Wind at Fontainebleau
c. 1860, oil on canvas-backed paper
Félix Ziem Donation, 1905 - Inv. PPP00279

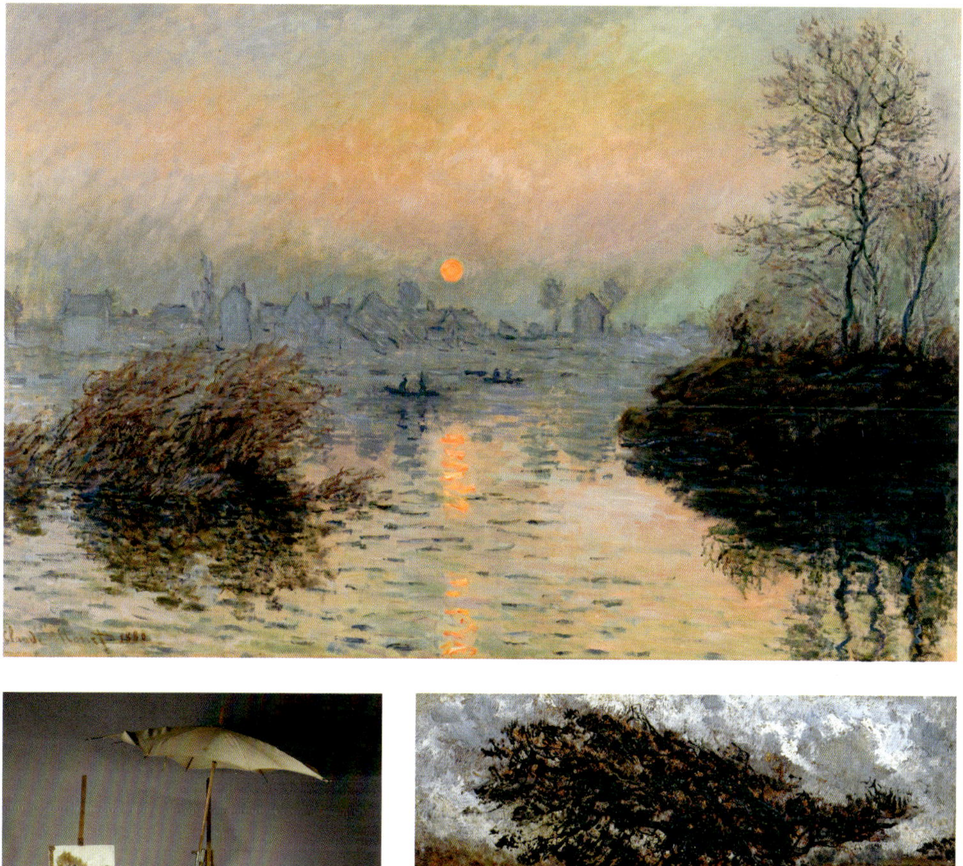

1

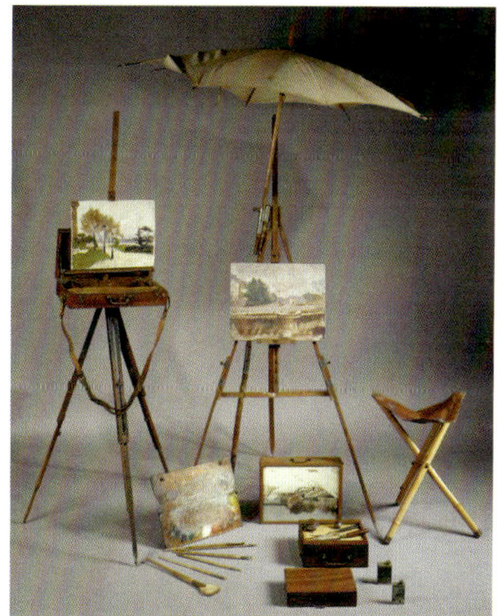

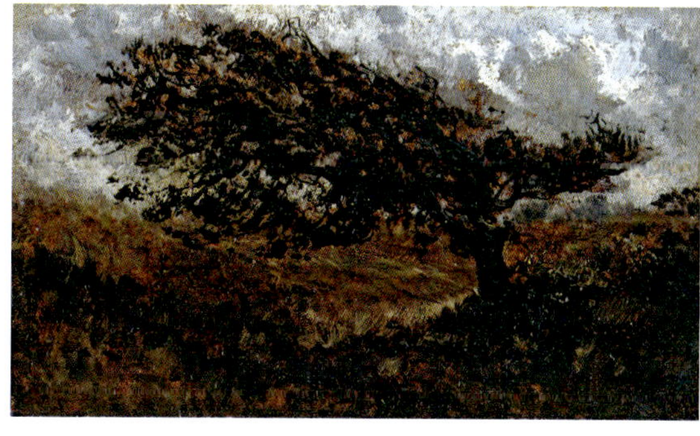

2 | 3

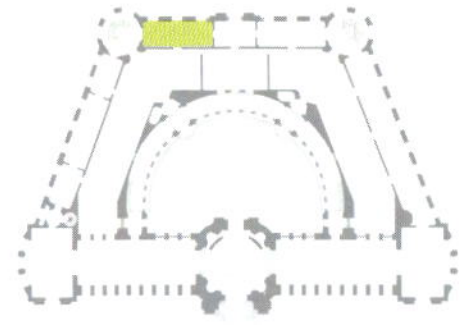

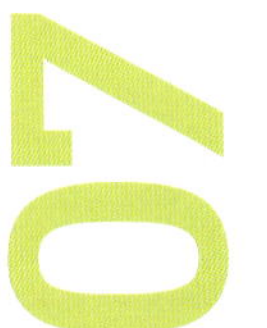

Rodin the unique

Auguste Rodin, the great sculptor of the second half of the 19th century, belongs to no school: with his formal daring - a face emerging from a block of raw marble, unfinished work shown to the public, a monument made of unpredictably accumulated assemblages, and countless other experiments - he was a precursor and an initiator. Passionately devoted to the materials of sculpture, fascinated by the relationship between sculpture, place and time, he opened up new horizons to an entire generation of sculptors, many of whom - Camille Claudel, Antoine Bourdelle, François Pompon and others - worked in his studio before going their separate ways. Yet his early years were far from easy and public recognition did not come until he was forty.

1 | **AUGUSTE RODIN (1840-1917)** Torso of a man

c. 1887-1888, bronze - After the clay original, a study for John the Baptist Preaching, c. 1878-79 - Gift of Sir Joseph Duveen, 1923
Inv. PPS01256

In about 1887 Rodin discovered in his studio a forgotten study for the large *John the Baptist* shown at the Salon in 1880: an unfired torso, split, crackled and incomplete. Delighted with his find and deciding to preserve its near-archaeological beauty, he made a mould and this extremely handsome casting. The bronze faithfully renders the rough surface of the dried and damaged original, while the greenish patina makes the piece look like an ancient fragment.

Rodin returned to the *Torso* in 1900, making a plaster proof to which he added legs - taken from another *John the Baptist* study - and thus creating his revolutionary *Walking Man*. This truncated statue in movement - it had neither head nor arms - was presented in the same year at the Pavillon de l'Alma, an exhibition venue independent of the Universal Exposition. In addition to its subtle daring, the *Walking Man* reveals a mature Rodin fascinated by the fragmentary, the assemblage and the effect of time on his work.

2 | **AUGUSTE RODIN (1840-1917)** Love and Psyche

c. 1885, marble, after the plaster model - Madame Thors Bequest, 1930 - Inv. PPS01463

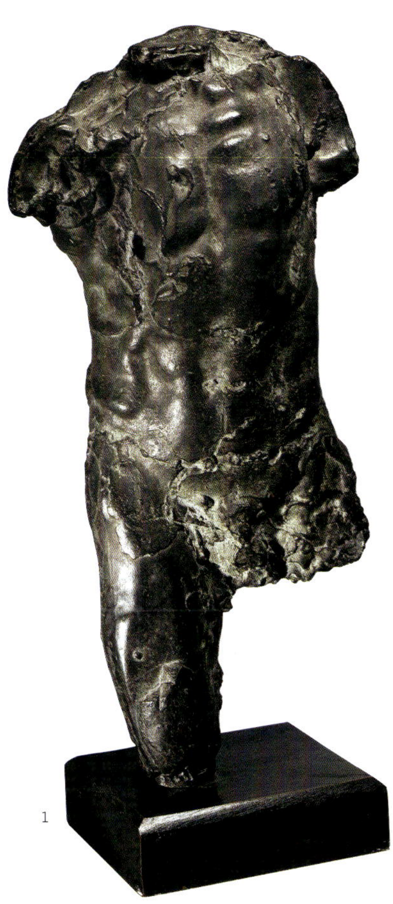
1

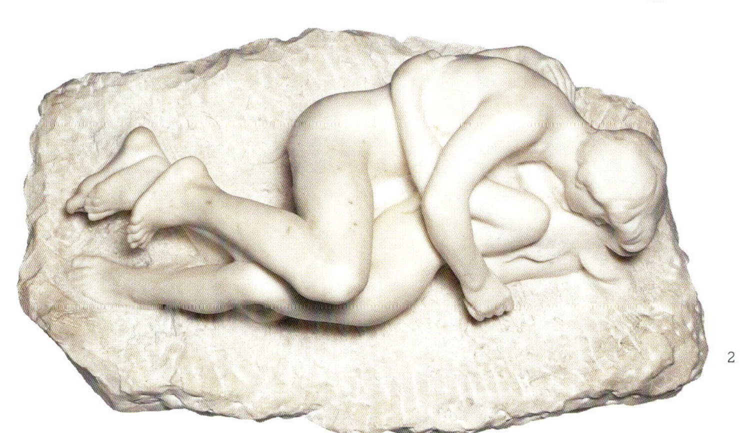
2

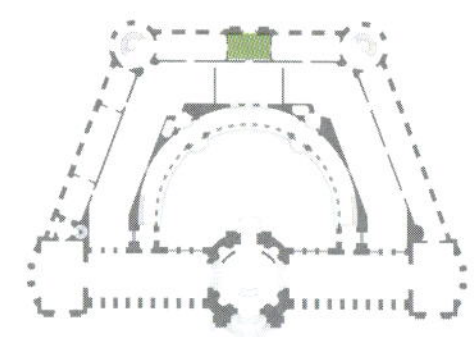

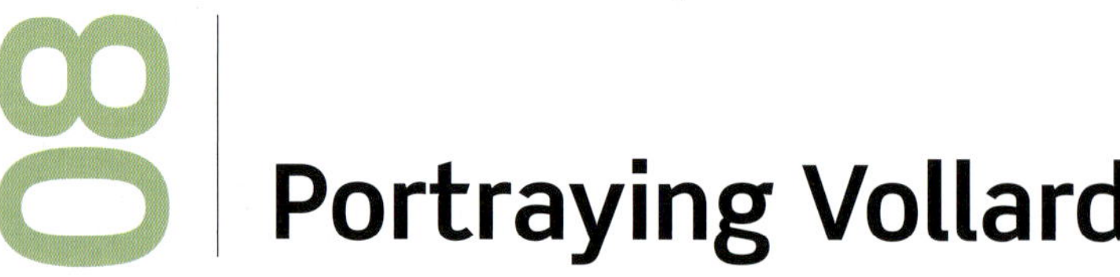

08 Portraying Vollard

1 | **PAUL CÉZANNE (1839-1906)** Portrait of Ambroise Vollard
1899, oil on canvas - Ambroise Vollard Bequest, 1945 - Inv. PPP02100

"I posed a number of times." With this simple sentence Ambroise Vollard begins the "My Portraits" chapter of his 1937 *Recollections of a Picture Dealer*. The book contains a host of delicious anecdotes about his sittings for different painters over the years: this was the giant - almost two metres tall - Creole who had no qualms about posing for Renoir wearing a red headscarf from his native Reunion Island or a flamboyant toreador's costume (Tokyo, Japanese Broadcasting Company).
Cézanne established his modus operandi in 1899 with endless sittings during which silence was de rigueur and Vollard had to stay as "motionless as an apple on a table". With Renoir, things were more relaxed: the sitter could speak and even move. Bonnard, knowing his subject's tendency to drift off to sleep, put a small cat on his lap to keep him awake.
Other artists selling via Vollard's Rue Lafitte gallery - Louis Valtat, Pablo Picasso, Émile Bernard, Jean-Louis Forain, Raoul Dufy and Georges Rouault - tried their hands too. Some of the portraits are veritable artistic manifestoes, notably those by Cézanne (Paris, Petit Palais) and Picasso (Moscow, Pushkin Museum), which provide striking evidence of the former's influence on the birth of Cubism.
Vollard was very much aware that in having his portrait painted by artists from his stable he was creating something for posterity - as his generosity to the Petit Palais, in the form of paintings, sculptures, ceramics, books, drawings and prints, confirms.

2 | **PIERRE-AUGUSTE RENOIR (1841-1919)**
Ambroise Vollard Wearing a Red Scarf
c. 1911, oil on canvas
Gift of Ambroise Vollard, 1928 - Inv. PPP00827

3 | **PIERRE BONNARD (1867-1947)**
Ambroise Vollard with a Cat
c. 1924, oil on canvas
Gift of the Vollard estate, 1950 - Inv. PPP03052

1

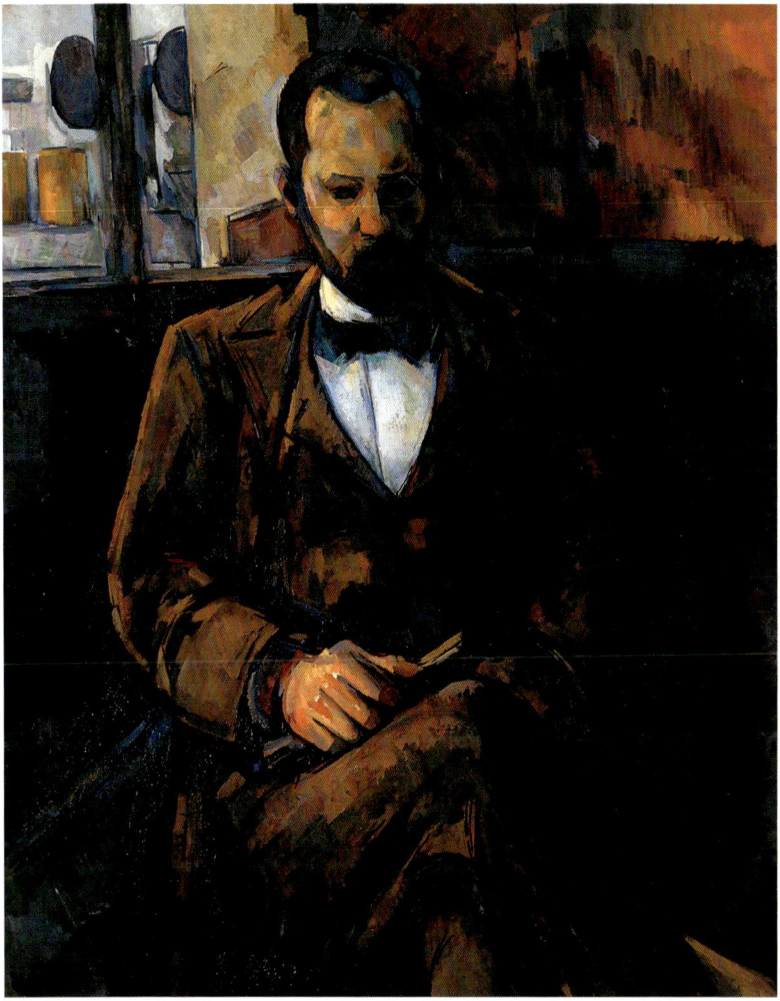

2 | 3

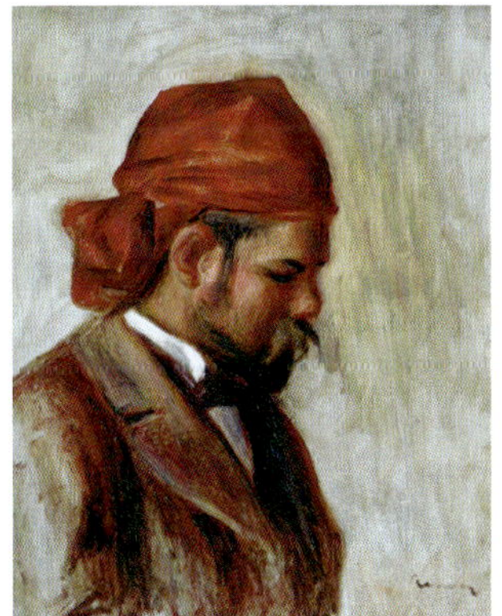

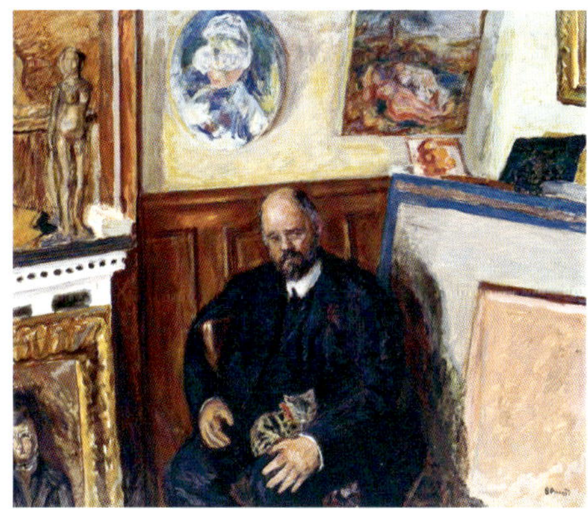

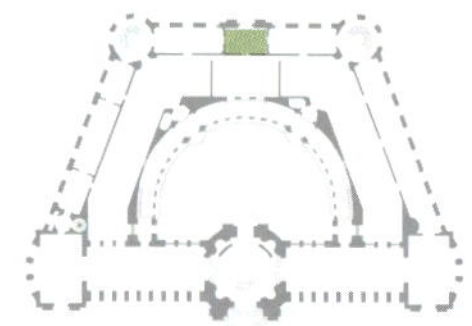

08 A step into modernity

The Industrial Revolution brought with it faith in progress and confidence in the future. Baudelaire was the first to speak of modernity, which he associated with a feeling of permanent change. With this notion there came a split between official art, still in the straitjacket of past practice, and artists demanding the right to express what they felt: "The reason the official Salons are so inferior," wrote Cézanne to Bernard in 1905, "is that their artists work strictly according to set procedures...They would do better to inject more personal emotion, observation and character." In freeing himself from the constraints of mere representation, the artist strove to express what Signac called "the will to art" and Kandinsky "interior beauty". With their deliberately arbitrary use of colour Gauguin and Van Gogh paved the way for the Fauves, while the Cubists radicalised Cézanne's approach to space and form. Little shown and little understood, these innovative movements finally found an audience when the Salons became more numerous and diverse. In 1884 came the Salon des Indépendants, with no jury and no prizes; and from 1890 the more selective Société Nationale des Beaux-Arts presented such artists as Maillol, Puvis de Chavannes and Rodin. However, it was the Salon d'Automne, inaugurated in 1903 at the Petit Palais, that first brought the great 19th-century innovators - Cézanne, Renoir, Redon, Lautrec and others - to the public eye.

1 | **ARISTIDE MAILLOL (1861-1944)** The Wave
c. 1891-1898, oil on canvas - Gift of Ambroise Vollard, 1937 - Inv. PPP02279
Maillol's career as a sculptor was preceded by ten years as a painter. Quickly shaking off the lessons of the Ecole des Beaux-Arts for those of Gauguin at Pont-Aven, he set out to abolish artistic frontiers: his nudes took the form of paintings, woodcuts, plaster sculptures and tapestries that gave concrete expression to his interest in the decorative arts.
The Wave borrowed its horizon-free approach to space from Gauguin and its ornamental curls of foam from Japonism. As in the metopes in the Parthenon, his woman bather, shaped out of the interplay of curves, seems to submit to the near-square format of the canvas. His use of matt paint is a further reference to architecture and, more specifically, to the murals then being given a new lease of life by Puvis de Chavannes.

2 | **PAUL GAUGUIN (1848-1903)** Jardinière
1886-1887, stoneware partially painted and glazed, incised and modelled decoration
Acquired with income accruing from the Dutuit bequest, 1994 - Inv. ODUT01787

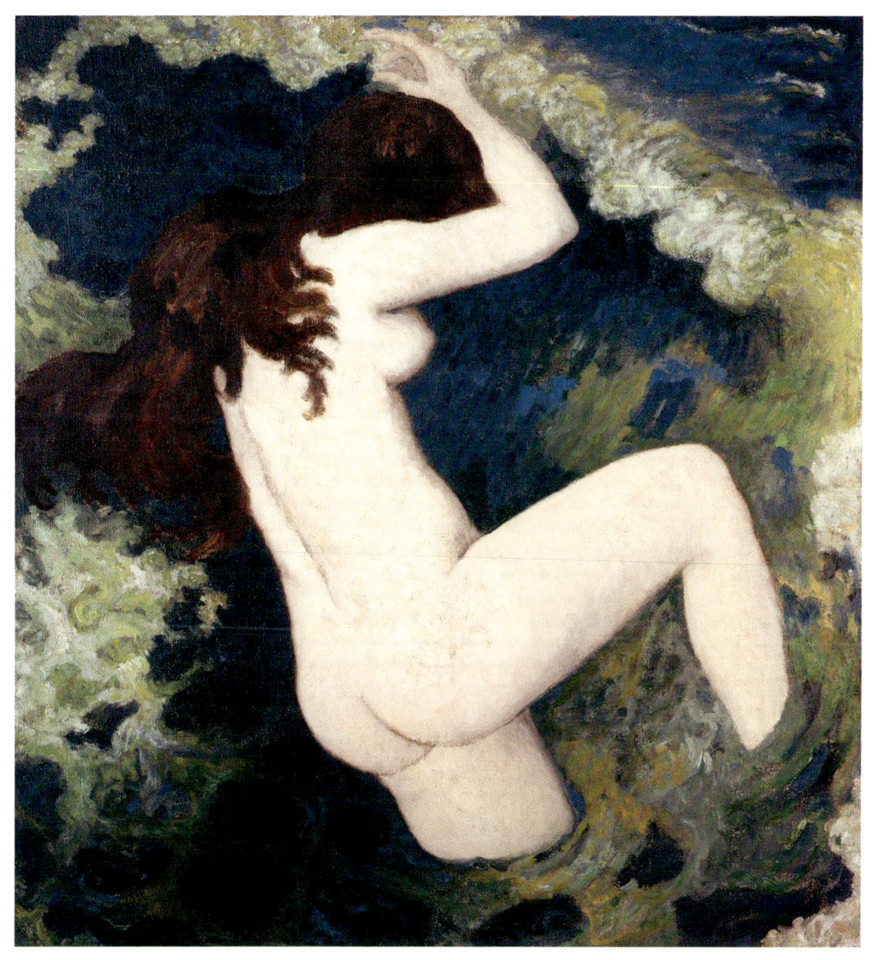
1

2

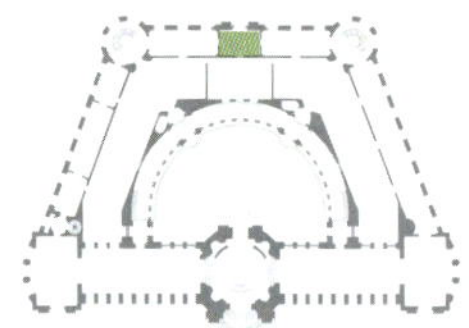

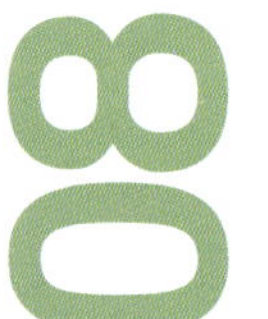

A step into modernity

1 | **PAUL CÉZANNE (1839-1906)** Three Bathers
1879-1882, oil on canvas - gift of Mr and Mrs Henri Matisse, 1936 - Inv. PPP02099

Cézanne made over two hundred paintings of male and female bathers, a subject he pursued from 1860 to 1906. The largest works occupied him for several years. As the compositions evolved, the emphasis moved from description to construction, with the figures becoming the components of a meticulously ordered pictorial assemblage. We know that the painter did not use studio models, preferring old sketches of nudes and the copies he had made of Titian and Rubens in the Louvre many years before.

Matisse considered the *Three Bathers* painting a landmark. He acquired it from Ambroise Vollard in 1899 and in a letter to the Petit Palais' director Raymond Escholier he spoke of its impact on his own explorations: "I've owned this canvas for thirty-seven years and know it fairly well - but not entirely, I hope. It has kept me going at critical points in my own adventure as an artist, and from it I have drawn my faith and perseverance."

Blonde, redhead and brunette: the Petit Palais' three female bathers are part of a pyramidal composition sharply outlined by the arch of the two trees. The use of a near-square format - repeated in several versions - enhances the impression of density and plenitude mentioned by that great admirer, Matisse. The first collectors to grasp the extent of the Cézanne revolution were themselves painters. Picasso was another admirer and collector of Cezanne *Bathers* and drew on them for his *Demoiselles d'Avignon* (New York, Museum of Modern Art).

2 | **ÉMILE-ANTOINE BOURDELLE (1861-1929)**
Penelope
Undated, bronze, after the plaster model, 1909
Original Petit Palais collection - Inv. PPS01524

3 | **MARY CASSATT (1844-1926), ANDRÉ METTHEY (1871-1920)** vase Children's Dance
c. 1905-1908, earthenware, gift of Ambroise Vollard, 1937
Inv. PPO01835

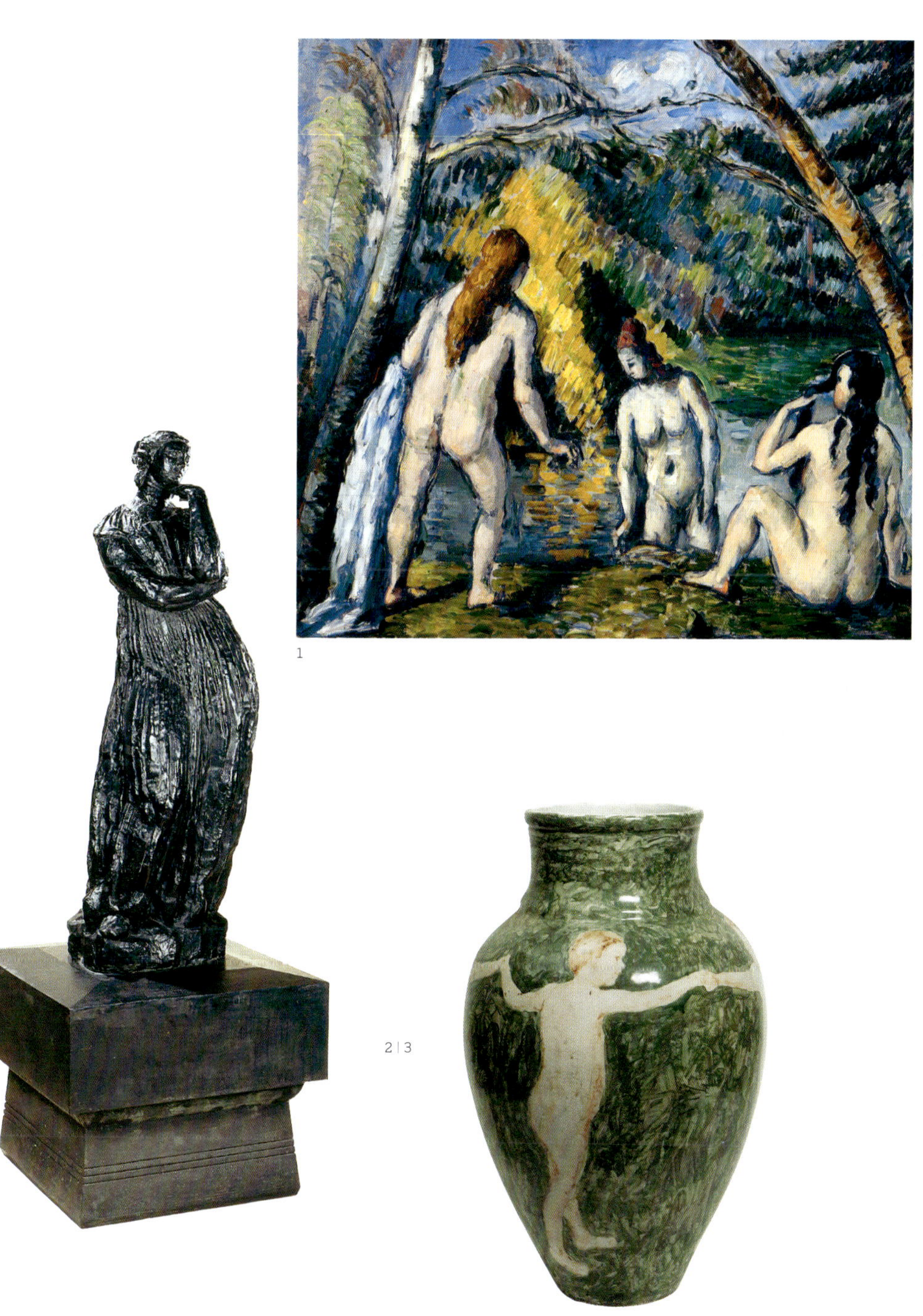

1

2 | 3

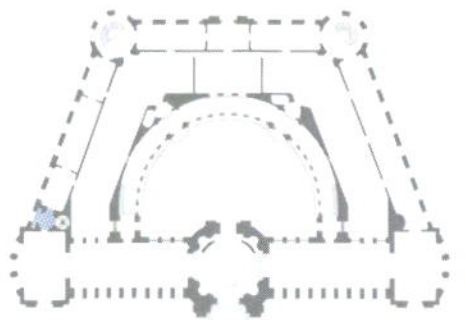

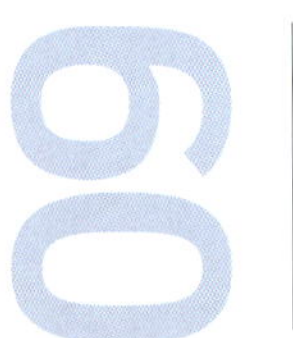

Bérain-style grotesques

In 1690-1720 grotesques, or arabesques, found new favour via the work of painters and decorators influenced by Jean Bérain (1640-1711). Designer of the king's private chambers, Bérain had borrowed this style of decoration from the Renaissance and it came to be named after him. Deriving from the Italian *grotte* ("subterranean ruins"), the grotesque was inspired by paintings in Nero's Domus Aurea, excavated in Rome.
The alternative term "arabesque" alludes to the use of complex tracery, reminiscent of Islamic art, to embellish panelling, sedan chairs, pottery and hangings, with a mix of little figures, animals, vases, colonnettes and foliage. The Gobelins and Beauvais tapestry workshops created their "Grotesques à fond jaune ou tabac d'Espagne", with their distinctive orange-brown ("Spanish tobacco") background, around 1690-1700 and several series of arabesque Months of the Year between 1694 and 1709.
Grotesques were also to be found in brass and tortoise-shell marquetry, notably by André-Charles Boulle (1642-1732). The metal and shell were glued together, cut with a jigsaw and then separated, offering two possibilities: brass figure inlaid on shell ground ("première partie") or the converse ("contrepartie"). The grotesques on Moustiers earthenware from Provence were produced using saturated cobalt blue on a pinkish-white ground, under a thick, glossy glaze.

1 | Sedan chair
Paris, c. 1700-1715, gilt, sculptured and painted wood - Tuck Donation, 1921 - Inv. OTUCK00059

The decoration of this elaborate yet functional object combines the arms of Duke Leopold I of Lorraine and his wife (1679-1729) Elisabeth-Charlotte d'Orléans (1676-1744), niece of Louis XIV. The sedan chair called attention to its proprietor in the street or in the vestibule of the townhouse he was visiting. The arabesques are reminiscent of certain works by ornamenter Sébastien Leclerc (1637-1714), with Fame, Victory, Mars and History hailing the military prowess of the dukes of Lorraine. The crowned cupids are a reminder of the couple's marriage in 1698. The chair was protected from the weather by a studded leather roof and panels either lacquered or coated with "vernis Martin" varnish.

2 | "Mazarin" kneehole desk
Cabinetmaker: **NICOLAS SAGEOT** - Mark: NICOLAS-SAGOET
Paris, c. 1700-1720, conifer wood, tortoiseshell and brass inlay, gilt bronze - Dutuit Bequest, 1902 - Inv. ODUT01500

3 | Dish
Moustiers, first half 18th century, earthenware - Dutuit Bequest, 1902 - Inv. ODUT01156

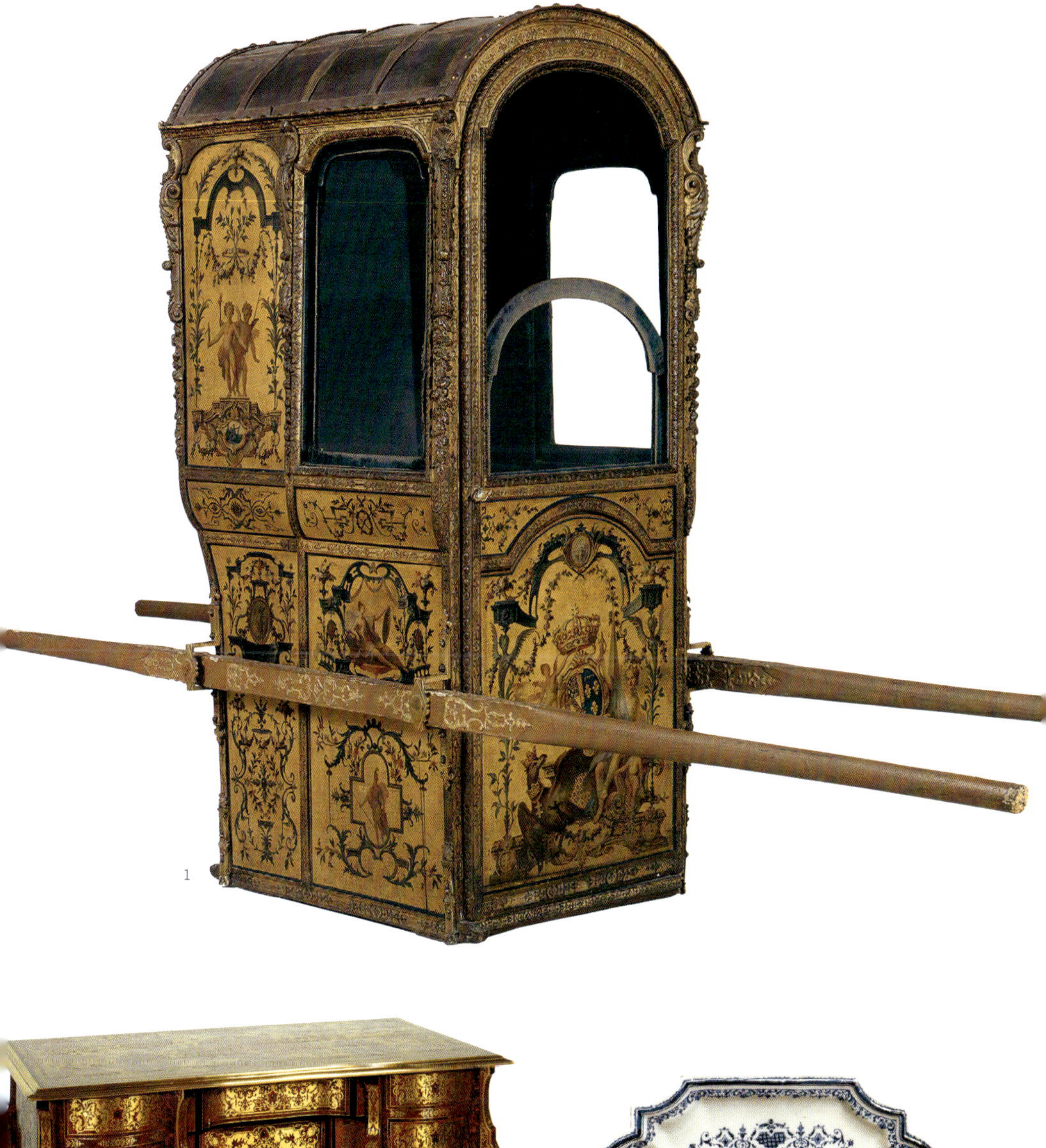

1

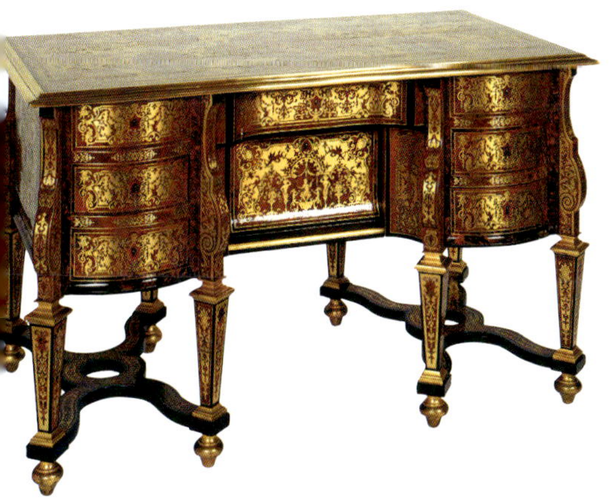

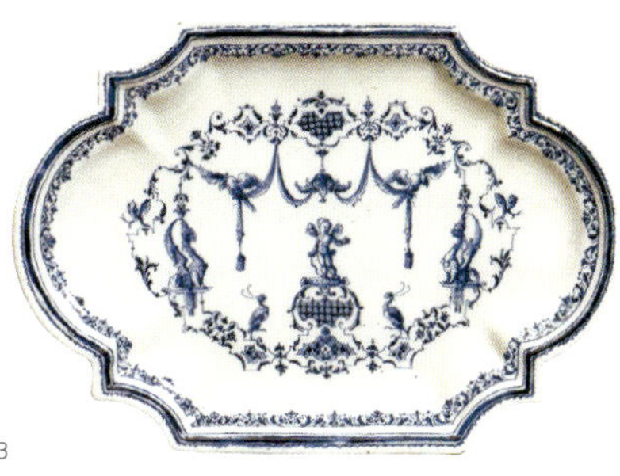

2 | 3

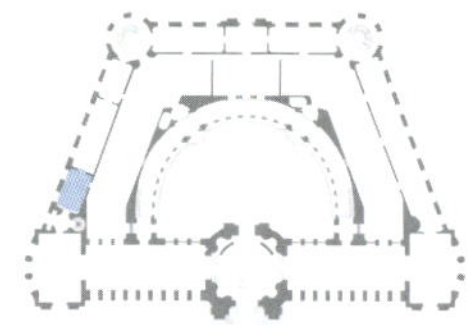

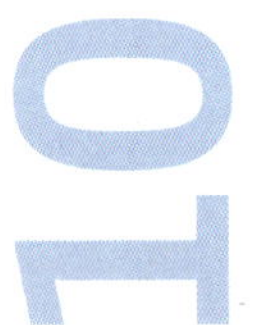

Rocaille furniture

The Regency of Philippe of Orléans (1715-1723) and the early part of the rule of Louis XV made up one of French furniture's golden ages, with the quest for elegance and comfort superbly served by the skill of the craftsmen of the time.
The body of the furniture is of oak or pine, and the veneer of imported woods. The marquetry offers geometrical or figurative decoration - bouquets, architecture, trophies - using woods of different colours, sometimes tinted. Frisage, a special marquetry technique, created diamond, rosette and butterfly wing patterns by reversing the grain of the wood on different panels. As a rule the marquetry has a frisage background using light-coloured woods - especially bloodwood and rosewood - with darker trim and foliated patterns of kingwood, palissander and amaranth.

1 | Secretaire: drawers behind sliding doors, writing table in drawer, cupboard
Attributed to the cabinetmaker **ROGER VAN DER CRUSE**, known as **LA CROIX** (1728-1794, qualified as master craftsman in 1755)
Paris, c. 1760, oak body, floral marquetry, rosewood and amaranth trim; gilt bronze fittings; brèche d'Alep marble - Acquired with income accruing from the Dutuit bequest, 1926 - Inv. ODUT01608

Roger Van der Cruse - the family name translates into French as "La Croix" - was long known only by the mysterious mark RVLC, cut into the wood of the piece by striking a stamp with a mallet. RVLC was at first keen on flower marquetry, later moving on to geometrical motifs: lattices, diamonds and overlapping circles. For his veneers he preferred such light-coloured woods as rose and lemon. He made several "secrétaires en armoire" with a slightly curved outline and sliding doors. This is doubtless one of the first models, with its main-drawer writing desk; later models were "à abattant" or "à cylindre". He worked for the cabinetmaker and dealer Pierre IV Migeon, supplier to the Court and Madame de Pompadour. Migeon pieces are slightly incurved and have geometrically decorated veneers of bloodwood, amaranth and kingwood, the butterfly wing pattern being frequent. Jacques Dubois also worked for Migeon, but in a more Rocaille spirit. His bronze appliqués are characteristic of his style.

2 | Bed table ("lying-in table")
Cabinetmaker **PIERRE IV MIGEON** (1701-1758)
Paris, c. 1750, pine frame, walnut surround; veneers of bloodwood, kingwood and amaranth; japan; gilt bronze and iron - Dutuit Bequest, 1902 - Inv. ODUT01520

3 | Writing table
Attributed to **JACQUES DUBOIS** (c. 1693-1763, qualified as master craftsman in 1742)
Paris, c. 1740-1760, rosewood and kingwood frisage marquetry, gilt bronze, black leather - Tuck Donation, 1921 - Inv. OTUCK00064

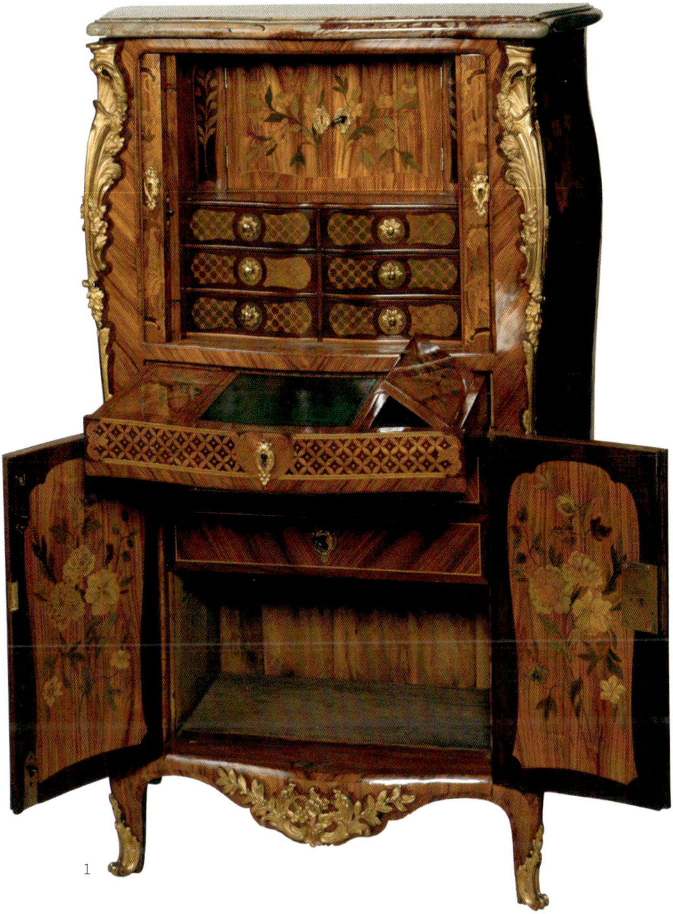

1

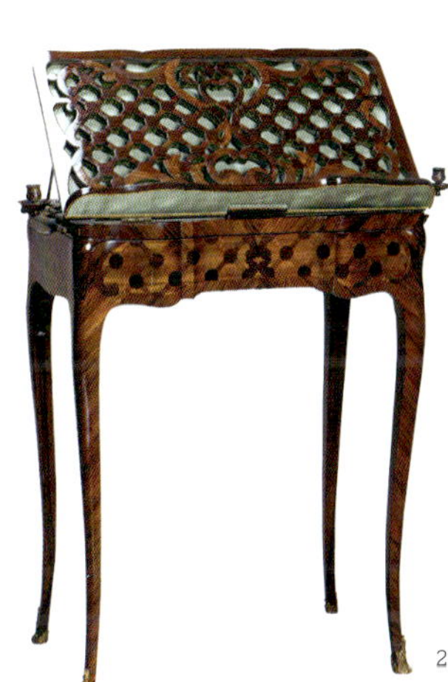

2

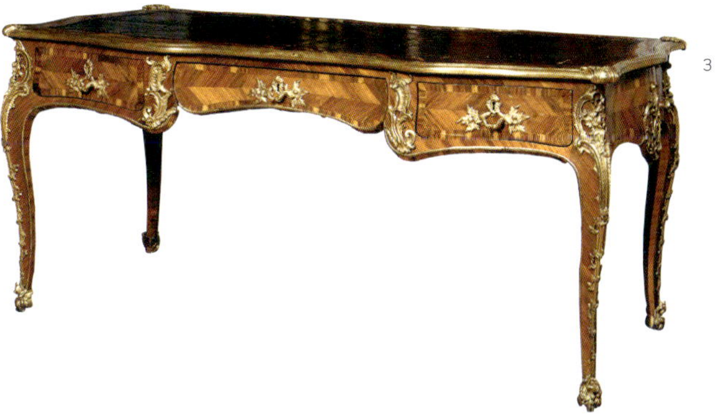

3

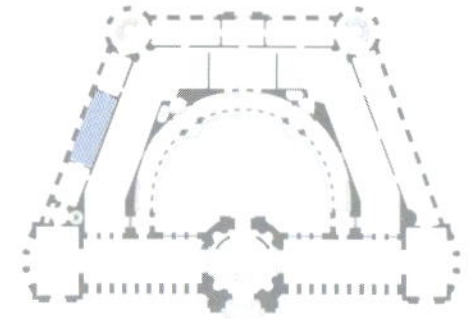

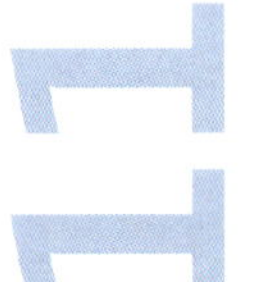

Tapestry

Tapestries are large woven panels used as wall decoration. The taut, parallel threads of the warp are interwoven with the threads of the weft, of various colours, so as to form patterns and images. Creating the tapestry on a loom, the weaver passes the weft back and forth with a shuttle, a bobbin with two pointed ends that must be changed with each new colour.
Established in 1662, the Royal Gobelins Tapestry Manufactory worked for the Crown, while the Beauvais workshops, opened in 1664, were furnishers to both the king and the wealthy. Other workshops in central France were known collectively as Aubusson, and also had a private clientele.
Much in demand for a time, exotic subjects - the story of the King of China in the late 17th century, for example - staged a brief comeback in 1767 with the "Russian Games" of Jean-Baptiste Le Prince, a former student of the painter François Boucher.
Made fashionable by Boucher, an idyllic vision of country life inspired pastoral scenes that lived on in tapestry-making until the end of the century via, for instance, cartoons produced by animal painter Jean-Baptiste Huet.
In the course of the 18th century the borders became imitations of gilded, sculpted frames or "alentours", surrounds that merged with the central scene in the form of garlands, scrolls and draperies. The wall hangings were increasingly accompanied by matching decoration for chairs.

1 | Transportation of Psyche by Zephyr to Cupid's Realm and Psyche Showing Her Sisters Her Gifts from Cupid – Tapestry from the Story of Psyche set (ill. following pages)
After cartoons by **FRANÇOIS BOUCHER** (1703-1770) - Beauvais, after 1741, wool and silk - Tuck Donation, 1921 - Inv. OTUCK00019
Under the artistic supervision of the painter Jean-Baptiste Oudry, the royal tapestry manufactory at Beauvais commissioned the greatest artists of the time - notably Boucher, but also Oudry himself - to provide the cartoons for six hangings.
The myth of Psyche was extremely popular in the 18th century. Jean van Orley and later his nephew Maximilien de Hase provided two versions for the Brussels manufactories; and in Paris, at the same time as Boucher was working on the Beauvais commission, the painter Natoire was completing a Cupid and Psyche series in the Princess de Soubise's oval drawing room.
Boucher's five contributions to the Story of Psyche were for impressive clients: the Spanish ambassador in 1744, the King of Sweden in 1745, the Infant Duke of Parma in 1748, Louis XV in 1758 and the King of Prussia in 1764.
The piece in the Petit Palais is a "rentrayage": two tapestries have been "invisibly mended" together.

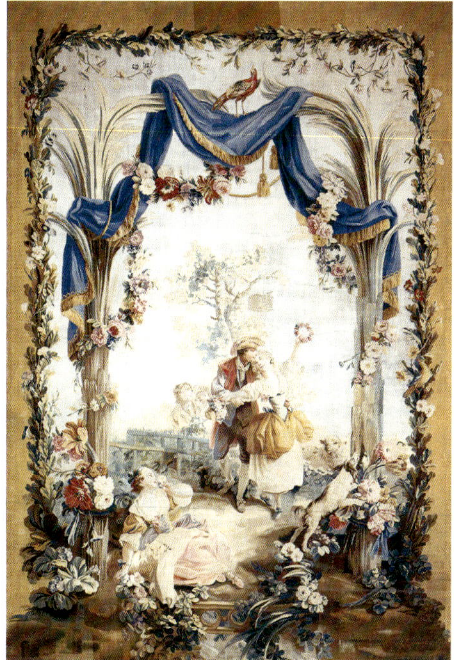

2 | The Dance
Tapestry from the set *Pastorales à draperies bleues et arabesques*
After cartoons by **JEAN-BAPTISTE HUET** (1745-1811)
Beauvais, c. 1780, wool and silk
Tuck Donation, 1921 - Inv. OTUCK00020

3 | The Return from the Hunt
Tapestry from the set of the History of the Emperor or King of China
After cartoons by **GUY-LOUIS VERNANSAL** (1648-1729), **JEAN-BAPTISTE BELIN DE FONTENAY** (1653-1715) and **JEAN-BAPTISTE MONNOYER** (1634-1699) - Beauvais, c. 1700, wool and silk - City of Paris Collection - Inv. PPO03526

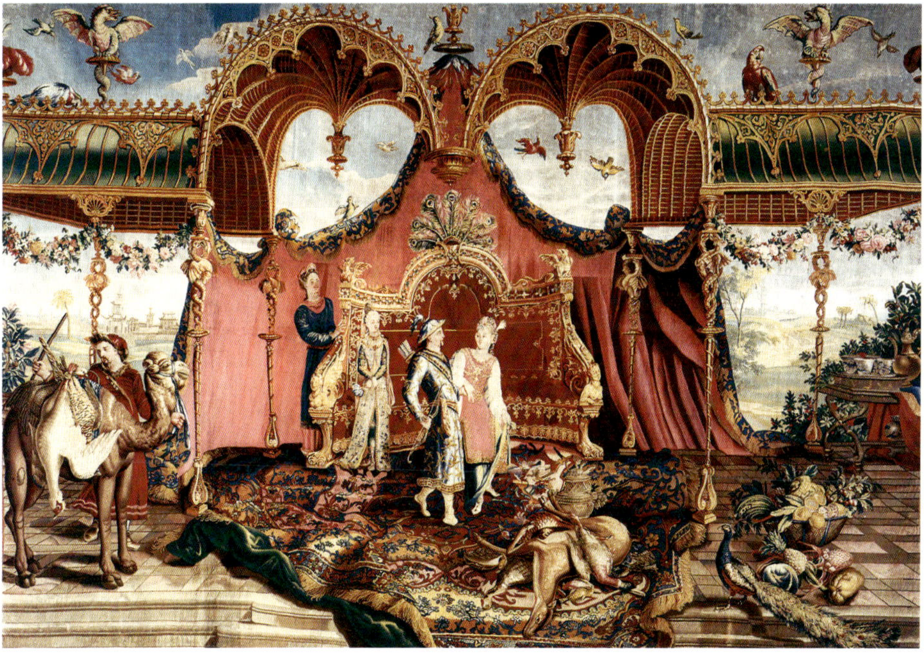

1 | Transportation of Psyche by Zephyr to Cupid's Realm and Psyche Showing Her Sisters Her Gifts from Cupid

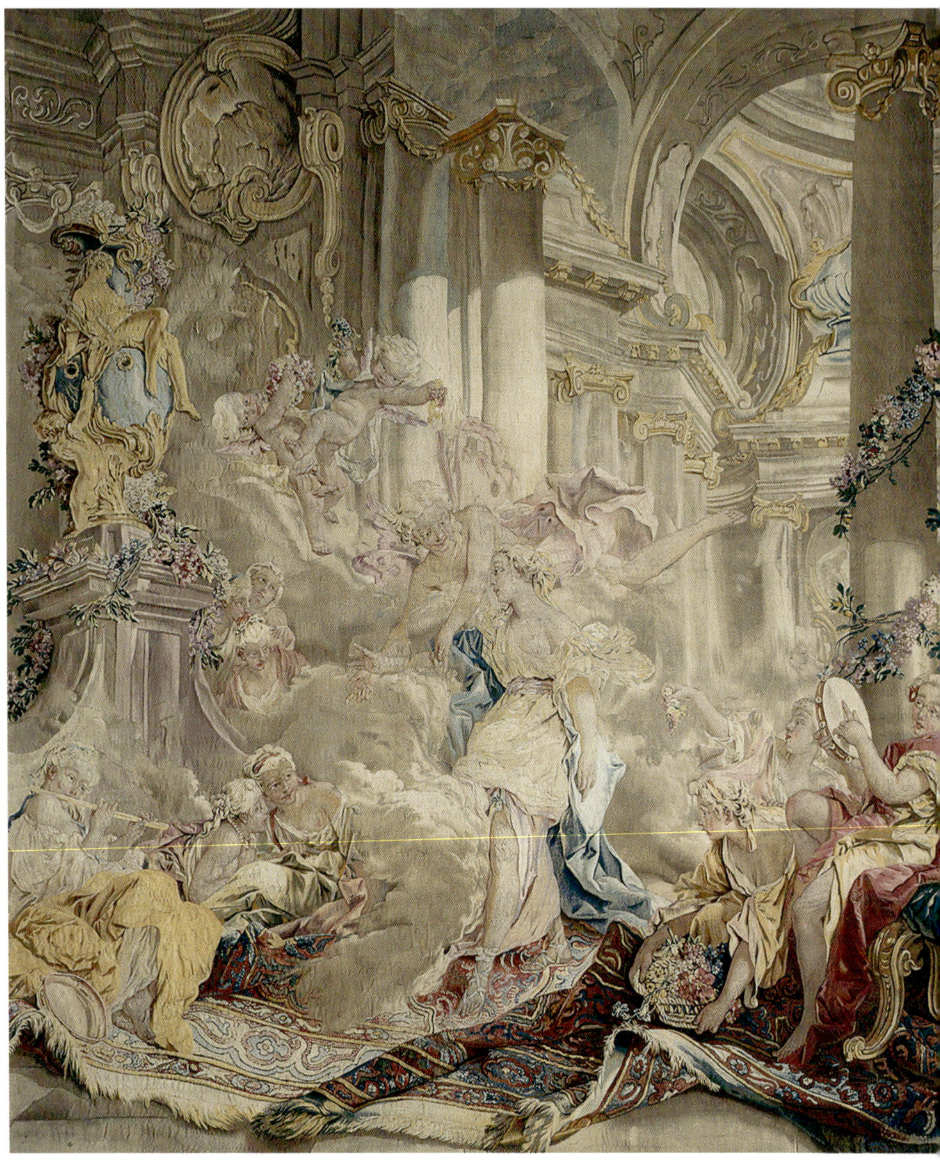

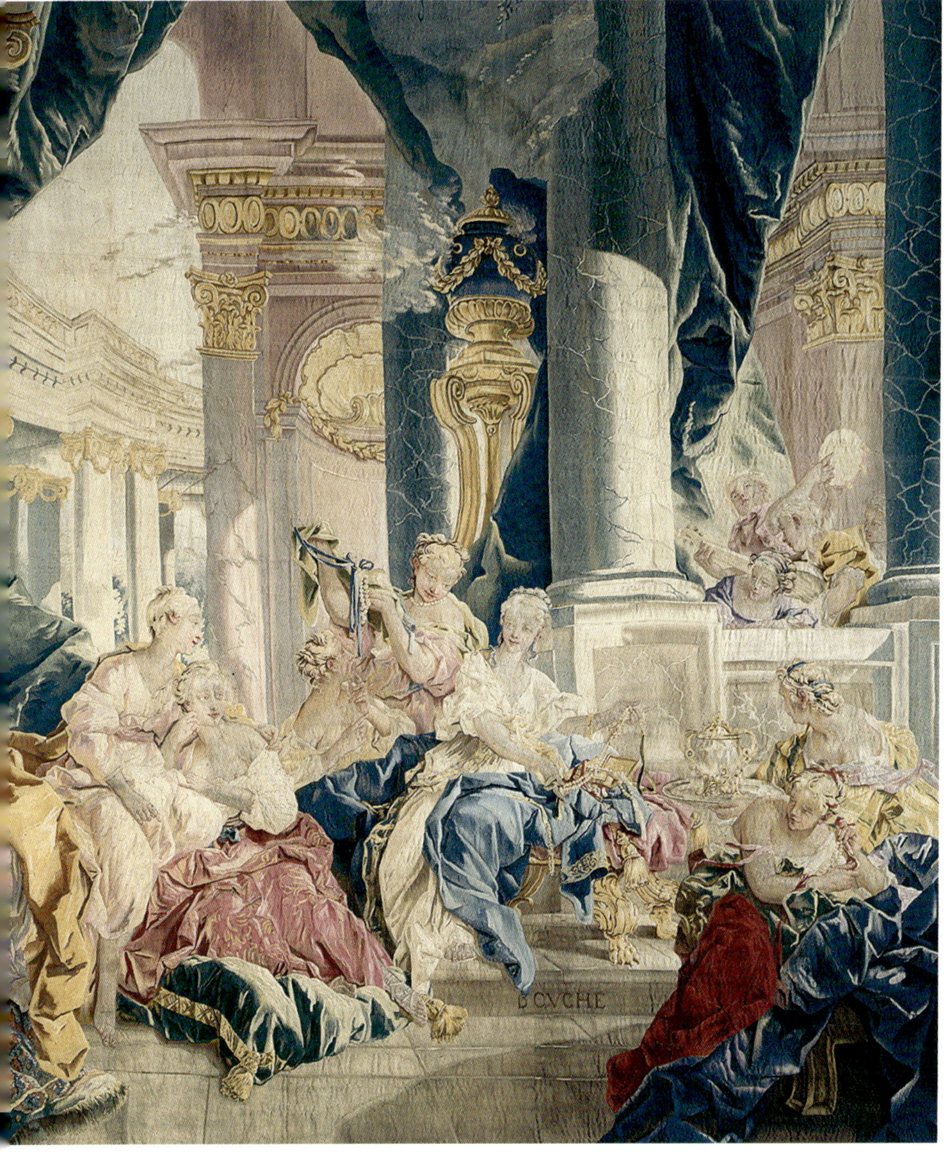
BOVCHE

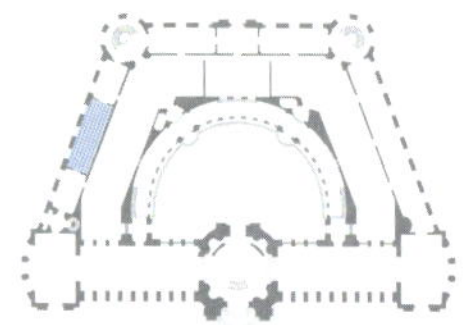

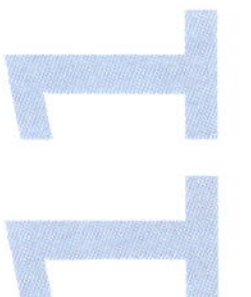

Sèvres porcelain

From 1753 onwards Louis XV oversaw the royal porcelain manufactory in Vincennes, whose pieces bore a "date letter" - a letter standing for a given year - surrounded by the interlaced L's that were the king's mark. In 1756 the workshops transferred to Sèvres.

The soft-paste Sèvres porcelain scratched easily, but was very handsome, with rich, clear colours. Unlike the hard-paste equivalent from China and Saxony, French soft-paste porcelain contained no fine, white kaolin: its clay was boosted with frit, an artificial mix that was vitrified then ground up.

One Sèvres speciality was the vividly coloured background. The most popular blues were the very dark lapis and, after 1753, celestial blue, a luminous turquoise much in demand in the 1760s and 1770s. Pink made its appearance in 1757.

Daring colour contrasts were not uncommon. From 1760 onwards a pink background was often accompanied by a strong apple green or lapis blue with gilt patterns. These patterns were "vermiculé", with random channels resembling worm tracks, or "caillouté" (pebbled). The use of gold was a prerogative of the royal manufactory.

1 | Rope festoon vase Attributed to the painter **JEAN-LOUIS MORIN** (1732-1787)
Sèvres, 1771, artificial soft-paste porcelain, celestial blue background, gilt, polychrome enamel -Tuck Donation, 1921 - Inv. OTUCK00110

The rope festoon vase appears in the Sèvres sales register in 1771 and the following years. Celestial blue was once again highly regarded, both for its vividness and its cost: it was made with aquamarine imported from Venice. One side bears a trophy of navigation instruments and aquatic plants, the other a port scene in the manner of Jean-Louis Morin, a painter of seascapes at the manufactory from 1754 to 1787.

A rope festoon vase was among the gifts given to the King of Sweden during his visit to France in 1771. English porcelain makers, Minton in particular, imitated this type of piece well into the 19th century.

2 | "Broc Roussel" ewer and basin
Sèvres, c. 1757-1765, artificial soft-paste porcelain, pink background, gilt, polychrome enamel
Tuck Donation, 1921 - Inv. OTUCK00098

3 | Cuvette Verdun flower vase
Painter: **XROUET-SECROIX**
Sèvres, 1760, artificial soft-paste porcelain, vermiculé pink background, gilt, polychrome enamel
Tuck Donation, 1921 - Inv. OTUCK00096

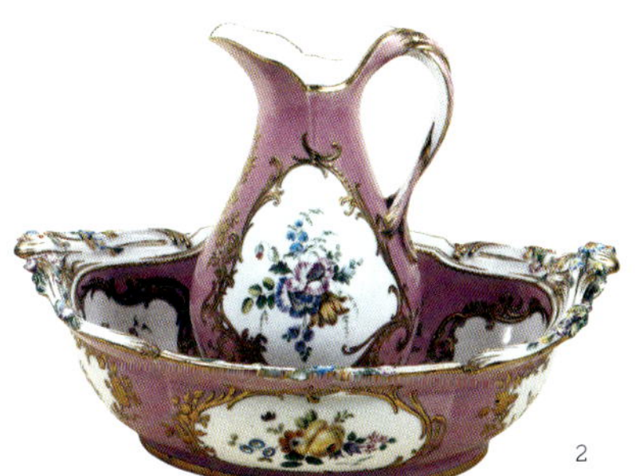

2

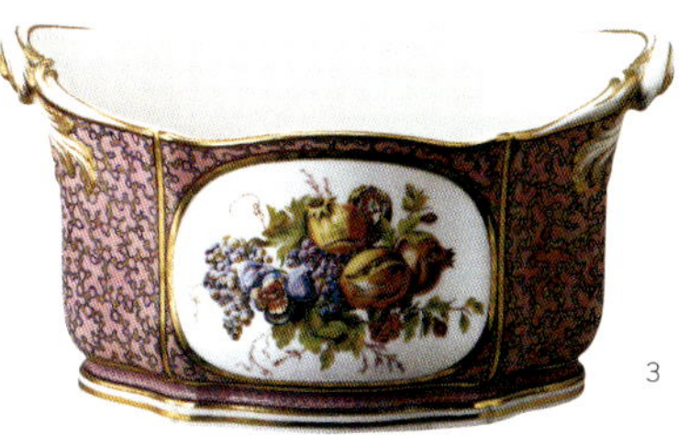

3

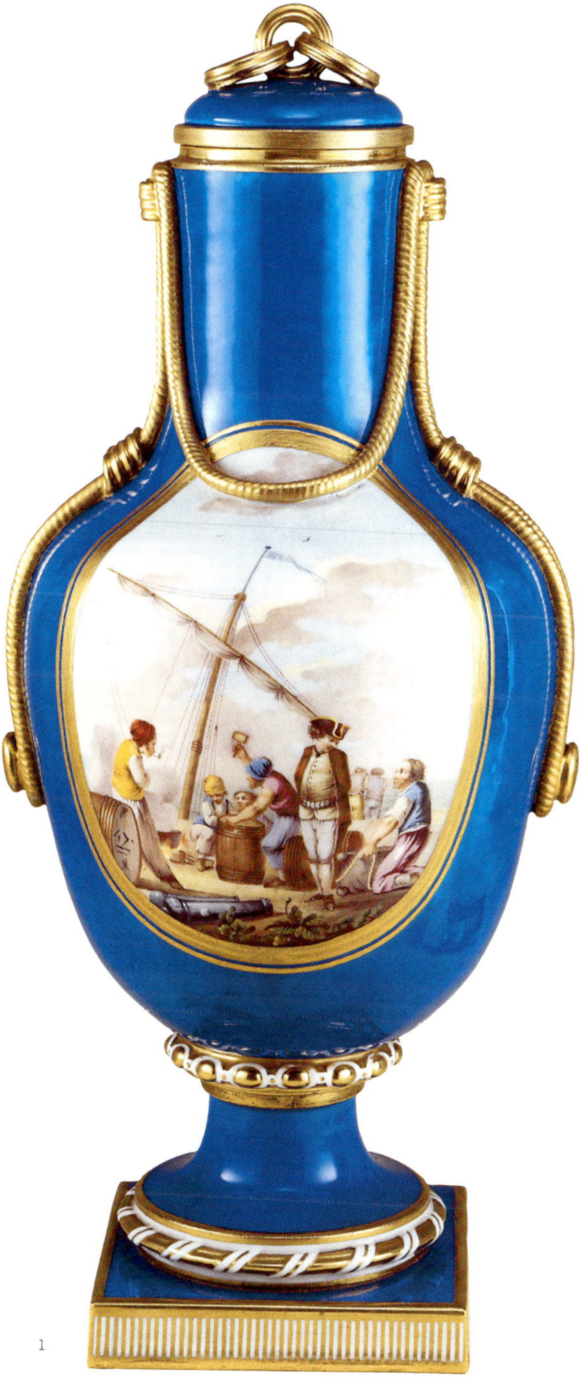

1

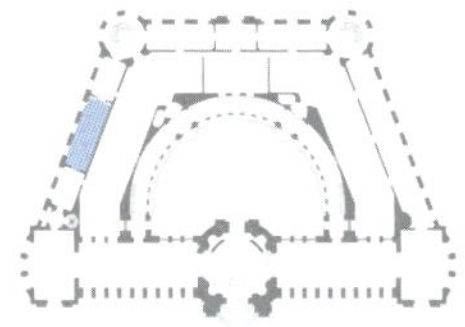

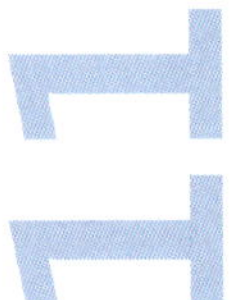

German porcelain

In 1708 Johann Friedrich Böttger (1682-1719), working in the service of Augustus II of Saxony, discovered the formula for hard-paste porcelain, a secret that had eluded Europeans for over a century. At the Meissen works, set up in 1710, Johann Gregorius Höroldt (1696-1775) used Chinese themes and port scenes to decorate porcelain ware.
Beginning in 1731, Johann Joachim Kändler (1706-1775) spent forty years turning out figurines reflecting current fashion: Chinese and Turkish themes, Commedia dell'Arte, pastoral subjects and animals. The misleadingly named "crinoline" pieces show ladies elegantly robed in enormous dresses decorated with stylised Indian flowers, the original inspiration actually being Japanese porcelain. The pug-dogs appearing in some pieces are a veiled reference to freemasonry. Highly typical of the Rocaille style, Kändler's work gradually supplanted that of the painting studios.

1 | Organ clock: The Monkey Concert
Clockmaker **JEAN MOISY** (1714-1782, , qualified as master craftsman in 1753)
Bronze fittings attributed to the goldsmith Jean-Claude Chambellan, known as Duplessis (c. 1690-1774)
Porcelain figurine models provided by Johann Joachim Kändler (1706-1775) and Peter Reinicke (1715-1768)
c. 1755-1760, gilt bronze, Vincennes soft-paste porcelain flowers, hard-paste Saxony porcelain figurines - Acquired with income accruing from the Dutuit Bequest, 1996 - Inv. ODUT01790

Porcelain of different kinds and from different sources was often used on the same piece: here, for example, soft-paste Vincennes flowers and hard-paste German figurines. At Vincennes the taste for flowers painted from the life peaked in 1751. The first monkey orchestras may have appeared at the Mennecy manufactory in France, after 1740, but they reached their apogee in Germany. At Meissen Johann Joachim Kändler created the model seen here in 1743, and reworked it in 1767 with his associate Peter Reinicke.
This exceptional piece was probably a private commission, perhaps via a leading *marchand-mercier* ("merchant of goods") like Lazare Duvaux, who sold a monkey orchestra to Madame de Pompadour in December 1753.

2 | Group: The Merchant of Hearts
Model by **JOHANN JOACHIM KÄNDLER** (1706-1775)
Meissen, c. 1738-1750, hard-paste porcelain, gilt, polychrome enamel - Tuck Donation, 1921 - Inv. OTUCK00129

3 | Figurine: Lady with Pug-dogs
Model by **JOHANN JOACHIM KÄNDLER** (1706-1775)
Meissen, c. 1744-1750, hard-paste porcelain, gilt, polychrome enamel - Tuck Donation, 1921 - Inv. OTUCK00127

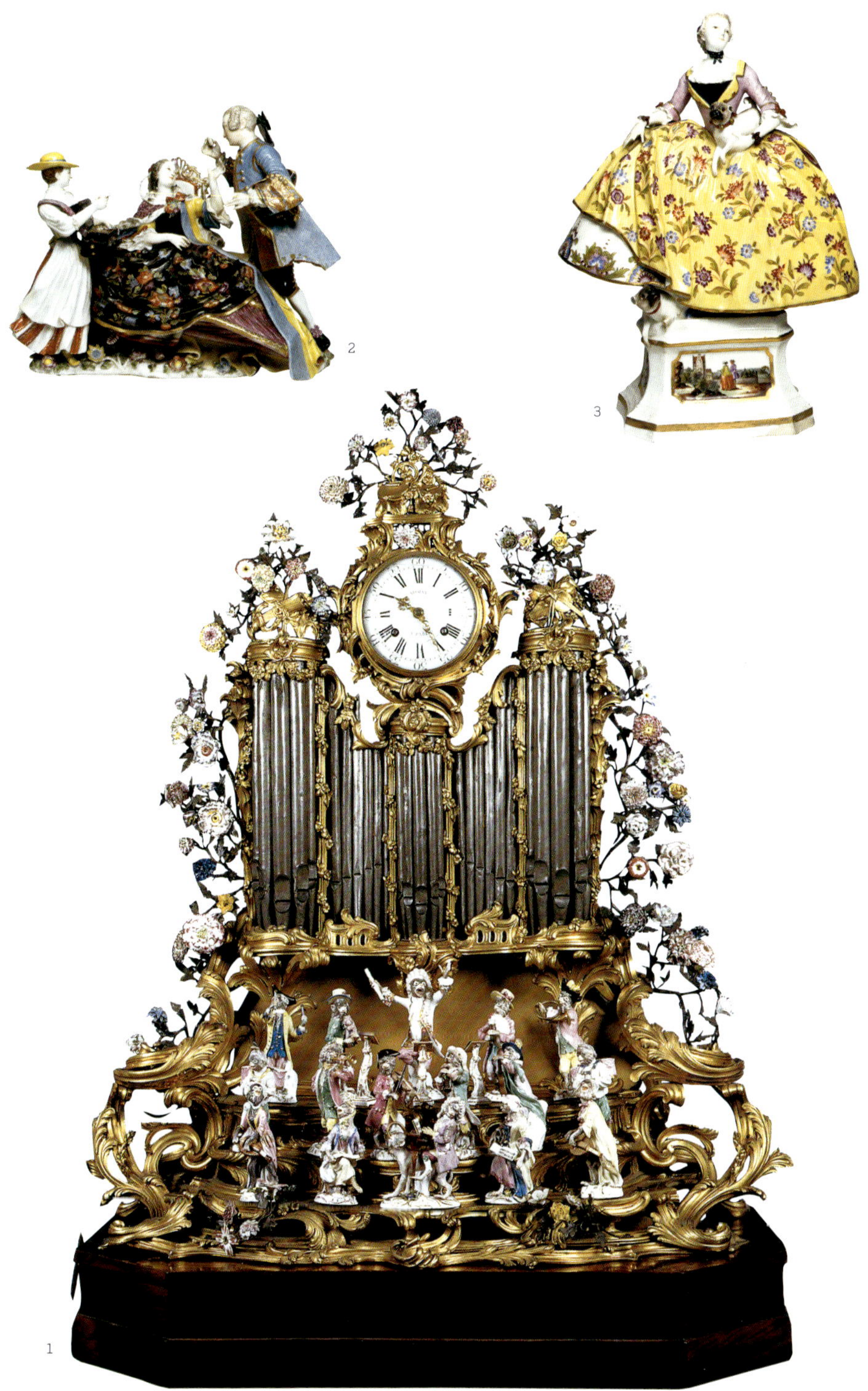

2

3

1

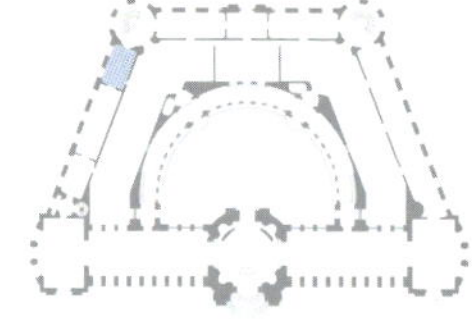

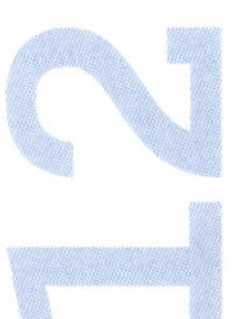

12 Transitional-style furniture and Louis XVI

In the closing years of the reign of Louis XV - from about 1760-1765 onwards - the convolutions of the Rocaille furniture so closely associated with the king's name began to evolve towards the more restrained straight lines of the Louis XVI style. Initially, however, the mix of the two trends resulted in the Transitional Style.

Especially characteristic of this period are the rectilinear pieces that conserve the earlier curved legs or feet. The frame of the breakfront chest of drawers seen here is all straight lines, but with a central projection of the facade. Less used than in the preceding period, the metal fittings illustrate the new decorative vocabulary: panels in the antique manner, pull rings and a cul de lampe with a vase motif.

Typical of the shift from Rocaille to Louis XVI, the work of cabinetmaker Pierre Roussel is well represented in the Petit Palais collection.

1 | "Bonheur du jour": combined writing table in drawer and toilet table
Workshop of cabinetmaker **RENÉ DUBOIS** (1737-1799)
Paris, c. 1775-1785, blue-lacquered wood decorated with beige monochrome cupids; gilt bronze - Dutuit Bequest, 1902 - Inv. ODUT01505

René Dubois (1737-1799) took over the workshop of his father Jacques (1693-1763), but abandoned Rocaille in favour of characteristic pieces with beige monochrome embellishments on green or blue backgrounds. The illustrations - port scenes, chinoiseries or trompe-l'oeil low reliefs of children at play - are reminiscent of the work of the engraver Louis-Félix de La Rue (1731-1765), himself influenced by the painter François Boucher (1703-1770).

The "bonheur du jour" is a lady's writing table with a raised back and a pull-out flap serving as a writing surface. Here the flap has been replaced by a drawer whose upper part pivots backwards to reveal a mirror and compartments for toilet articles.

2 | Chest of drawers
PIERRE I ROUSSEL (Paris 1723-1782, qualified as master craftsman in 1745)
Paris, c. 1765-1770, wood marquetry on green-tinted sycamore, bronze - Dutuit Bequest, 1902 - Inv. ODUT01507

3 | Secretaire "à abattant", low cupboard
Attributed to the workshop of **RENÉ DUBOIS** (1737-1799, qualified as master craftsman in 1755)
Paris, c. 1770-1780, lacquered wood with trompe-l'oeil monochrome decorations, rosewood marquetry, leather
Dutuit Bequest, 1902 - Inv. ODUT01506

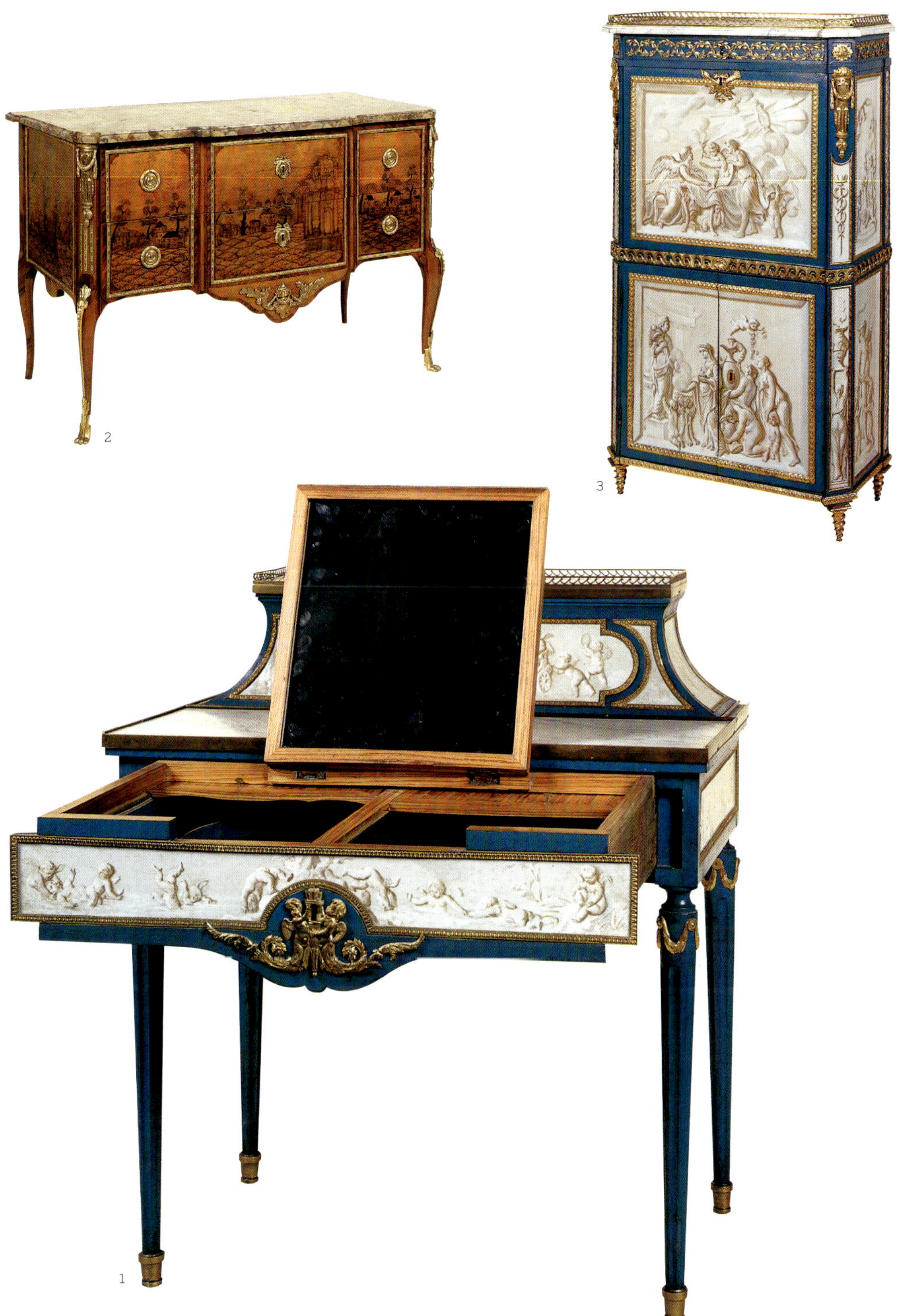

2

3

1

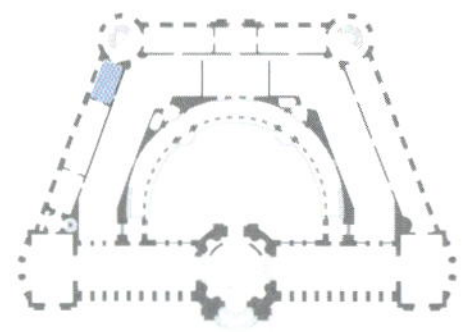

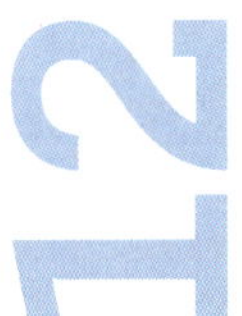

Responding to nature

The accession of Louis XVI in 1774 was in itself of no great significance in the history of painting, but between 1770-1789 the discipline underwent rapid, radical changes that endured until well after the Revolution. This shift in taste was marked by greater sensitivity and an austerity that helped shape the Neoclassical movement headed by Jacques-Louis David (1748-1825), one of whose early works can be seen in Room 12. Especially perceptible in the field of landscape, the new sensitivity is well illustrated by the oeuvre of Hubert Robert, one of the period's great landscape painters. During a long stay in Rome (1754-1765) early in his career, Robert built up a repertoire of ruins he drew on all his life - and which earned him the sobriquet of "Robert of the Ruins".

HUBERT ROBERT (1733-1790) Washerwomen in the Grounds of a Château

c. 1775, oil on canvas - Dutuit Bequest, 1902 - Inv. PDUT00881

This work shows that Hubert Robert was much more than just a painter of ruins, for it throws light on another of his activities: as "designer of the king's gardens", he worked especially at Versailles and Rambouillet. He was also much in demand among the nobility and the wealthy financiers of the time and created many famous gardens around Paris, notably that of Méréville, since destroyed. His work was characterised by a highly personal use of terraces, galleries, ponds, fountains, magnificent staircases and avenues offering a variety of views.

In *Washerwomen in the Grounds of a Château* Hubert Robert portrays a garden similar to those he himself created: nature taken in hand by art and craft to create a setting for human activity. This is the type of painting Proust had in mind in his two references to Robert in *Remembrance of Things Past*. Here Robert contrasts the majesty of the garden with the everyday character of a scene showing a pool being used for washing clothes. Superb proportions, delicately handled atmosphere and the charm of the good life are all conveyed with the flair that characterises his work: fluidity of touch, clarity of colour, silvery highlighting, skilful use of glazes and overlaid colours, play of light and a witty liveliness of execution.

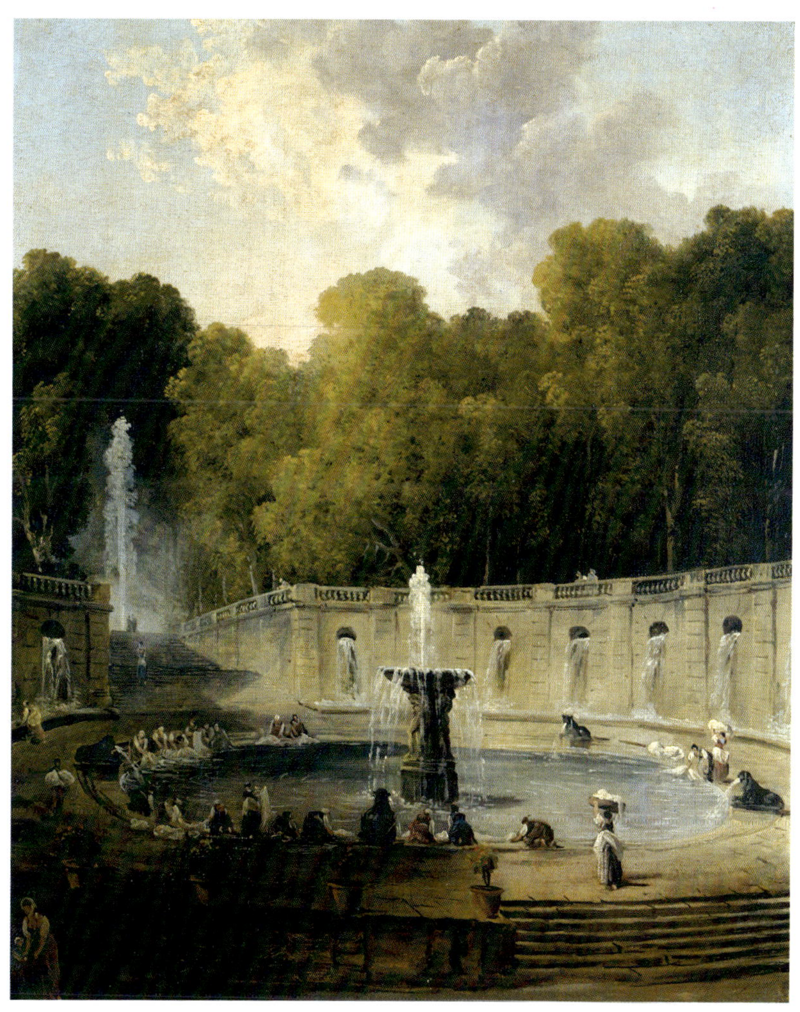

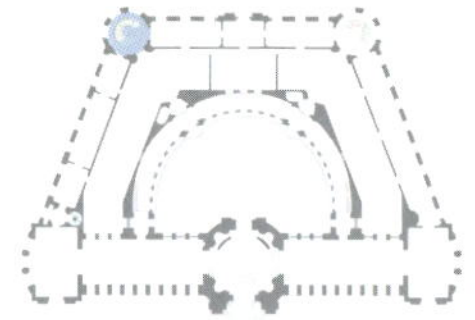

Decorative painting

The pictures in Room 13 illustrate two aspects of the decorative painting of the 18th century: the end-of-the-century landscapes with ruins and relics of antiquity typified by Hubert Robert (1733-1808) and the chinoiseries of Jean Pillement (1728-1808). The latter was one of the leading figures of the Chinoiserie movement, which had its golden age in the 18th century, spreading from France to the whole of Europe. Antoine Watteau (1684-1721) can be considered the main instigator of this new taste, which made China the pretext for the portrayal of an unreal, deliciously absurd world totally lacking in substance.
Born in Lyon, Pillement completed his apprenticeship in Paris. In 1743 he was working as a designer at the Gobelins tapestry works and would become official painter to Queen Marie-Antoinette. Principally a landscape painter, he also, early in his career, specialised in the drawing of chinoiseries. He travelled widely and this, together with engravings of his works, made his Chinese figures and flowers and his delicate intertwinings of vegetal and animal motifs an inspiration for the decorative art of his time, both in France and abroad. Pillement pursued the Rocaille style under Louis XVI and it could be said of him, as the Goncourt brothers so aptly said of Boucher, that he made "China one of the Rococo's provinces".

JEAN PILLEMENT (1728-1808) Chinoiserie

Between 1765-1767, oil on canvas - Gift of Count and Countess Andrzej Mniszech, 1901 - Inv. PPP00442

Pillement is thought to have painted this work during his stay in Warsaw in 1765-67, together with the three other panels in Room 13. They were commissioned by King Stanislas-Auguste Poniatowski, who appointed him First Court Painter.
Here he plays on the contrast between the Chinese figures and a decorative setting whose motifs - the medallion with its vegetal border and the overarching greenery - are very much in the occidental Rococo spirit. His pretty little medallion landscapes illustrate perfectly his skill in their effortless merging of flowers, leaves and real or totally whimsical branches, all in his personal "Chinese" style. The overall atmosphere of enchantment is heightened by the clarity, lightness and freshness of his colours.

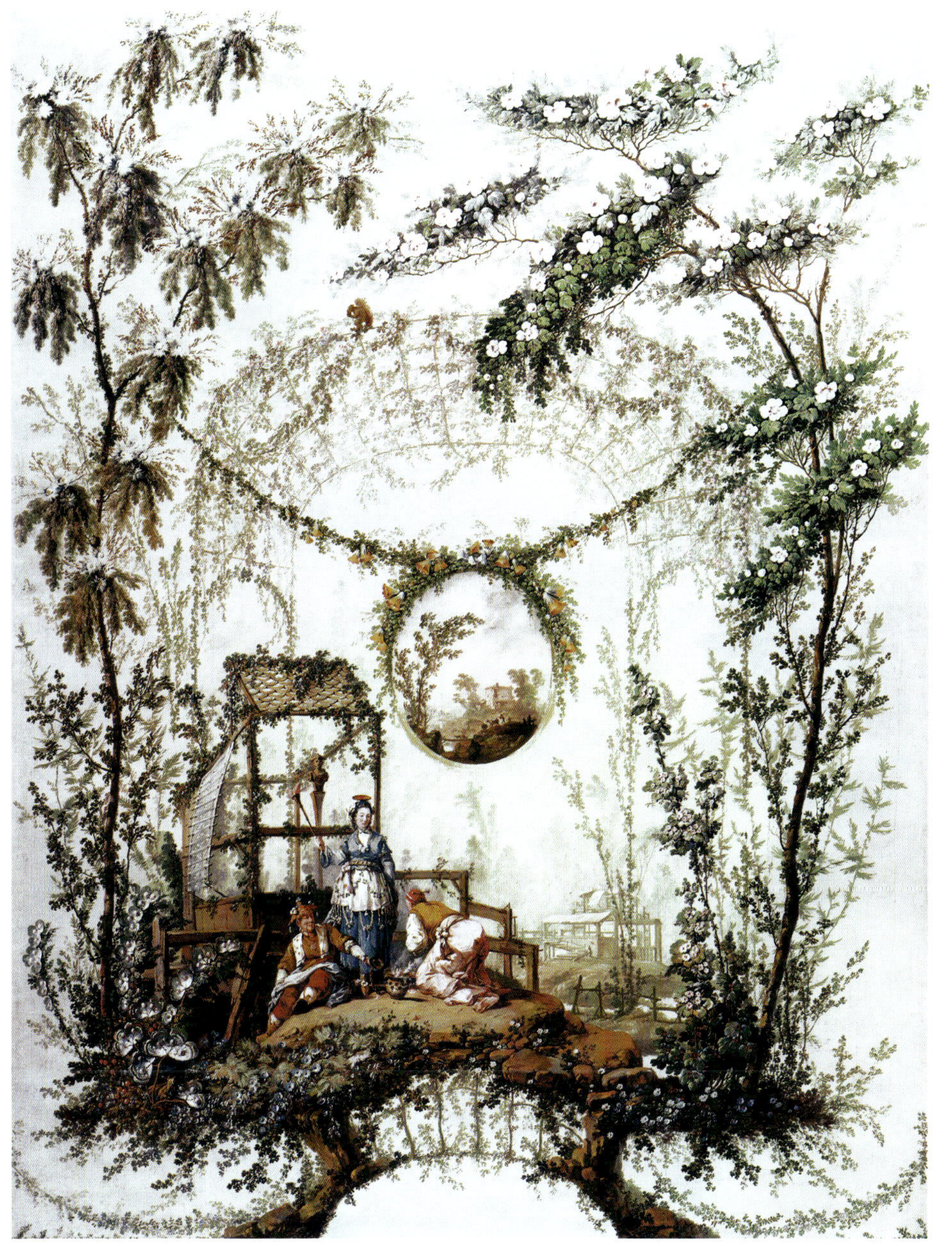

Ground floor

Rooms 14-40

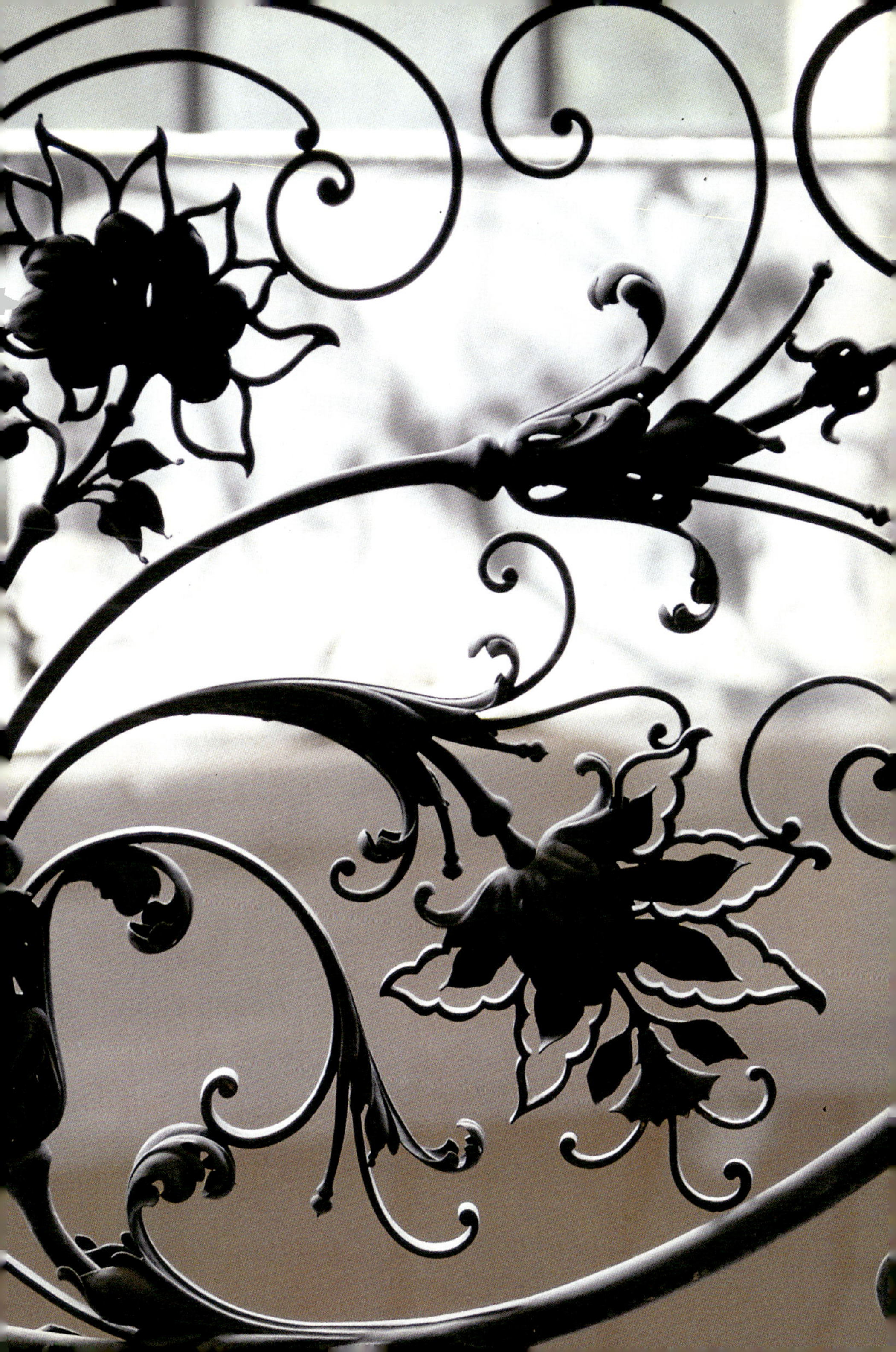

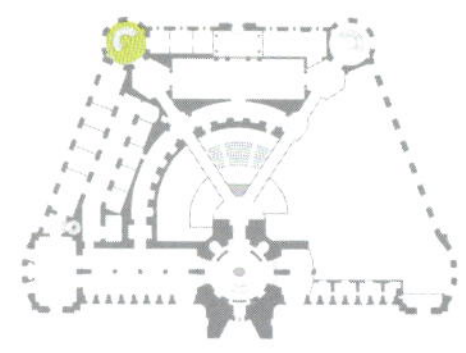

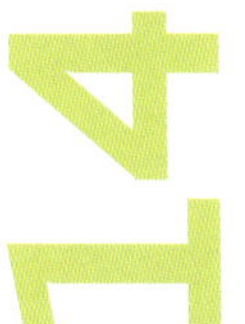

Creative torment

Born into a family of modest means in Valenciennes, Jean-Baptiste Carpeaux quickly became aware of his own genius and of the sheer hard work required to become famous. Despite his talent as a painter, he became the great sculptor of the Second Empire, using painting only for preliminary work and relaxation. After ten years' striving he won the Grand Prix de Rome and the works he sent back from Italy brought him his first Paris successes: *Young Fisherman with a Shell* (Salon of 1858) and *Ugolino* (Salon of 1861).

On his return to France he created part of the ornamentation for the Pavillon de Flore at the Tuileries. Appointed teacher of drawing for the Imperial Prince, Carpeaux left us a veritable gallery of portraits of his time. The years 1867-69 saw his fame at its peak: *The Dance*, a group of naked bacchantes at the entrance to the new Opera House, created an uproar.

His failing health and a growing paranoia fed by certain members of his circle made his last years a hell on earth. Revealing outlets for his unhappiness, the self-portraits he painted at this time show him increasingly haggard.

The collapse of the Second Empire in 1870 cost him many clients, and he died in 1875. Paradoxically it is the joie de vivre of his sculpture that symbolises even today the reign of Napoleon III.

1 | **JEAN-BAPTISTE CARPEAUX (1827-1875)** Ugolino

Patinated plaster, 1862(?) - Gift of Louise Clément-Carpeaux, daughter of the artist, 1938 - Inv. PPS01573

Completed in 1861, *Ugolino* marks the culmination of Carpeaux's period of study at the Académie de France in Rome. This is already the work of a master. The subject is taken from Dante's *Divine Comedy*: Ugolino, the tyrannical ruler of Pisa, is shown in chains in the Tower of Hunger with his children. Seeing him biting his hands in despair, his children, as an act of filial piety, ask him to consume them instead. The work makes no secret of its borrowing from the classical models Carpeaux had seen in Italy: the intertwining of the bodies is inspired by the Belvedere Laocoon, with Ugolino's musculature and expression reminiscent of Michelangelo. The swirl and skill of the composition are the hallmark of Carpeaux's groups. It is said that he personally applied the patina to this plaster so as to prepare the appearance of the work before it was cast as a state commission.

2 | **JEAN-BAPTISTE CARPEAUX** Self-portrait

1874, oil on canvas

Gift of Louise Clément-Carpeaux, daughter of the artist, 1938 - Inv. PPP02075

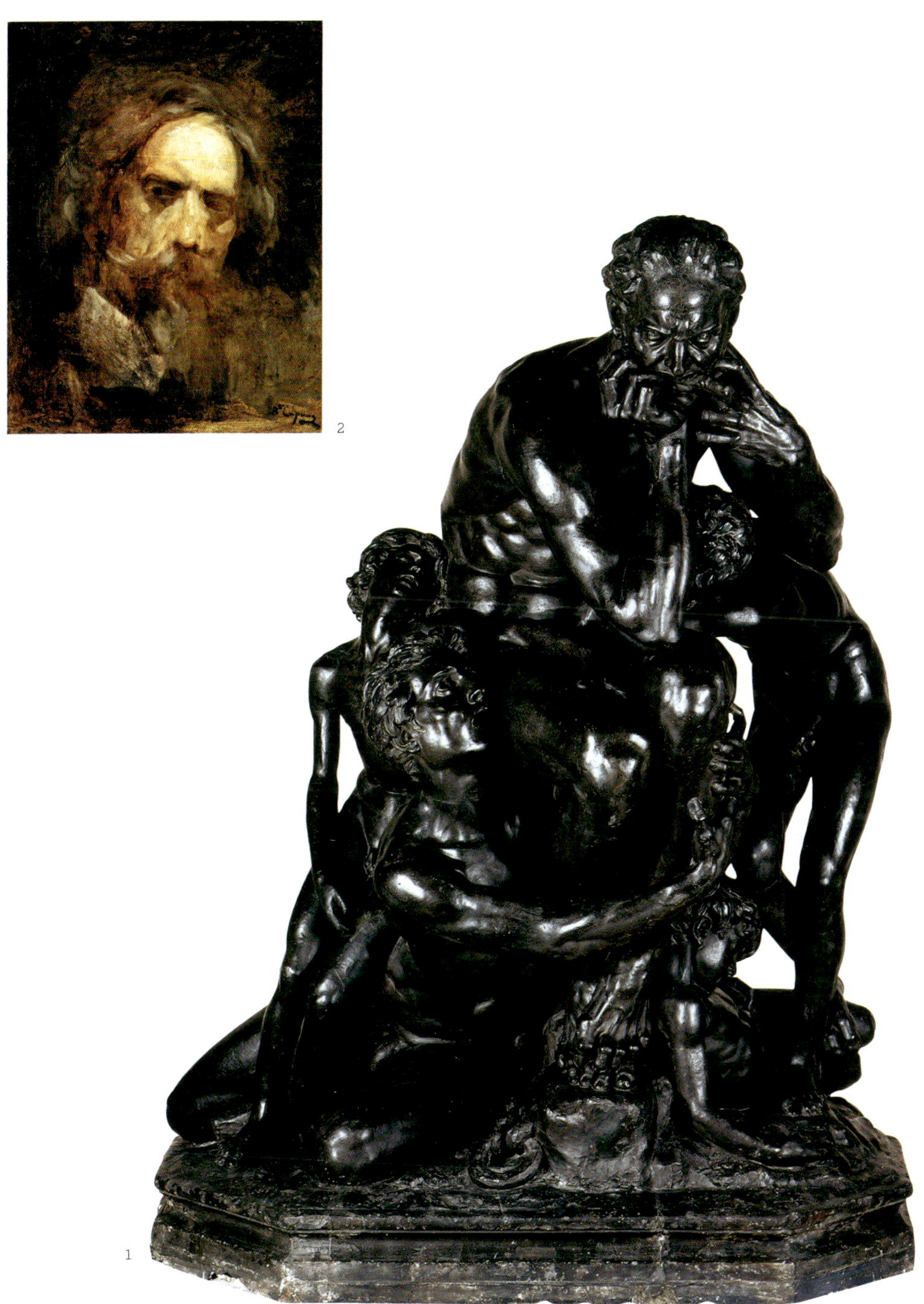

2

1

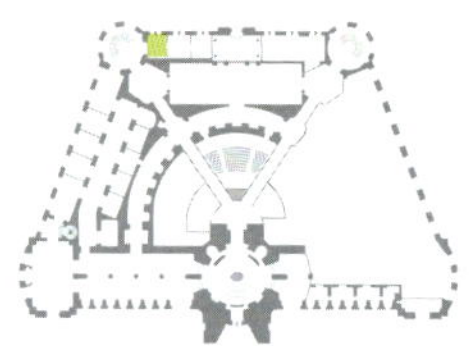

The Mosselman Family

1 | **ALFRED DE DREUX (1810-1860)** The Mosselman Family
1848, oil on canvas - Acquired with income accruing from the Dutuit bequest, 1970 - Inv. PDUT01178

As a young man Alfred Dedreux trained under Géricault, whose love of horses he shared and whose romantic spirit he inherited. He met with artistic success from the very first, from 1831 until his last Salon in 1859. A court painter under the July Monarchy, he opted for the more aristocratic De Dreux form of his name, accompanied Louis-Philippe on a state visit to London in 1844 and later followed the Orléans household into exile in England.

Alfred Mosselman (1810-69), brother-in-law of the Belgian ambassador in France, was among his illustrious clients. De Dreux decorated his Paris residence with hunting scenes. The Mosselman fortune came from its mines and zinc foundries in Belgium.

Executed for the 1848 Salon, just before the period of exile, this large painting celebrates a certain lifestyle in its portrait of the society drive on the Champs-Elysées. The family stands around Eugénie Mosselman as she sits in a "petit duc" carriage drawn by Shetland ponies. The elegantly simple outdoor costumes are painted in a pinkish-white shade over which plays the contrasting light of the clearing.

In this highly accomplished work De Dreux shows himself an clever portraitist, but above all an authentic animal painter: the horses and dogs seem to be playing an active part in the scene. With its distant prospect broken up by trees and luxuriant vegetation, the setting suggests the clearings of Barbizon and the verdant landscapes of English painting.

2 | **JEAN-BAPTISTE CARPEAUX (1827-1875)** Mademoiselle Fiocre
Plaster bust, c. 1870
Gift of Louise Clément-Carpeaux, 1938 - Inv. PPS01536

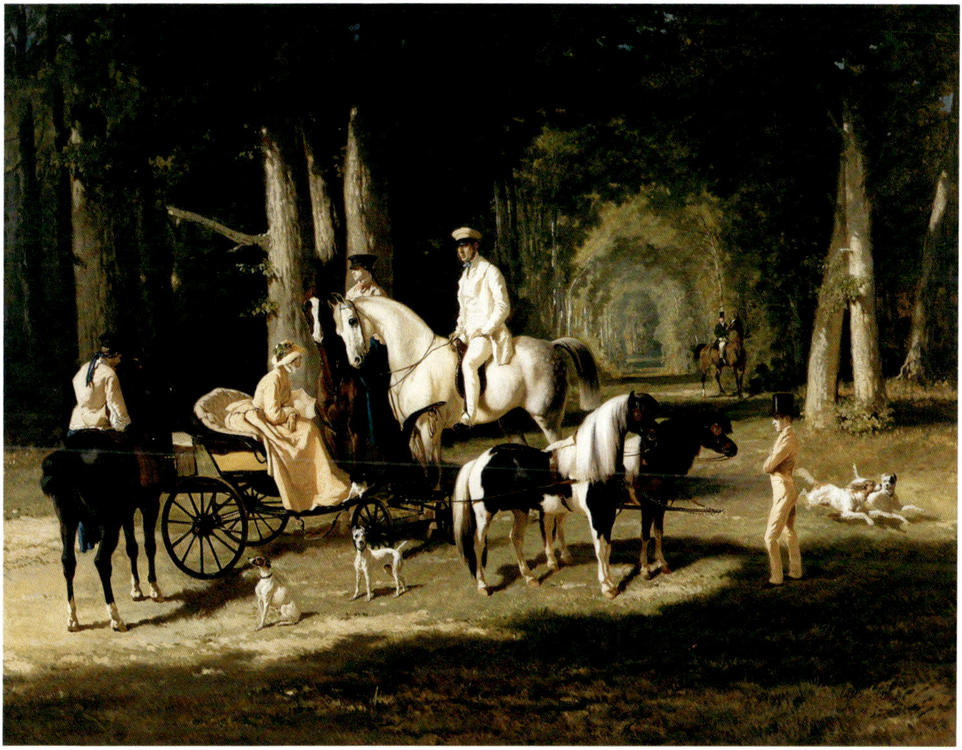

1

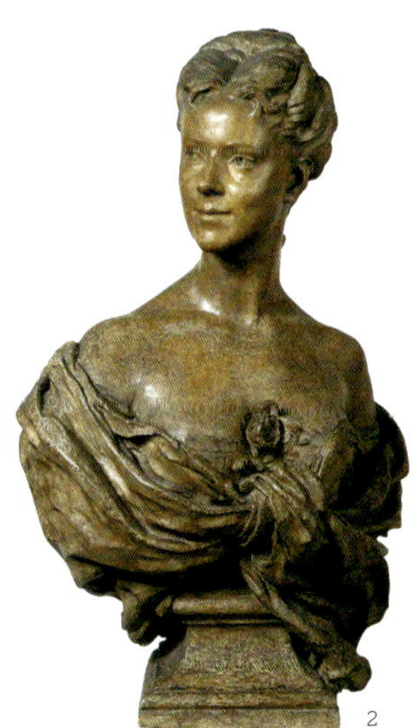

2

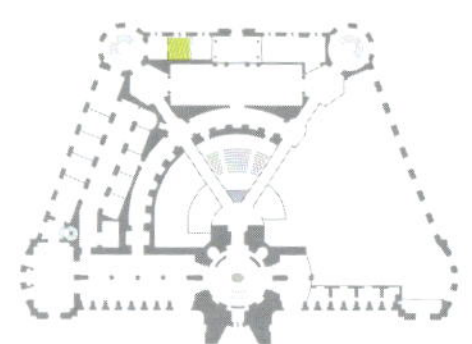

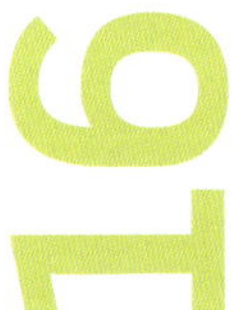

16 The last of the dandies

Particularly well represented in the Petit Palais collection, the painted portrait became enormously popular in the mid-19th century. The economic rise of the middle classes increased the clientele, while the portrait itself evolved towards greater simplicity and truthfulness. As resolute chroniclers of the times, the Realist artists opted for the *genre portrait* with its emphasis less on the person than on a social type and a lifestyle. Thus it was that Daumier explored the life of the "little people" of Paris in all their humanity. Courbet, Millet and Ribot drew on an intimate knowledge of the rural world to which their families belonged. In the 1870s it was sculpture's turn to cut free of the academic portrait in search of a more psychological and personal interpretation of the subject - a trend that became more marked late in the century in the work of Rodin and Camille Claudel.

ÉDOUARD MANET (1832-1883) Portrait of Théodore Duret

1868, oil on canvas - Gift of Théodore Duret, 1908 - Inv. PPP00485

This portrait was painted on Manet's return from a trip to Spain, during which he had met Théodore Duret (1838-1929).Described by Manet as "the last of the dandies", this cognac merchant, art lover and great traveller remained a firm friend of the painter, of whom he wrote a biography published in 1926. Directly influenced by the art of Velázquez, Manet here sets his model in an abstract space, opting for a thick, forthright brushstroke despite the smallness of the format. The still life placed in the right-hand corner brings a bright touch of colour to the dark harmony of the painting.

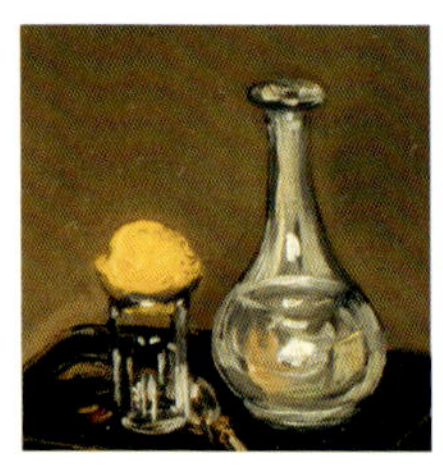

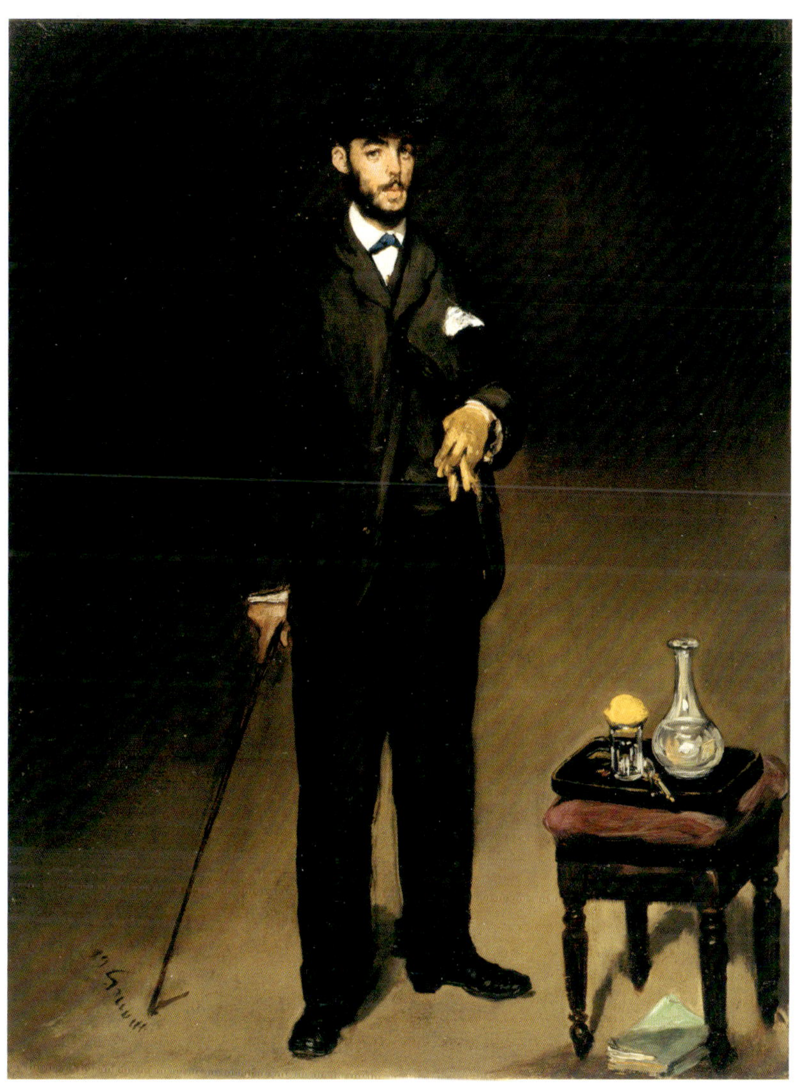

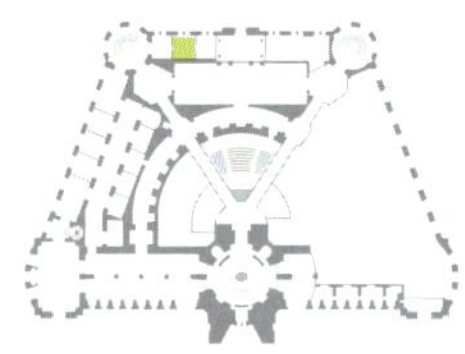

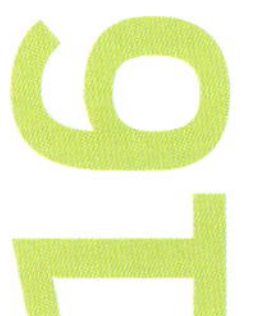

Roman Odalisque

JEAN-BAPTISTE-CAMILLE COROT (1796-1875) Roman Odalisque

1843, oil on canvas-backed paper - Purchased 1934 - Inv. PDUT01158

Marietta was painted during Corot's third and last stay in Rome, in 1843. The term "odalisque" was first applied to this study of a reclining woman in the catalogue for the posthumous sale of the artist's studio in 1875. There is nothing Turkish about the model, whose first name is carefully noted in the upper left part of the composition, yet the twist of the body, with its stress on the curve of the breast and the hip, does recall the *odalisques* of Ingres. Here Corot achieves a harmonious balance between the echo of the classical example and the simplicity of modern life. Marietta's face is treated with the directness of a true portrait and the way she looks straight at the painter gives her a very concrete presence.

Corot was proud of this nude and especially of the subtly accurate distinction between the values of skin and sheet. The Italianate interior is handled with real economy as a purely pictorial space, depthless and reduced to three horizontal strips. This starkness is part of the unique character of a study testifying to the diversity of the artist's ways of working.

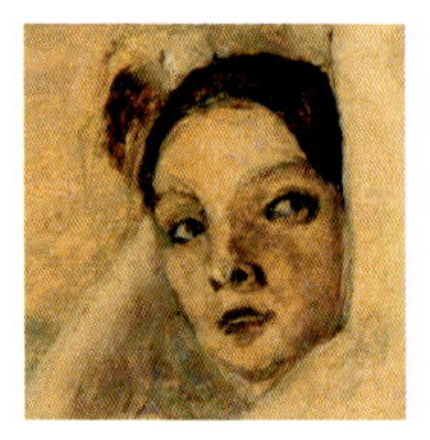

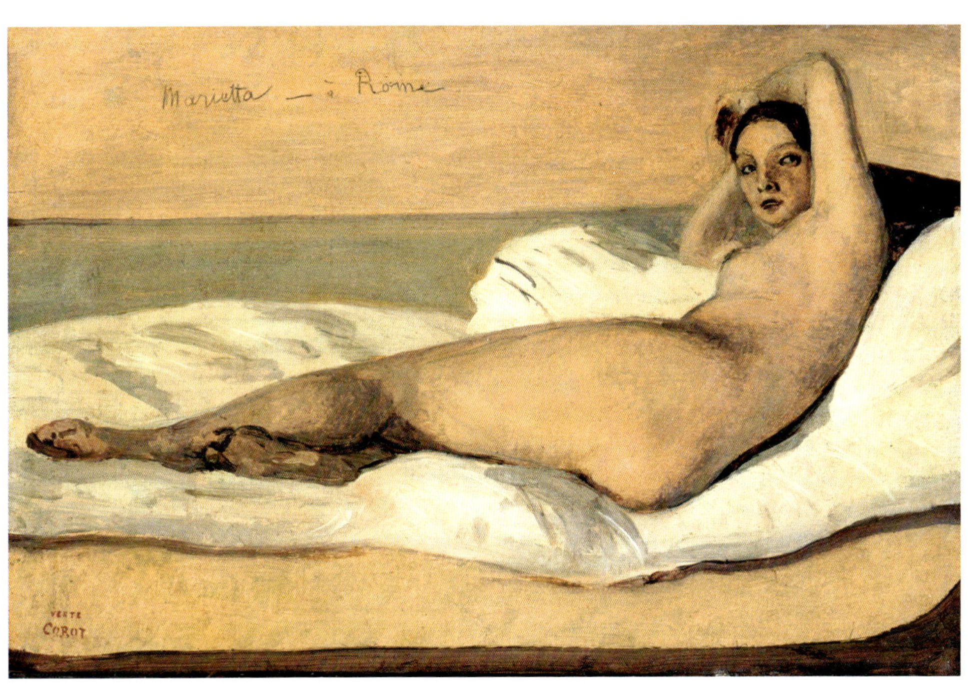
Marietta — à Rome
VENTE
COROT

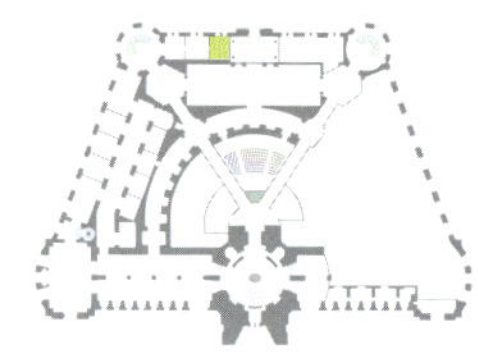

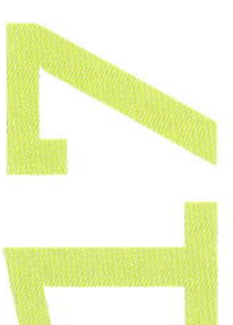

17 Intimate portraits

1 | **LOUIS-LÉOPOLD BOILLY (1761-1845)** Portrait of Miss Athénaïs d'Albenas
1807, oil on canvas - Acquired with income accruing from the Dutuit bequest, 1999 - Inv. PDUT01983

This is the graceful, minutely detailed portrait of the daughter of Jean-Joseph d'Albenas, who made a name for himself during the American war of Independence, before settling in Toulouse. In accepting the commission Boilly acknowledged the period's growing interest in childhood.

Although influenced by the English fashion for portraits in a landscape setting, the work hews to the rules of Classicism: the landscape is a simple backdrop of the kind later used by early studio photographers. With its pretty, clouded sky and succession of light and dark planes, it leads the eye from the hill to the little bridge and the waterfall in the foreground.

Athénaïs is dressed like an adult in a high-waisted, light-coloured dress with puffed sleeves; only the shortening of the ankle-length hem betrays its adaptation to her age. The light slanting in from above is different from that of the landscape, and in fact matches the lighting in the studio where the girl posed.

2 | **VICTOR-LOUIS MOTTEZ (1809-1897)** Portrait of Julie Mottez
1842, oil on canvas - Gift of Henri Mottez, 1906 - Inv. PPP00440

Mottez is considered one of Ingres' best pupils. Although inclined towards religious painting because of his Christian beliefs and affection for the mural, he was a much sought-after portraitist. The influence of his master is evident in this portrait of his wife, Julie Odevaere (1805-1845): we note the perfect drawing of the bejewelled hands, the attention to the texture of the fabrics, the expressionlessness of a face marked only by a faint smile. The emphasis on austere elegance is very much in line with the middle class fashion of the 1840s.

3 | **BARON JEAN-ANTOINE GROS (1771-1835)**
Portrait of Jacques Amalric
1804, oil on canvas
Acquired with income accruing from the Dutuit bequest, 1982 - Inv. PDUT01303

1

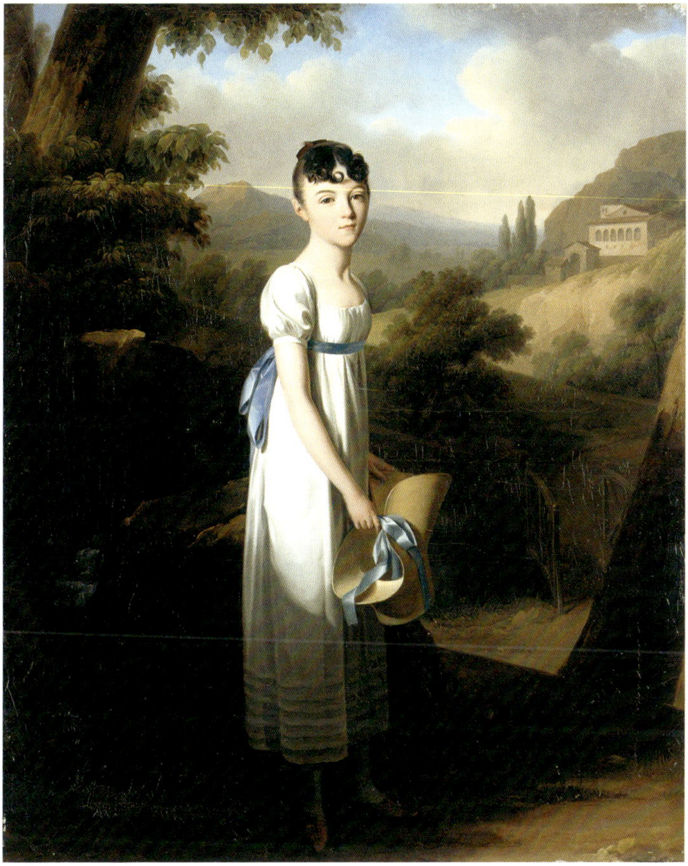

2 | 3

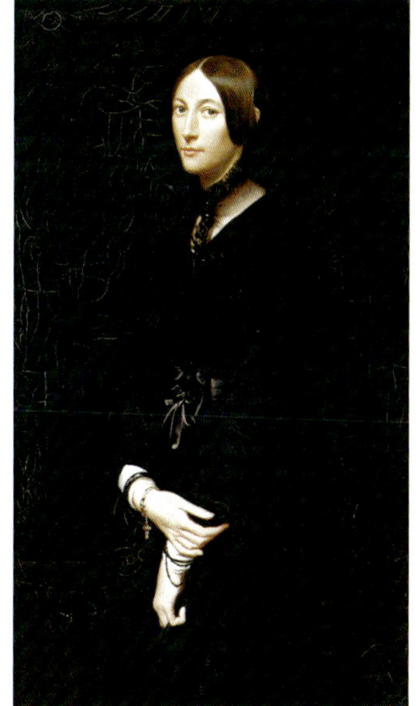

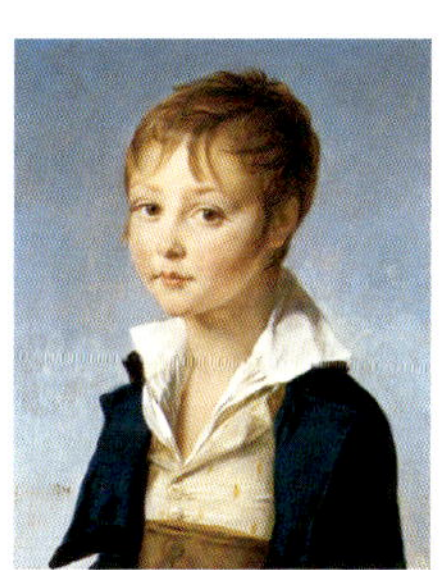

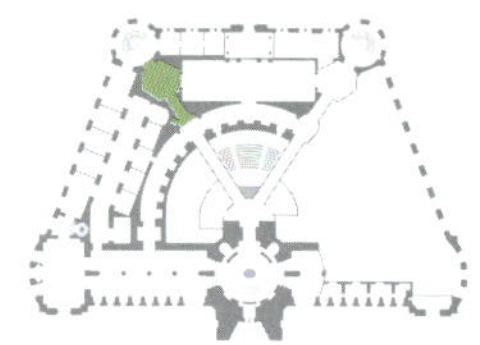

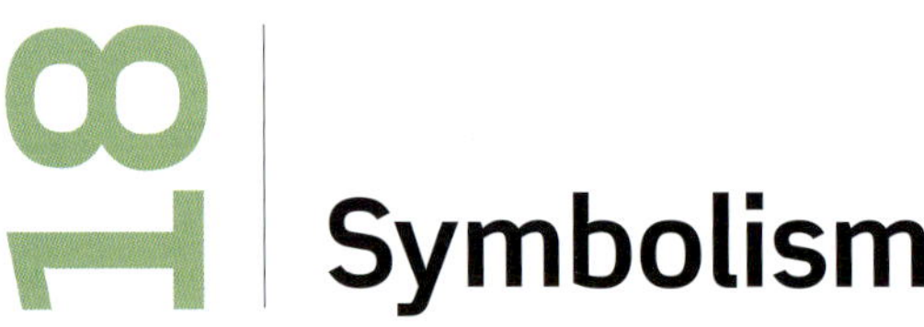

18 Symbolism

A movement both artistic and literary, Symbolism appeared with the Pre-Raphaelites in the England of the mid-19th century before extending to the rest of Europe. Opposed to industrialism and Naturalism, it advocated an idealist aesthetic founded on a quest for what Gustave Moreau called "inner feeling" and a mysticism drawing on sacred texts and legends. In France Moreau (1826-1898) and Puvis de Chavannes (1824-1898) were the heralds of a movement Jean Moréas defined in a manifesto in 1886 – the year when Gauguin's first visit to Martinique led to his break with Impressionism.

There is no single style common to the Symbolist artists. Nevertheless all of them were in search of correspondences Maurice Denis described as "the passionate equivalent of a received sensation". Interested in polychromy, Symbolist sculptors like Rosso, Cros and Dalpayrat tried out new techniques heralding the aesthetic explorations of Art Nouveau (see Alaphilippe, Room 1).

The presentation of the Petit Palais' Symbolist collection follows three lines of interest: the spiritual quest (Moreau, Gallé, Lemaire), Woman and the ambivalence of desire and death (Bartholomé, Fantin-Latour, Bigot) and subjective landscape (Ménard, Brokman, Le Sidaner, Lévy-Dhurmer). The Carabin vitrine offers a range of items relating to Symbolist decorative art (see also the Armand Point casket, Room 1).

PAUL GRANDHOMME (1851-1944) after **GUSTAVE MOREAU (1826-1898)** Europa

1897, enamel painted on copper, flecks of gold leaf, gold highlighting - Purchased 2003 - Inv. PPO03703

Gustave Moreau's originality lies in the sophistication and skill he brings to a highly personal mingling of mythology, Biblical references and Oriental legends. His subtle pictorial language uses singular colour combinations, often accompanied by great graphic precision and obsessive attention to detail. With Thesmar, Feuillâtre and Armand Point, Grandhomme was one of the late-19th-century artists who revived the art of enamel, forgotten or disparaged since the Middle Ages. Alone or working with Étienne Garnier (1848-1908?), he concentrated almost exclusively on the interpretation of pictures by Moreau, working in a delicately precious vein in close harmony with the subtle poetry of the originals.

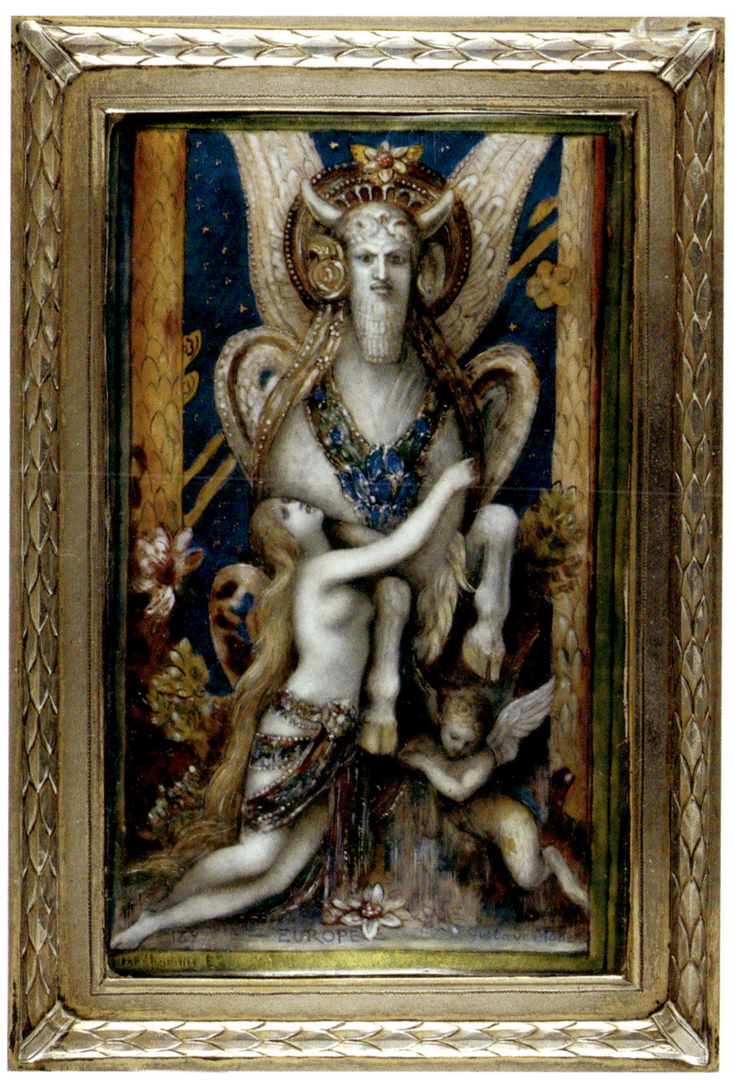
EUROPE

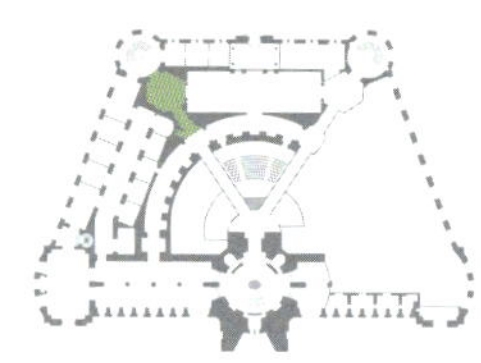

18 Henry Cros, seeker after polychromy

Born in Narbonne into a cultivated but unconventional family, Henry Cros was the son of a philosophy teacher and brother of the poet-inventor Charles Cros. A man of discretion, he divided his time between art and research. He made his debut as a sculptor and medallion-maker at the Salon in 1861, then showed at the Salon des Refusés in 1863.

Seeking to reconcile relief and colour, Cros returned to the early wax techniques, which unfortunately gave very fragile results. In 1884, in association with Charles Henry, he published *L'encaustique et les autres procédés de peinture chez les anciens, histoire et technique* ("Wax and Other Painting Methods of Old: History and Techniques"). His observation of the antiquities in the Louvre led him to a more durable method of moulding, using glass paste, but he jealously guarded the secret of the tinted low reliefs that would inspire the Art Nouveau master glassmakers Dammouse, Decorchemont and Despret. To encourage him in his research, in 1891 the Sèvres porcelain factory provided him with his own studio.

His painting, with its experimental additions of wax and spirit to the pigments, was part of an overall creative agenda, as were the host of drawings that reveal all the diversity of his sources of inspiration. The works in wax show scenes of medieval life borrowed from the illuminations in old books of hours. Ancient statuary was also a major contributing factor in his work. Without falling into the trap of pastiche, he succeeded in creating a kind of ideal, timeless beauty characterised by suppleness, soft colours and slightly blurred contours. From 1893 onwards he focused more on allegorical and symbolist themes, while still tirelessly pursuing his experiments with polychromy.

1 | **HENRY CROS (1840-1907)**
Ariadne's Thread
c. 1889. Oil on panel - Acquired with income accruing from the Dutuit bequest, 2005 - Inv. PDUT02157

2 | **HENRY CROS (1840-1907)**
Bust of Marie Cros
c. 1895. Glass paste
Gift of Jacques Zoubaloff, 1916 - Inv. PPO01144

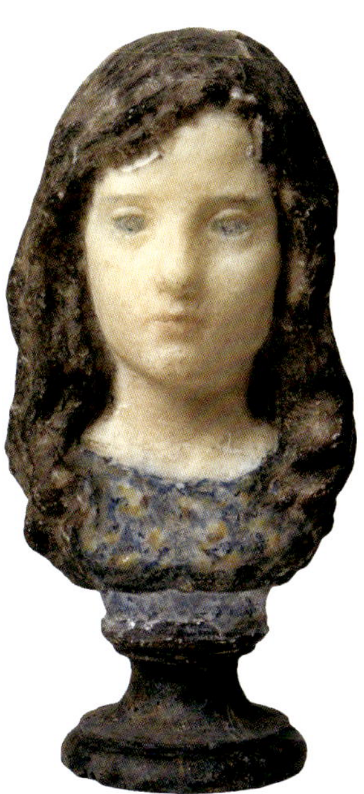

1 | 2

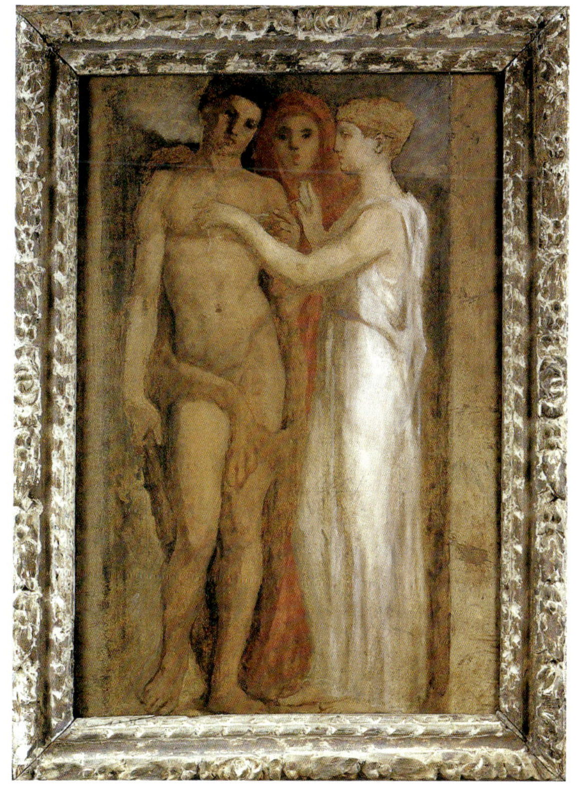

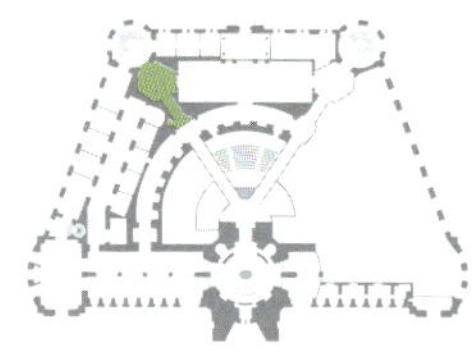

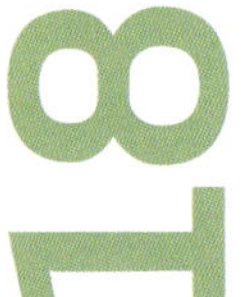

A master of wood

FRANÇOIS-RUPERT CARABIN (1862-1932) Vitrine

1895, walnut, metal, glass and ceramic - Commission, 1893 - Inv. OGAL00040

A celebration of art and design, this "vitrine for objets d'art" was shown in 1895 at the Salon of the Société Nationale des Beaux-Arts. Two naked women symbolising Softwood and Hardwood support the projecting glass-covered top. One of the sculpted side panels shows Ceramics above a niche in which Clay sleeps; the other is occupied by Metal buried deep in the earth and Flame, whose upswept hair forms a "plume of fire". On the back is an allegory of Stone holding a hammer and chisel. Carabin has portrayed himself as a grimacing mask spying - as in *Suzanne and the Old Men* - on the modern beauties on the front of the piece.

This vitrine exemplifies Carabin's notion of cabinetmaking. He appreciated walnut for its density, strength and fineness of grain: as a proponent of the craft revival he urged the use of "native" as opposed to "exotic" woods, castigated "the abominable contemporary trash known as veneer" and criticised Art Nouveau artists for "giving matter to a shape rather than shape to matter". The female caryatid, the emblem of the fantasies and fears of the turn of the century, is everywhere present in his work: to an extent verging on the obsessional he used as his sole model a woman with piled-up hair whom he stretched, flexed and bent in order to obtain the desired decorative and structural function. The vitrine houses a range of items - semi-precious stones, enamelware, objects made of glass paste, etc - meeting the postulates of Symbolist and Ideistic decorative art. Many of them come from the former City of Paris Musée des Arts Décoratifs at the Musée Galliera.

FRANÇOIS-RUPERT CARABIN (1862-1932)
Self-portrait (detail of the mask under the central section)
Ceramic

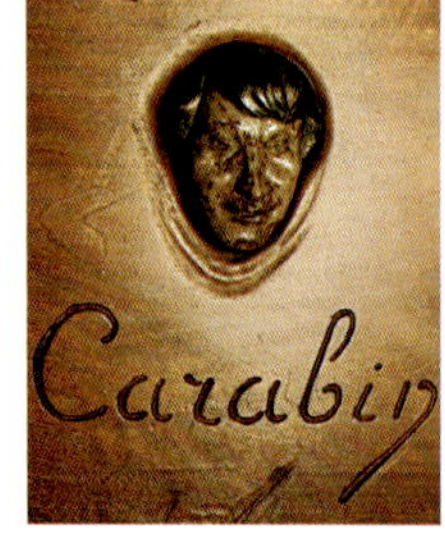

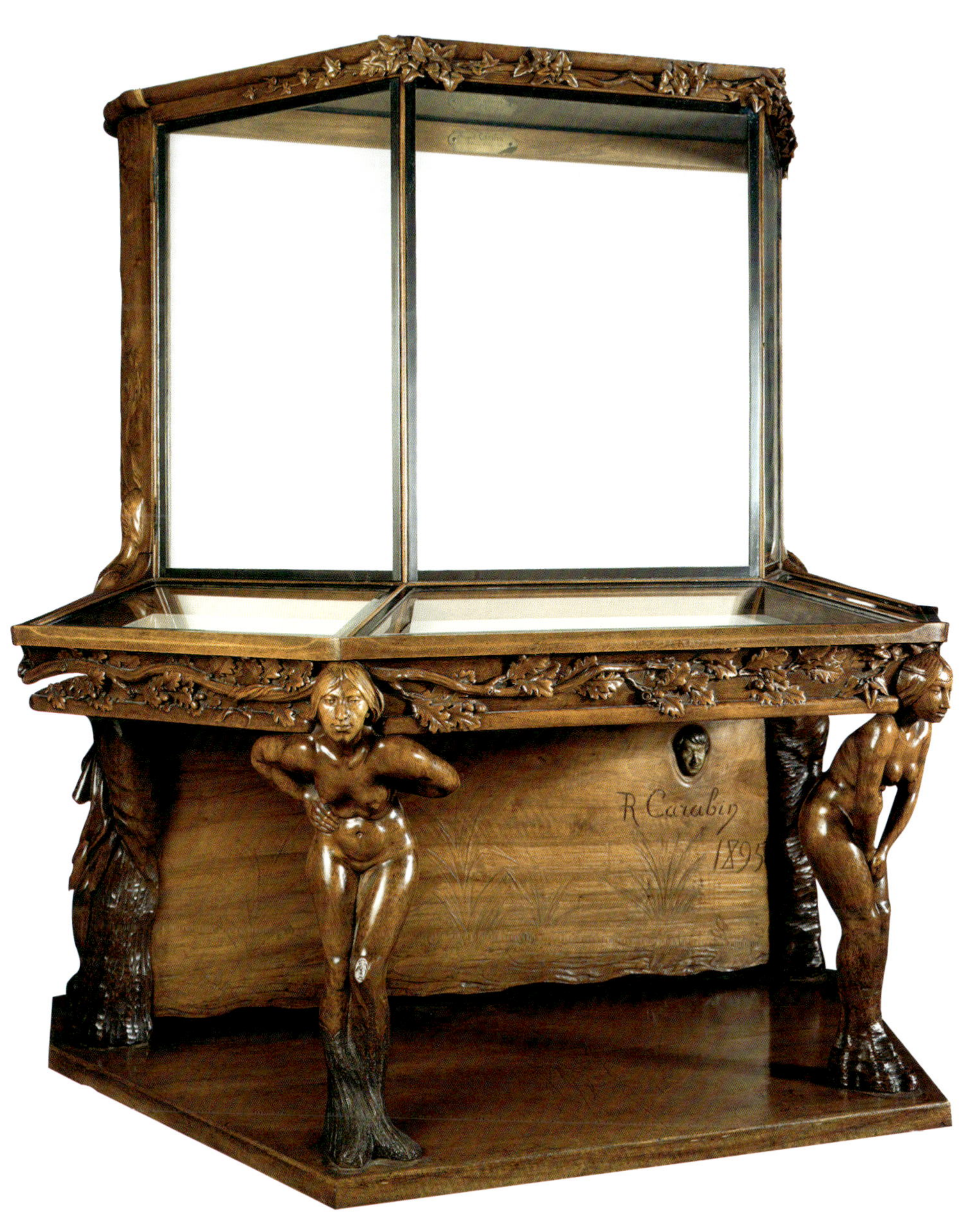
R Carabin
1895

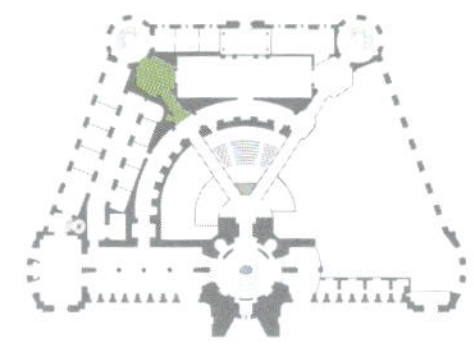

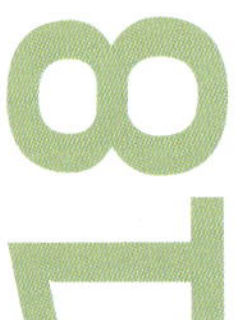

The art of pastel

Highly valued during the 18th century, when it was used for portraits, then abandoned in the Neoclassical period, pastel made a real comeback in the second half of the 19th century. Following Delacroix, a number of landscape artists, Huet and Boudin among them, regularly made plein air pastel studies that freed the medium from the straitjacket of the portrait. In turn it was fruitfully rediscovered by Realists like Millet and Lhermitte, and a Society of Pastellists was formed in 1885 after the split in the earlier Society of Pastellists and Watercolourists. Among its members were such representatives of the avant-garde as Degas and Toulouse-Lautrec, and more traditional, Symbolist or academic artists like Albert Besnard, the society's first president, and his successor Henri Gervex. Lending itself to both rapidity and virtuosity, pastel became a universally prized medium.

The Petit Palais has a substantial collection of some two hundred works illustrating the pastel in all its diversity, notably Impressionism with Morisot, Cassatt, Gauguin, Renoir, Degas and Guillaumin, and Symbolism with Redon, Osbert, Ménard, Roussel, Léandre and Lévy-Dhurmer.

ODILON REDON (1840-1916) The Birth of Venus

c. 1912, pastel on paper - Gift of Jacques Zoubaloff, 1916 - Inv. PPD01220

Somewhat unwillingly associated with the Symbolist movement, Odilon Redon began as a maker of monochromes: the charcoal drawings and lithographs he called his "Noirs" ("Blacks"). Colour only made its appearance in his oeuvre around 1894, notably with the use of pastel: similar to charcoal in its velvety dustiness and extreme fragility, this was the perfect medium for the move to a new, violently intense use of colour. In some cases he reworked earlier "Noirs" like *The Old Angel* in colour, but he also undertook such new subjects as the birth of Venus, butterflies and bouquets of flowers, in which iridescent effects - skies, water, mother of pearl, insect wings and silken petals - chimed perfectly with the texture of pastel.

This *Birth of Venus* is dated c. 1912, when he was using the model Alphonsine Zabé, recommended to him by Maurice Denis.

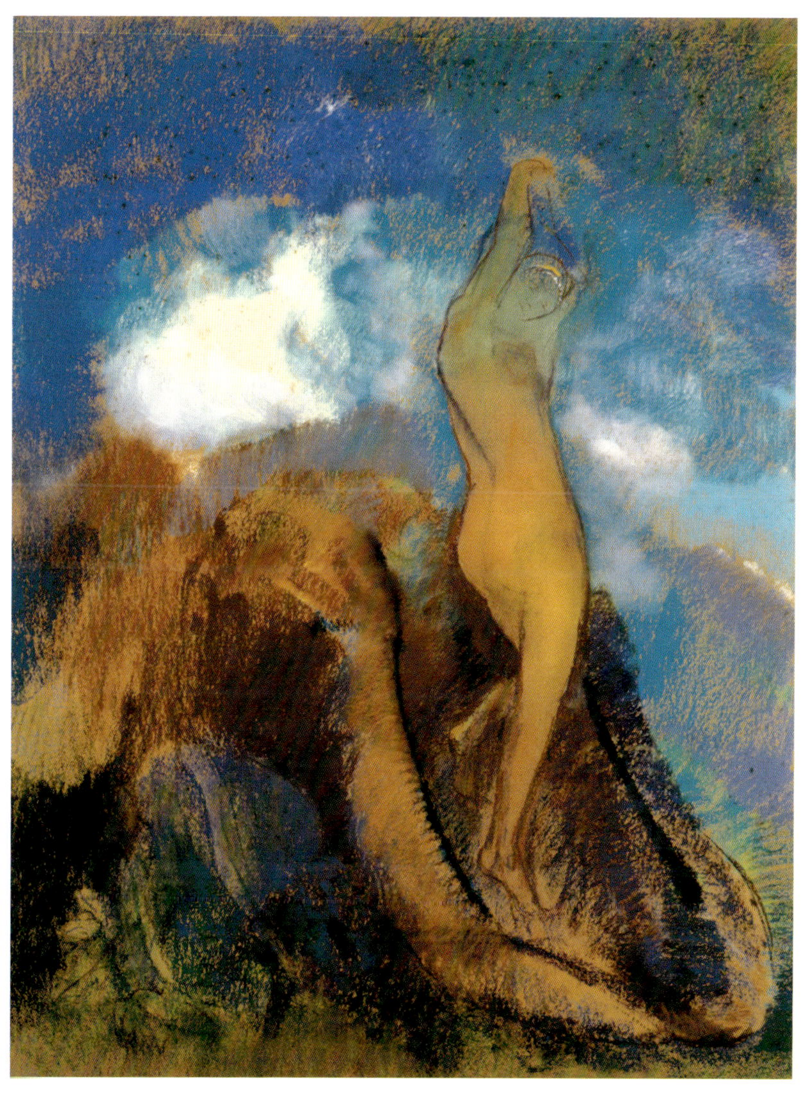

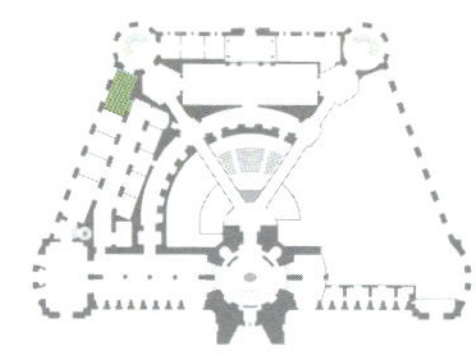

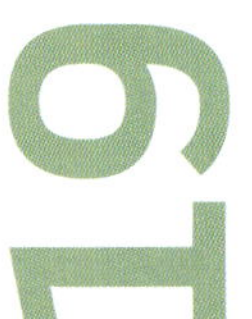

A singular creator

Carriès (1855-1894) is the very archetype of the independent artist: partially self-taught and fascinated by all sort of materials and techniques, he enjoyed great success with private collectors, specialising in commissioned portraits and series of busts mixing realism and fancy. He was especially interested in surfaces, endlessly experimenting with patina recipes as he sought strangely shimmering effects. For his bronzes he worked extensively with the founder Pierre Bingen, their association beginning in 1883.
In 1888 he moved to Puisaye in eastern central France to work in stoneware, beginning with simple pots and making ceramic versions of his works in plaster. In 1890 the wealthy American artist Winaretta Singer commissioned a *Monumental Door* - actually an enamelled stoneware door frame - based on a project by Eugène Grasset. Carriès produced a model seething with disturbing creatures, but had difficulty overseeing the making of the work and died of tuberculosis at the age of thirty-nine. The contents of his studio were recovered by his friend Georges Hoentschel, who donated them to the City of Paris ten years later.

1 | **JEAN CARRIÈS (1855-1894)** My Portrait
c. 1887-1888, wax - Gift of Georges Hoentschel, 1904 - Inv. PPS00387
Jean Carriès was about thirty-two when he made this self-portrait; wax was one of his favourite materials, but few sculptors of the time dared to use it on such a scale. Partially stamped in a mould and partially hand-modelled, the stained wax is set either on a plaster and hemp core or a jigsawed wooden armature.
The piece is extremely realistic. Carriès had had mouldings made of hands - maybe his own - and his torso "with a smock and arms", and he doubtless used them here. At the same time, this is an idealised portrait in which the artist has surrounded himself with things important to him: a death mask known as "Carriès' mother", a whimsical figure reminiscent of the imaginary busts he created, and two odd animals heralding those on the *Monumental Door*.

2 | **JEAN CARRIÈS (1855-1894)** Large vase with ornamental base
Glazed stoneware, 1889-1894
Gift of Georges Hoentschel, 1904 - Inv. PPS000414

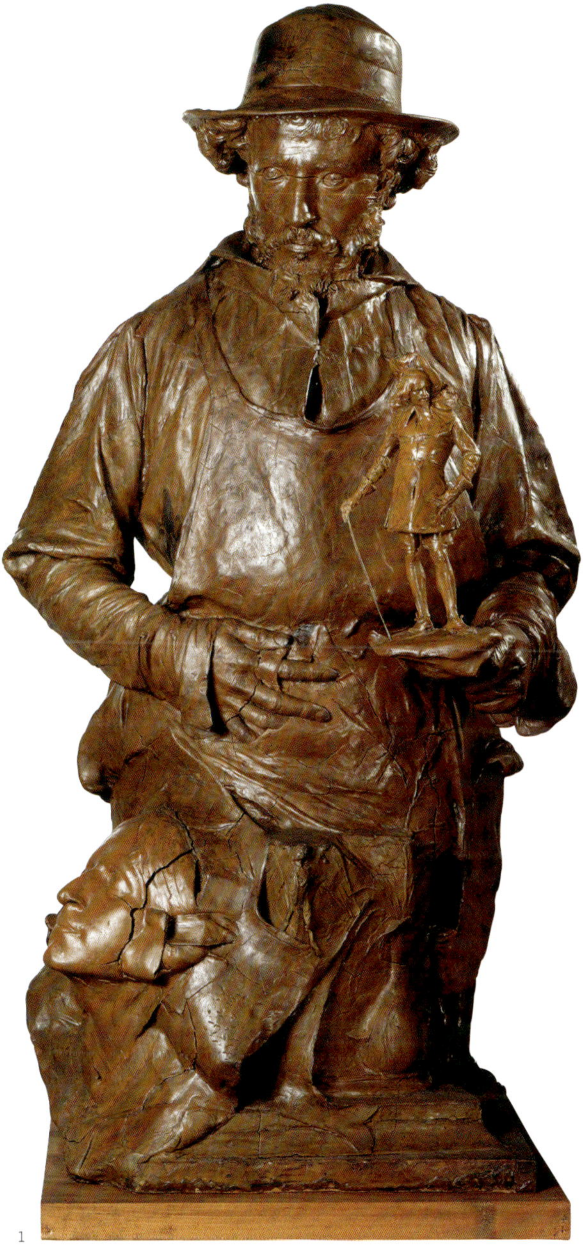

1

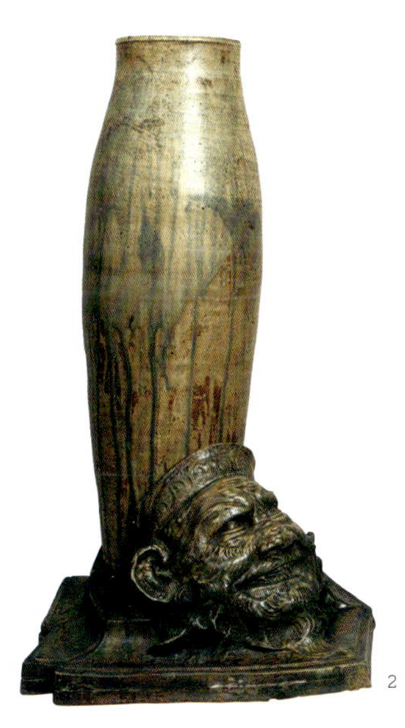

2

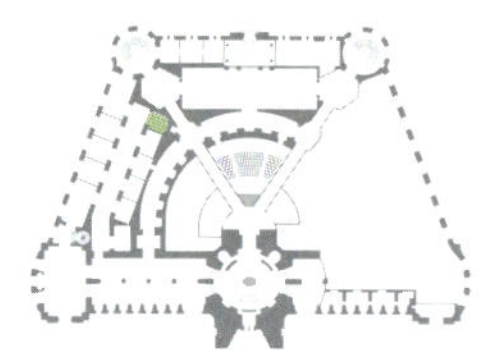

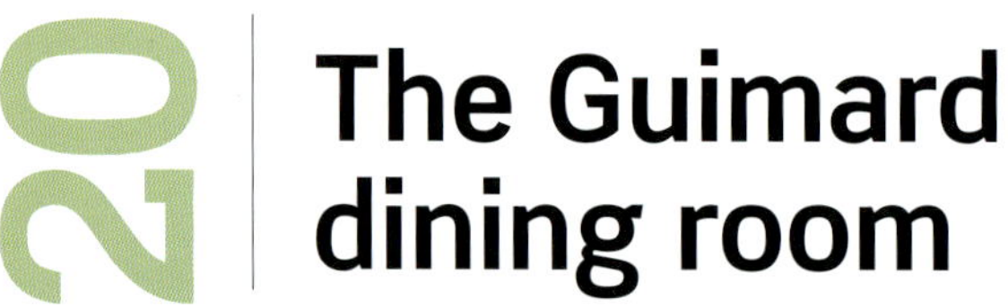

20 The Guimard dining room

The architect and interior designer Hector Guimard (1867-1942) was one of France's leading exponents of Art Nouveau. He studied at the Ecole des Arts Décoratifs in Paris in 1883-85, became interested in architecture and was influenced by Viollet-le-Duc's functionalist and rationalist theories. He was admitted to the Ecole des Beaux-Arts in Paris in 1885, but failed the final examination. On a trip to Belgium in 1895 he met the architect Victor Horta, whose aesthetic concerns - the designing of a "total work of art", and the expressive value of line - were very similar to his own.

In Paris he mainly built apartment blocks and townhouses, but the "Guimard style" also found expression in the Metro station entrances commissioned from him in 1900. Made of cast iron, wrought iron and glass, these structures drew their inspiration from vegetal forms, discreetly hinted at via their green colour and sinuous lines.

1 | **HECTOR GUIMARD (1867-1942)** Hôtel Guimard: The first-floor dining room

Photograph by Stan Ries - Gift of Madame Guimard, 1948 - Inv. PPPH00026

In May 1909, shortly after his marriage to the American-born painter Adeline Oppenheim, Hector Guimard had a townhouse built on land he had bought at 122 Avenue Mozart in Paris. The ground floor was given over to a reception room and his architecture studio and the first floor to a dining room and an elliptical living room. The décor - panelling, cornices, furniture, ironwork, lights and fabrics - was entirely Guimard's work. For the furniture and woodwork he used pear wood, whose shine and soft grain were especially suited to his supple, elegant line.

The dining room has been restored and faithfully recreated. Among the wooden items matched to the room's oval shape are a sideboard and a silver cabinet in which are presented ceramics by Dalpayrat (on loan from the Dalpayrat collection) together with solid silver plate by Henri Husson. The dining chairs are decorated with repoussé leather and marked "OG" (Oppenheim/Guimard) in lettering designed by Guimard himself.

2 | **PAUL PHILIPPON (active between 1893-1919)**
Vase, c. 1909
Gilt chased bronze, after a model by Guimard - Acquired 1993 with funds accruing from the Dutuit bequest - Inv. ODUT01783

3 | **HECTOR GUIMARD (1867-1942)**
Chair, c 1909
Pear wood, leather
Gift of Madame Guimard, 1948 - Inv. PPO03499

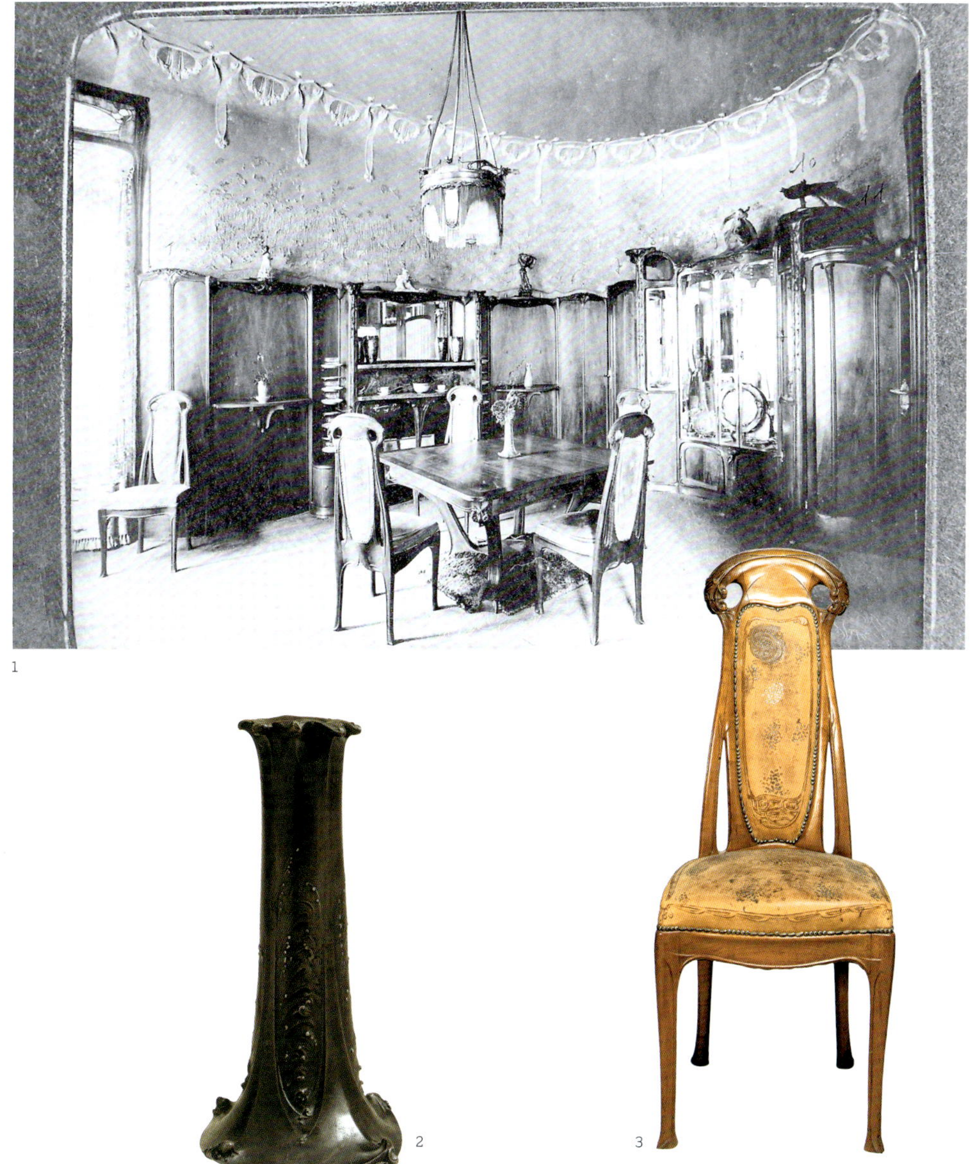

1

2

3

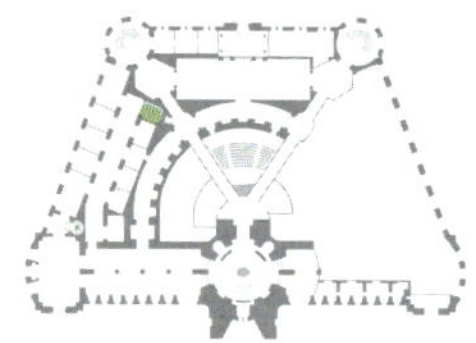

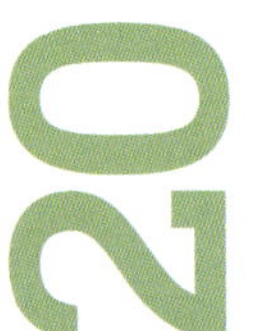

Fouquet jewellery

In 1895 Georges Fouquet succeeded his father Alphonse, who had founded his jewellery business in 1860. Working with such innovators as Alphonse Mucha (1860-1939) and Charles Desrosiers, Fouquet utterly transformed the jeweller's art. From Mucha, a Czech-born painter and designer now mainly remembered for his elegantly sinuous poster work, he commissioned a number of remarkable pieces including a bracelet for Sarah Bernhardt. He also entrusted him, in 1900, with the decoration of his new store at 6 Rue Royale, now recreated at the Musée Carnavalet. Desrosiers, who had studied with Grasset, designed more everyday jewellery for him.
The striking features of Fouquet jewellery are its decorative character and clarity of design. His pieces were often outlined with brilliants in a way that highlighted the central motif. Following René Lalique, he cared little for precious stones, preferring a range of materials - glass, ivory, horn, translucent enamels, opals and baroque pearls - chosen for their shape and colour. His formal inspiration came mainly from the plant and animal world.

1 | **GEORGES FOUQUET (1862-1957)** Waterfall pendant

c. 1900 - Mount based on a model by Mucha, décor after Desrosiers - Gold, enamel "à jour" with flecks of gold, opals, diamonds and baroque pearl - Purchased 1937 - Inv. PPO03570

Portrayed with gold-flecked enamel - specks of jeweller's foil are set into the enamel to heighten its brightness and luminosity - the waterfall is studded with diamonds in an eloquent suggestion of droplets. It is set in a splendid landscape of opal rocks in a kind of crazy-paving pattern.

2 | **GEORGES FOUQUET (1862-1957)** Byzantine comb

c. 1905 - After a model by Mucha - Tortoiseshell, cloisonné enamel "à jour" with gold and opals - Purchased 1937 - Inv. PPO03583

Here Fouquet makes extensive use of the enamel "à jour" technique, in which the layer of cloisonné enamel is not set on a base: this heightens its colour and translucency.

3 | **GEORGES FOUQUET (1862-1957)** Sycamore pendant

Between 1905-1910, enamel "à jour", gold cloisonné, two peridots, baroque pearl
Purchased 1937 - Inv. PPO03575

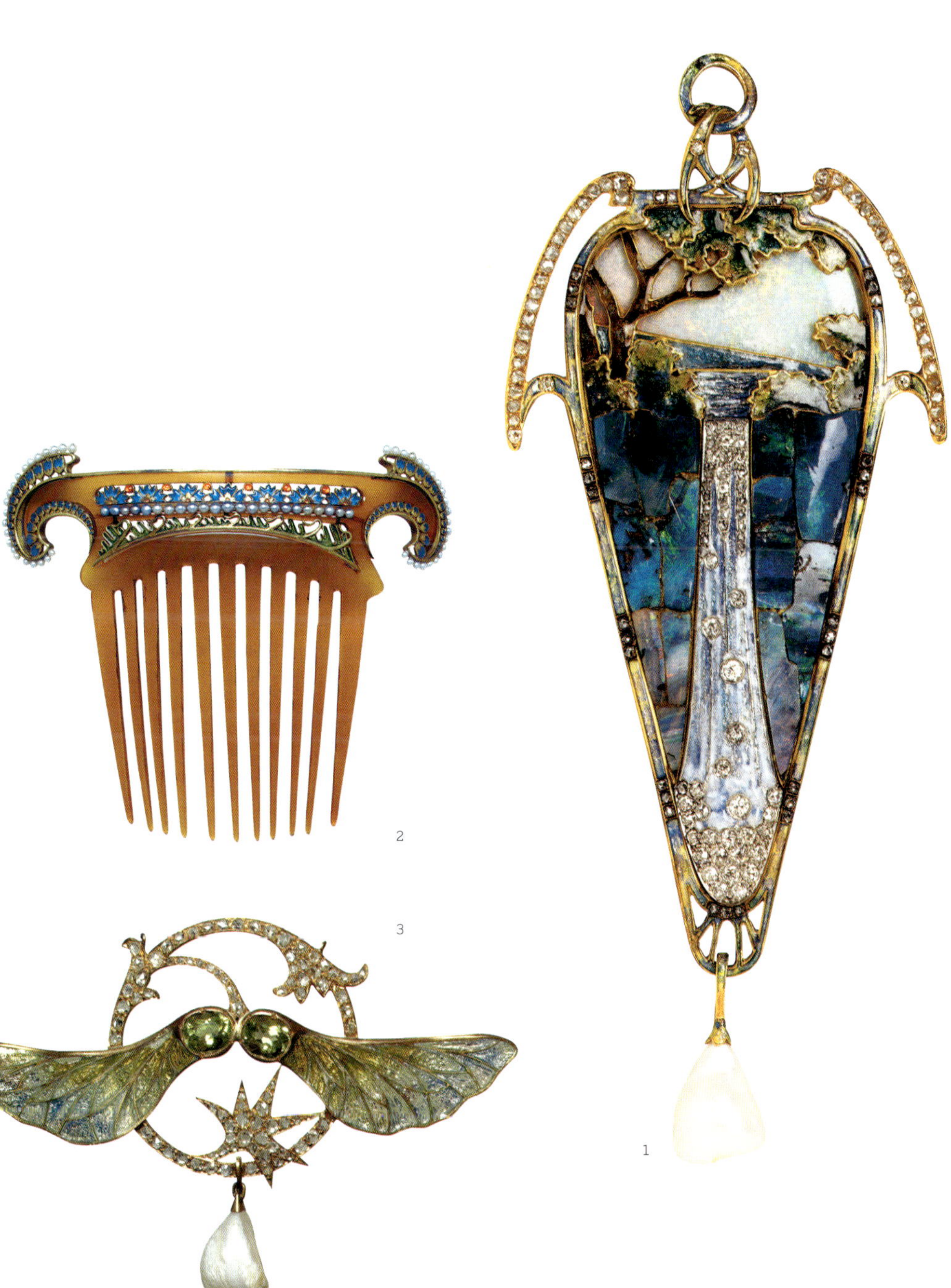

2

3

1

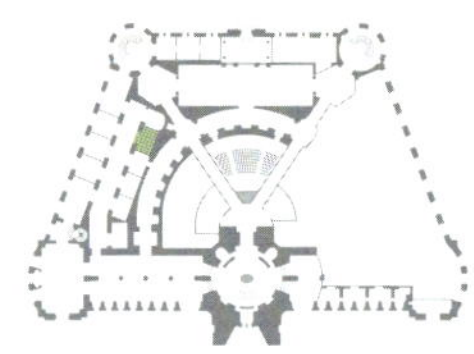

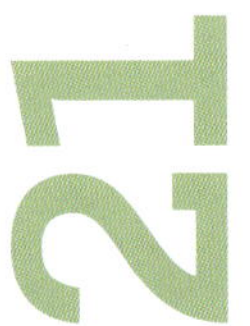

The library of Dr Vaquez

In the 1890s the Nabis, a group of young artists trained at the Académie Julian in Paris, reacted against Realism by taking Gauguin as their inspiration for a new artistic approach. Their aim, they said, was "to decorate the banal walls of human edifices with thoughts, dreams and ideas", make art available to all and bring beauty to the useful. Their names were Pierre Bonnard, Maurice Denis, Ker-Xavier Roussel, Paul Sérusier, Félix Vallotton and Édouard Vuillard. Well after the group broke up in 1900 these artists were still painting murals for apartments and public spaces: in 1925, for example, Maurice Denis marouflaged onto the cupola of the Petit Palais' southeast staircase a canvas titled *History of the Arts in France*.

ÉDOUARD VUILLARD (1868-1940) Intimacy, Music, Choosing a Book, Work

Four panels for the apartment of Dr Vaquez, 1896 - Glue-based paint on canvas - Gift of Madame Vaquez, 1936 - Inv. PPP02439, 02440, 02441 and 02442

These four panels decorated a small room - probably the library - in the Paris apartment of the cardiologist Henri Vaquez (1860-1936), doctor of Alphonse Daudet and Marcel Proust and a passionate lover of modern art.

In this small, intimate space Vuillard opted for subtle interplay between the paintings and the wallpaper around them. The deliberately unidentifiable silhouettes are imaginary doubles of the occupants, merging into the multicoloured backdrop of fabrics and wallpaper reminiscent of the "millefleurs" tapestries of the late Middle Ages.

The artist has painted a world closed off by the squared ceiling and the edging of the carpet, and muted by a limited colour range made up mostly of purple, brown and green. The matt finish, intended to accentuate the simplicity of the interior and avoid any impression of depth, was obtained by using glue-based paint.

Consummate examples of the artist's concern with the relationship between painting and the decorative arts, these panels, whose subjects dissolve into the interplay of colour areas, herald the pictorial revolutions of the early 20th century: the beginnings of Abstraction and Matisse's decorative paintings.

Choosing a Book

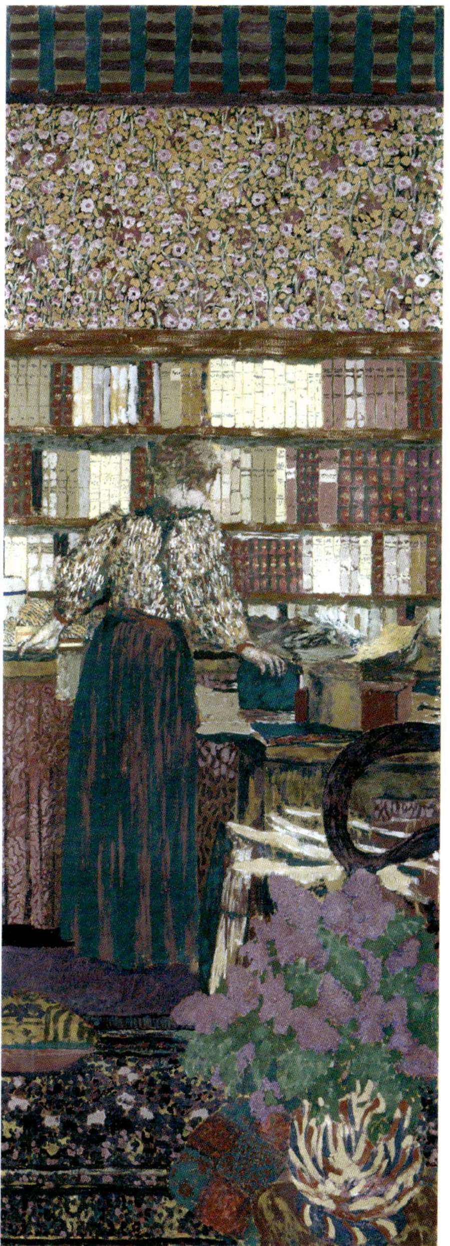

Work

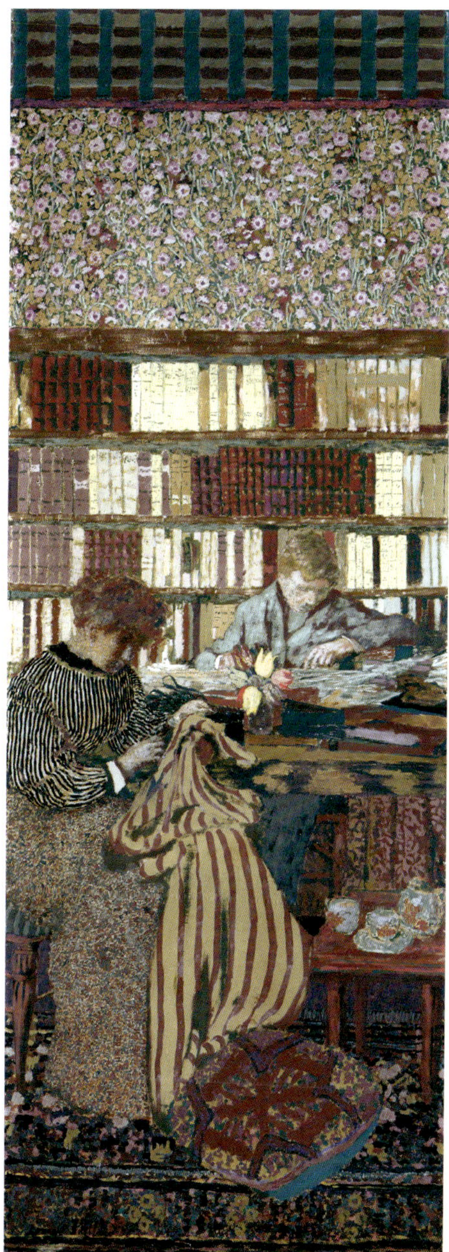

Music

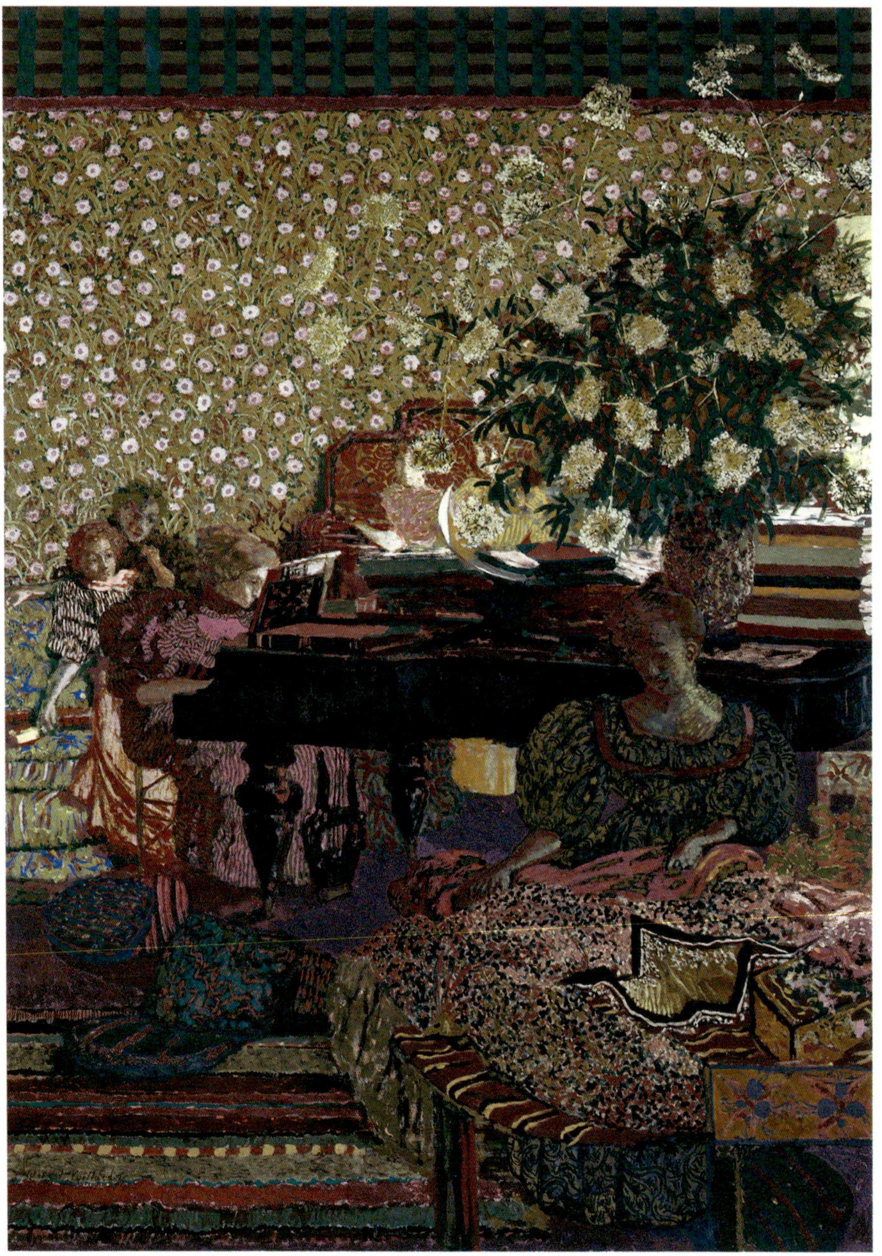

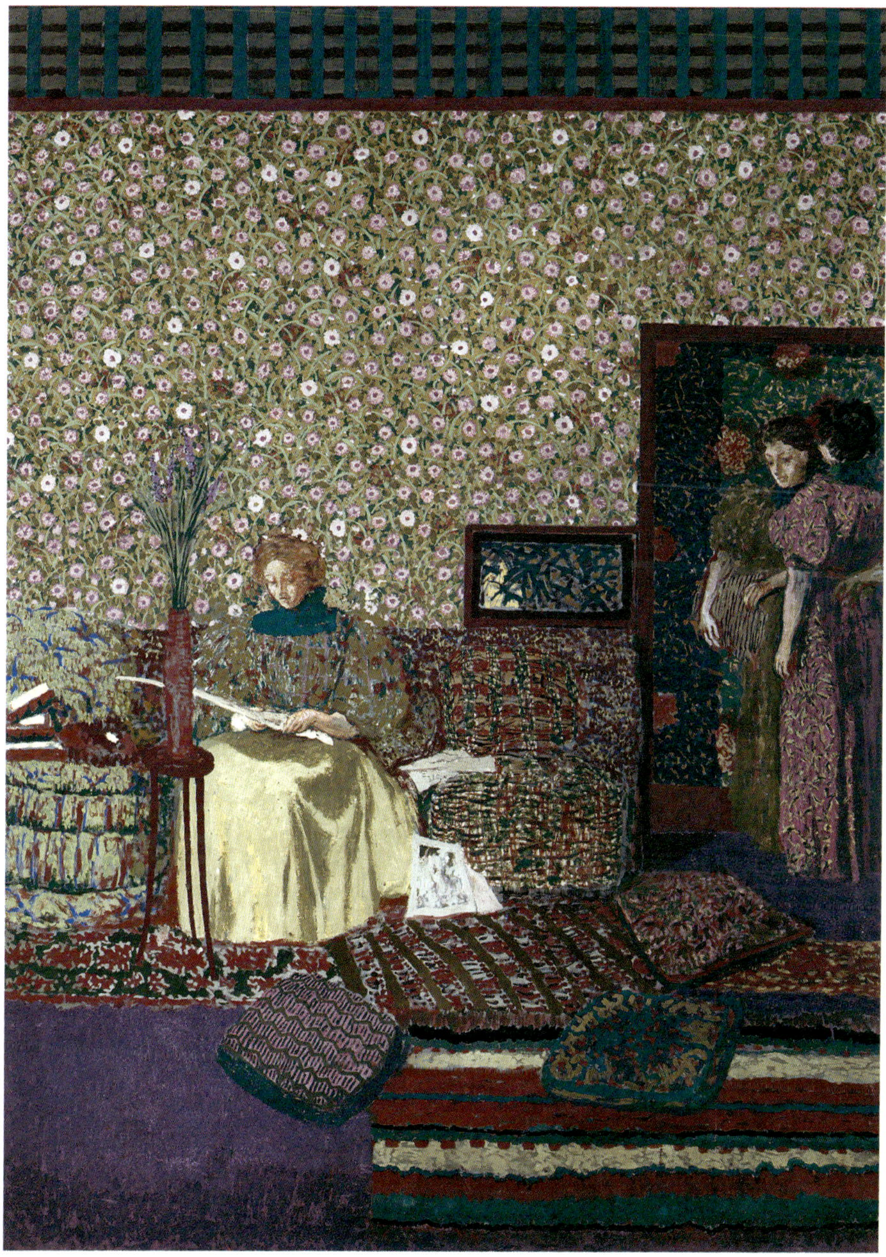

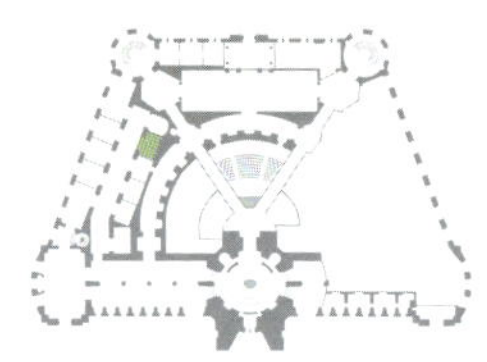

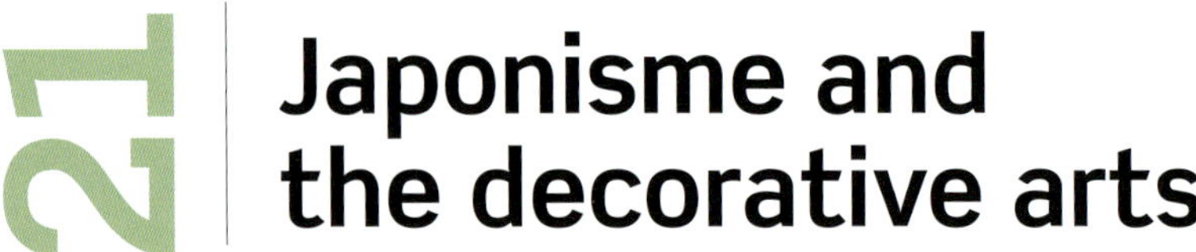

21 Japonisme and the decorative arts

During the second half of the 19th century, international trade and the Universal Expositions led to what the Goncourt brothers called "Chinoiserie" and "Japonaiserie" making themselves felt at every social level.

In the decorative arts the Chinese and Japanese influence brought profound change in terms of form, decoration and materials. Chinese celadon ware inspired Bracquemond's sumptuous "Animals" table setting, with its engraved underglaze decoration. Japanese ceramics were a major influence for Carriès and Hoentschel, both especially interested in stoneware for its substance and texture. Gallé borrowed blue, red and gold motifs from Imari porcelain for a Rocaille jardinière and decorated a square, glazed glass vase with a praying mantis and chrysanthemums of Japanese inspiration.

1 | **FÉLIX BRACQUEMOND (1833-1914)** Fruit bowl. Rousseau dinner service

Model created in 1866, produced 1866-1875, earthenware - Acquired with income accruing from the Dutuit bequest, 2002 - Inv. PPO03727

Comprising over two hundred pieces, the Rousseau dinner service resulted from the association between the printmaker Félix Bracquemond and the dealer Eugène Rousseau. First made in 1866 at the Creil and Montereau works, it was reproduced until the mid-20th century. Bracquemond made an enormous quantity of plant, bird and animal-inspired etchings grouped together on twenty-eight plates; these were cut out and transferred onto the earthenware.

The patterns are mostly tripartite: a main subject and two smaller secondary ones. The drawing is simple and the colours strong, leaving a major role to the white of the surface. The shapes are more traditional and draw on Rococo models in imitation of 18th-century porcelain. The edges are moulded, with blue comb decoration.

In his review of the 1871 International Exhibition in London, Mallarmé paid tribute to "this admirable, unique dinner service, decorated by Bracquemond with Japanese motifs borrowed from the barnyard and the fishtank: the handsomest recent crockery I have had the privilege of seeing."

2 | **FÉLIX BRACQUEMOND (1833-1914)**

Cock, ray, plants and pheasant. Plate no. 9 for the Rousseau service

1866, etching and drypoint on papier japon

Acquired with income accruing from the Dutuit bequest, 2003 - Inv. GDUT11021

1

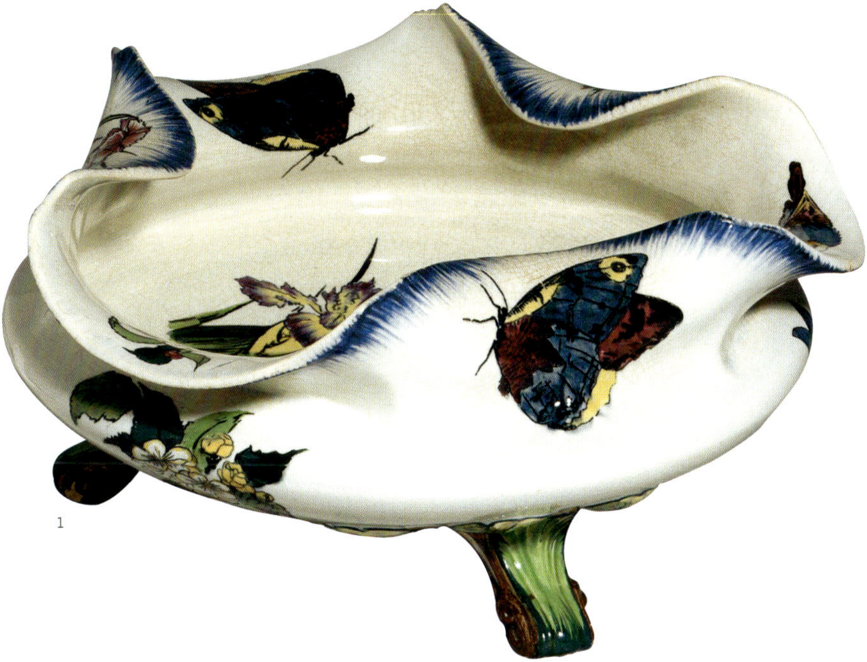

2

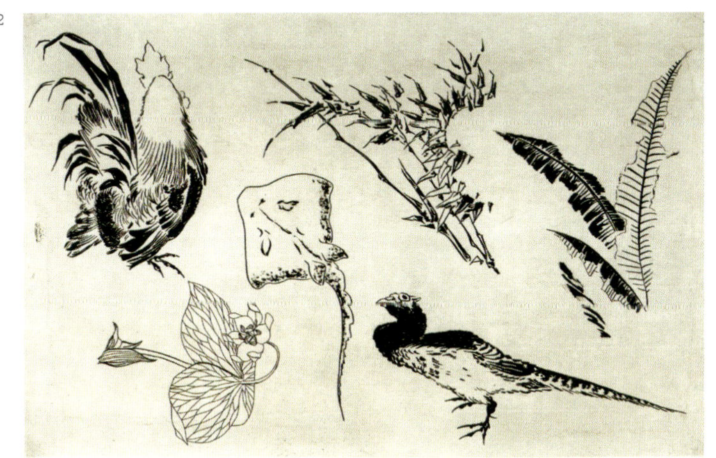

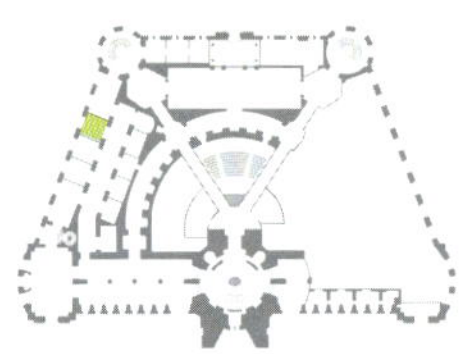

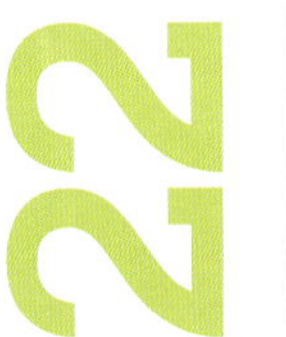

Reinventing the past

19th-century thinking was marked by the awakening of a historical national consciousness. France became passionately interested in the recent upheavals of the Revolution and the Empire, periods which became the basis for political analysis and commitment. With the education of the masses in mind, the Third Republic - established after the events of 1870 - fostered the cult of great men. The study of man's origins also became a major concern and had its own influence on the arts: Cormon, for example, portrayed the activities of our earliest ancestors on the walls of the lecture theatre at the Museum d'histoire naturelle in Paris.

As they broadened their retrospective repertoire to include new historical periods, artists - for the theatre and, soon, for the cinema - showed real inventiveness in the way they played on the dramatic aspects of the past. Particular attention was given to faces, costumes and settings as a way of achieving maximum credibility. At the same time they borrowed as needs be from a range of styles looking back to the more or less distant past. This eclecticism points up a certain tension between the identitarian historical concerns of a positivist century and the difficulty of cutting free from established models.

1 | **JAMES TISSOT (1836-1902)** The Prodigal Son: the Departure (ill. following pages)
1863, oil on canvas - Acquired with income accruing from the Dutuit bequest, 1985 - Inv. PDUT01453

A painter of modern life and elegant women, Tissot divided his time between Paris and London. Using the codes of genre painting he also produced appealing Historical canvases. In Venice in search of inspiration in 1862, he wrote to his friend Degas that he was working on the theme of the Prodigal Son as recounted in the gospel of St Luke. The result was two large Gothic Revival works in very different styles: *The Departure*, with its strong, luminous colours, is a direct reference to Venice as seen by Carpaccio in 1490. The work's charm lies in the exuberant costumes and handsome décors, with the Biblical message a strictly secondary consideration.

2 | **FERNAND-ANNE PIESTRE,** known as **CORMON (1845-1924)** The Hunt
Study for the palaeontology lecture theatre at the Museum d'histoire naturelle in Paris - 1897, oil on canvas
Acquired with income accruing from the Dutuit bequest, 1984
Inv. PDUT01393

3 | **FERNAND-ANNE PIESTRE,** known as **CORMON (1845-1924)** The Crab Eaters
Study for the palaeontology lecture theatre at the Museum d'histoire naturelle in Paris - 1897, oil on canvas
Acquired with income accruing from the Dutuit bequest, 1984
Inv. PDUT01390

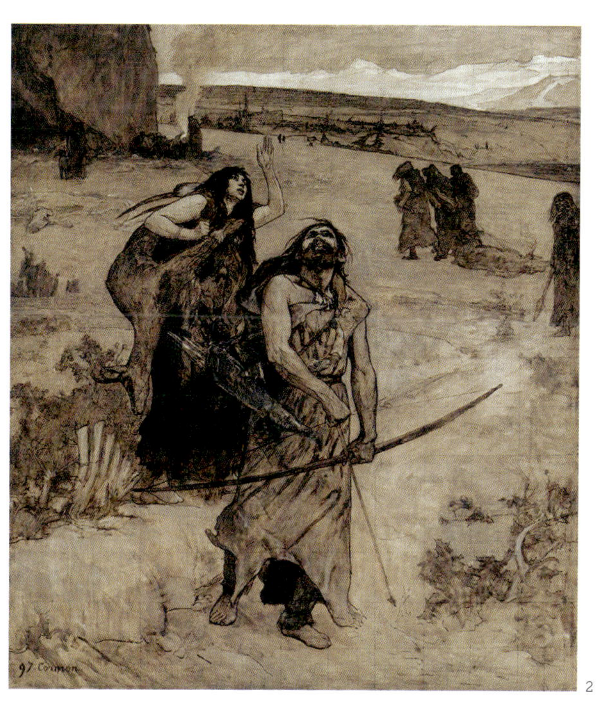

2

3

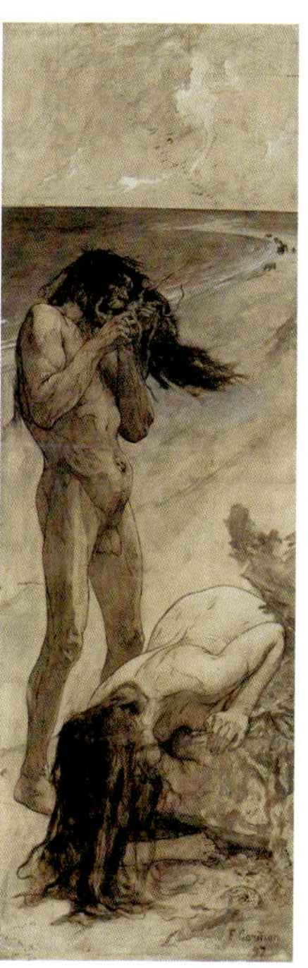

1 | The Prodigal Son: the Departure

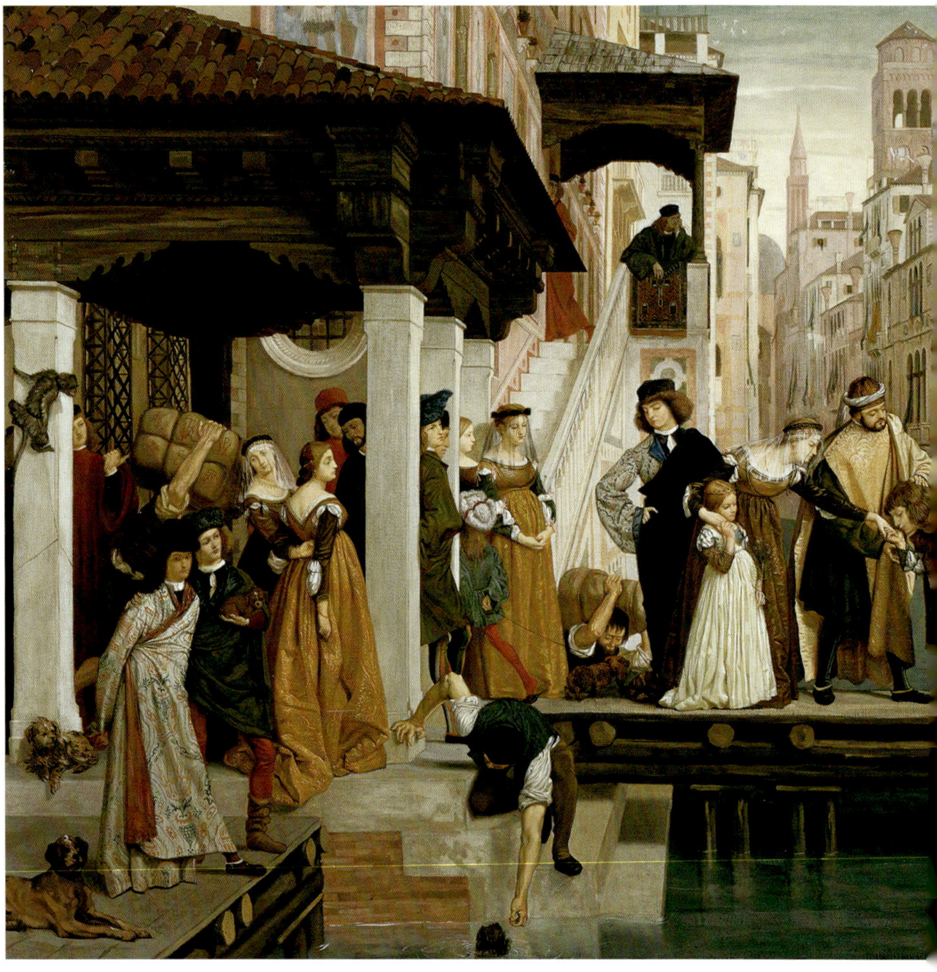

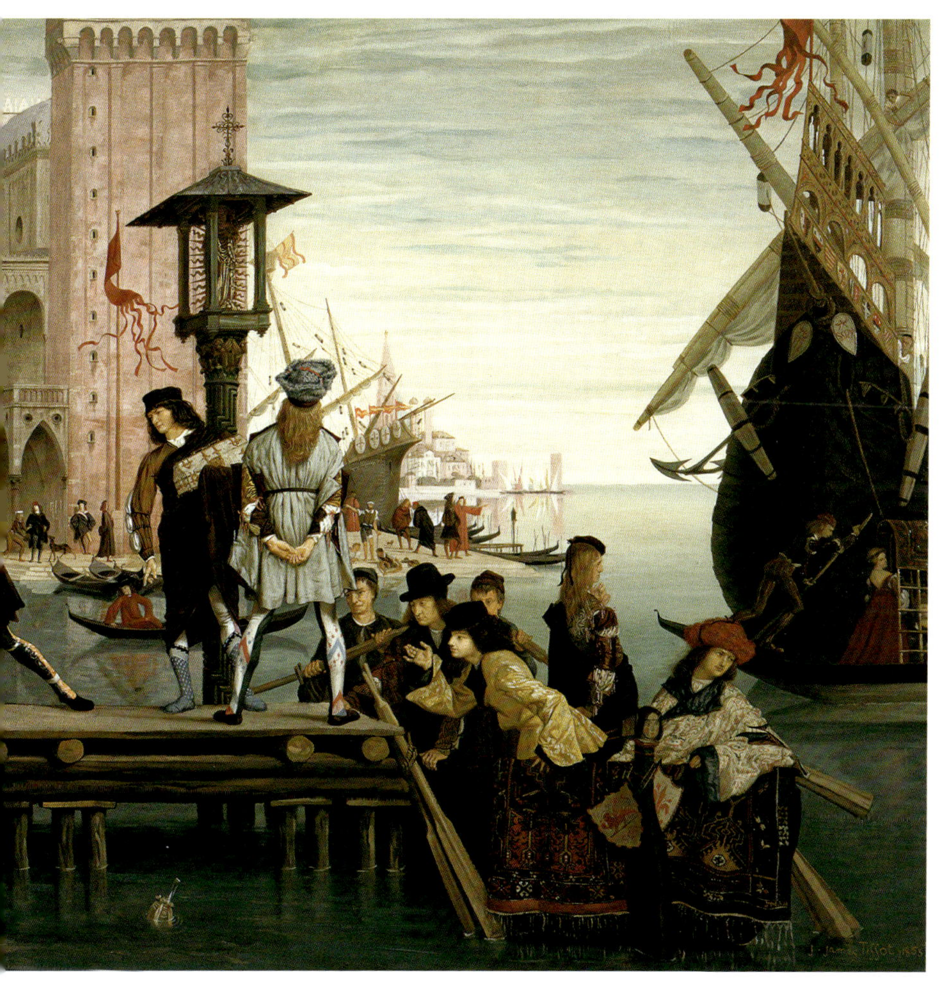

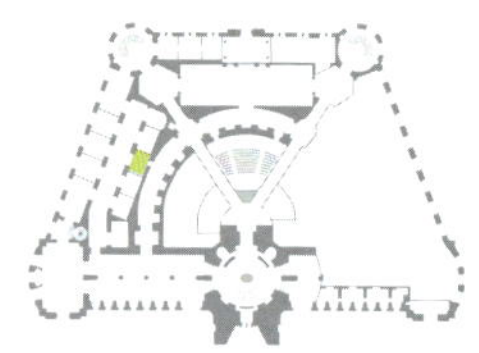

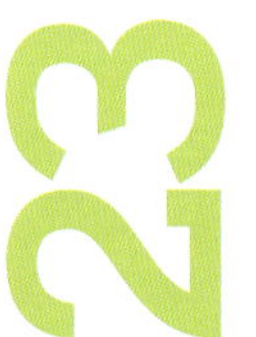

The Romantic spirit

This room brings together some of the great names of French Romanticism, a movement that focused on the individual and his emotions. Often with a solid classical training behind them, the Romantic artists drew on new sources of inspiration.
Louis Boulanger, intimate friend and quasi-official illustrator of Victor Hugo, sought his tragic heroes in Shakespeare. Travel, which was no longer limited to Italy, honed their sensibilities: Géricault, for example, preferred England, staying only briefly in Italy and finding the life of the streets there more inspiring than the ancient ruins. Following in the footsteps of Delacroix, Chassériau remembered his journey to North Africa for the Oriental tone of his religious compositions in the churches of Paris.
The Restoration brought Christian art a new lease of life and religious subjects returned in force to the Salon. Granet, a medieval architecture enthusiast, achieved great success with his delicate paintings of the interiors of churches and monasteries.
Romanticism's subjective approach to nature as direct individual experience contributed to the coming of the modern landscape. The Romantic spirit lived on late into the century in the work of such singular artists as Gustave Doré (Room 6).

EUGÈNE DELACROIX (1798-1863) Combat of the Giaour and the Pasha
1835, oil on canvas - Acquired with income accruing from the Dutuit bequest, 1963 - Inv. PDUT01162
Delacroix remains one of Romanticism's tutelary figures. His first contact with the Orient was through the highly coloured poetry of Byron. The reality came with his visit to Morocco in 1832 and his way of painting was profoundly affected by exposure to a host of new sensations.
This canvas is inspired by Byron's story of the thwarted love affair between a Venetian, the Giaour ("non-Muslim") and a slave girl from the Pasha's harem. Delacroix shows us in all its violence the final, hand-to-hand combat between the rivals. The beauty of the costumes and the intensity of the colours hark back to his still recent memories of Moroccan experience.

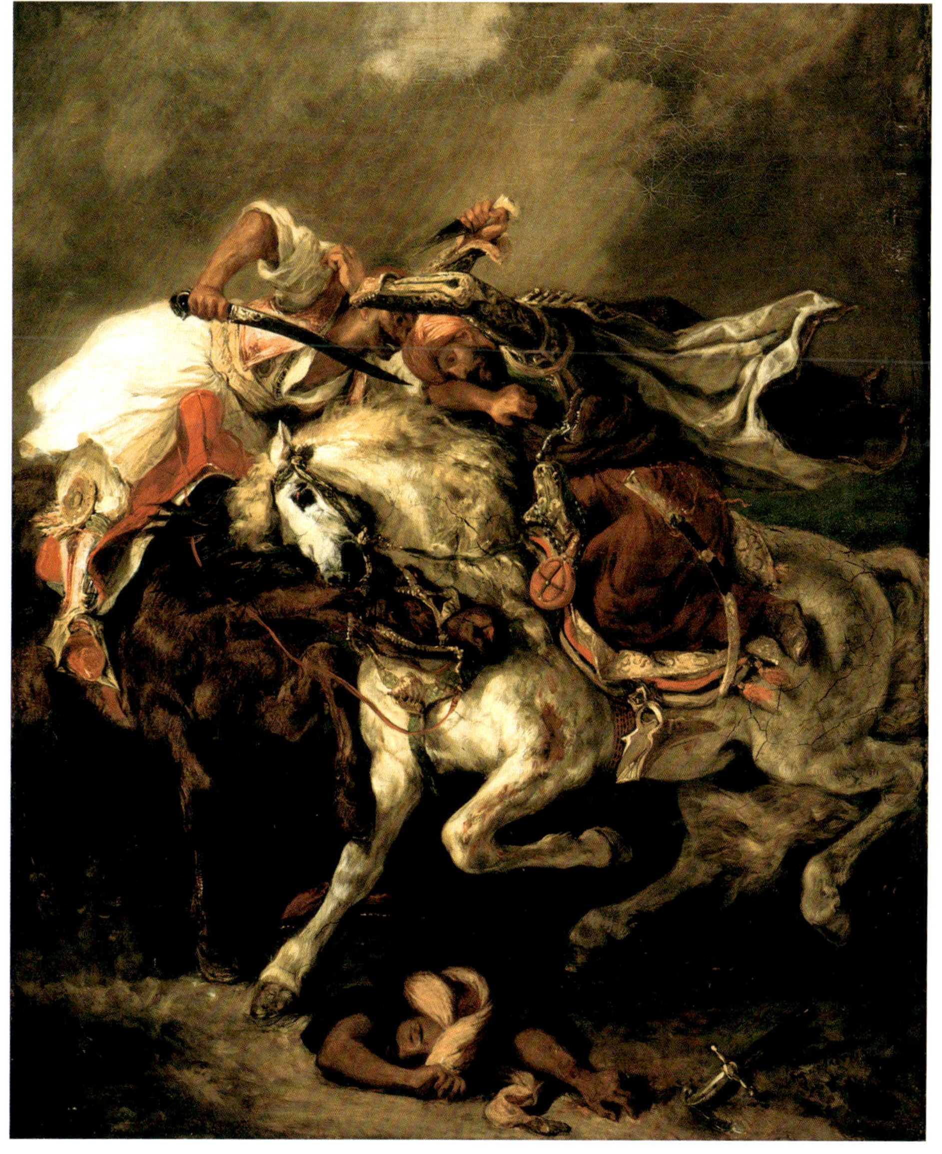

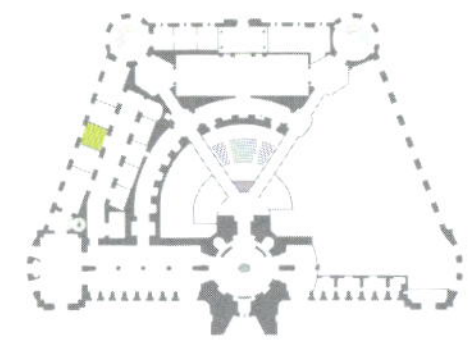

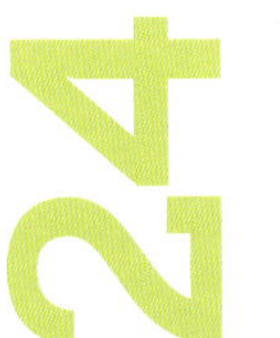

The Troubadour Style

After a long period in oblivion, medieval art made a comeback in the second half of the 18th century. In Paris the Musée des Monuments Français, created during the Revolution in the evocative setting of the medieval monastery of the Petits-Augustins, was the gathering point for works from plundered churches and the mansions of the aristocracy. This new museum provided artists with a formal repertory different from that of Greece and Rome, which until then had been the unchallenged benchmark.

The so-called Troubadour style, which came to full flower in 1802-1824, was the visible outcome of this new passion. Ingres focused on French history until the time of Henri IV, Granet produced sentimental anecdotes of the lives of kings and great men of France, Chauvin offered knights in armour traversing Italian landscapes, and Sermezy replaced the deities of Olympus with heroes from novels of chivalry, pages and minstrels. The same elaborate fancifulness was brought to the lives of the old masters: Raphael and Leonardo da Vinci as seen through the Ingres filter and versions of Van Dyck by Ducis and Roqueplan.

The movement also made its presence felt in the decorative arts, with the "Cathedral" style bringing Gothic motifs to furniture, goldsmithing, bookbinding and clockmaking. In the *cabinet gothique* of the Countess d'Osmond the chairbacks were ornamented with unicorns and three-lobed arcatures.

1 | **JEAN-AUGUSTE-DOMINIQUE INGRES (1780-1867)** Death of Leonardo da Vinci
Rome, 1818, oil on canvas - Acquired with income accruing from the Dutuit bequest, 1968 - Inv. PDUT01165

In a single painting Ingres succeeds in conveying the sublime emotion of this fictive episode - the painter dying in the arms of François I, King of France - and the more anecdotal impact of the secondary figures and their picturesque evocation of the period.

Ingres' style, which for Baudelaire held a "weird" charm, combines meticulous references to classical art with the mouthwatering interplay of colour that gives it its strange beauty.

2 | **JACOB-DESMALTER (1770-1841)** Chairs from the "cabinet gothique" of the Countess d'Osmond
c. 1820
Purchased 1990 - Inv. PPO03509 and PPO03510

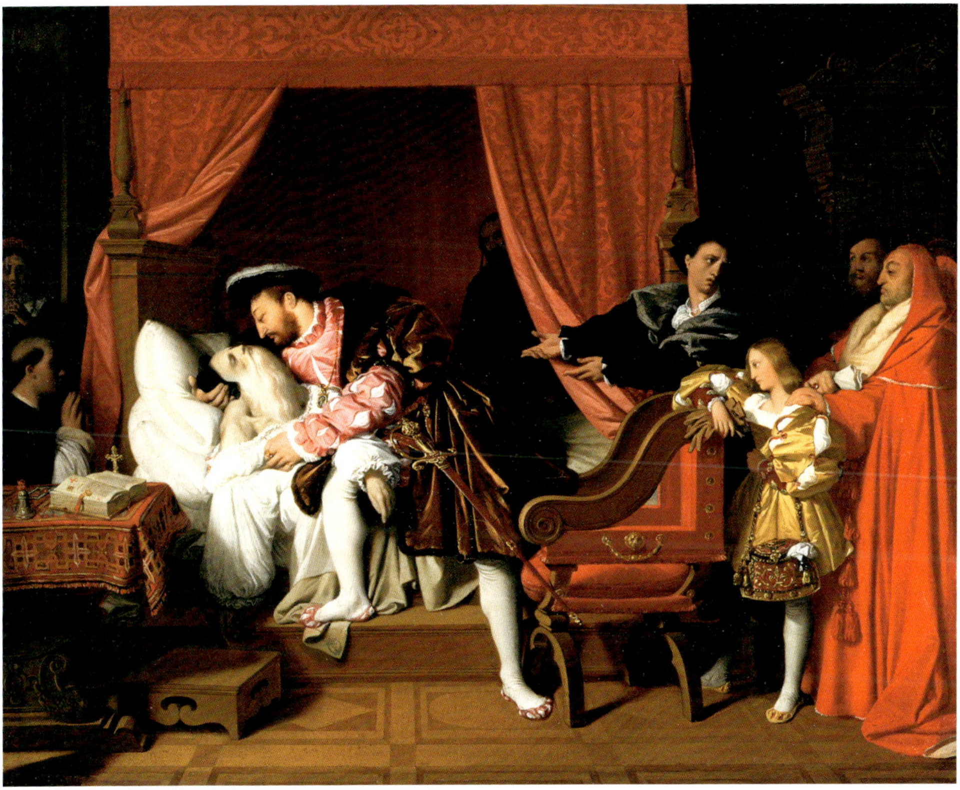

1

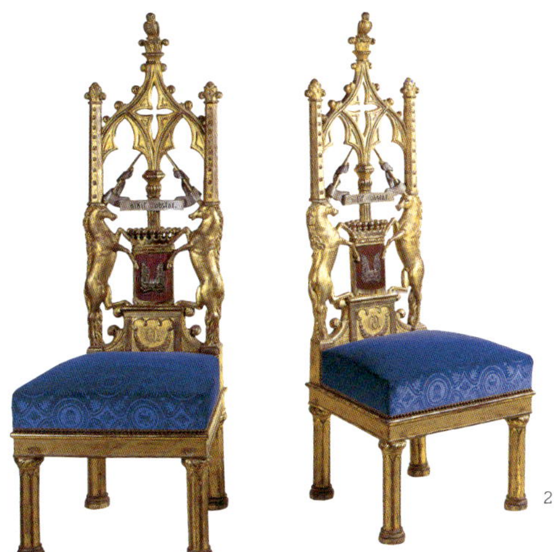

2

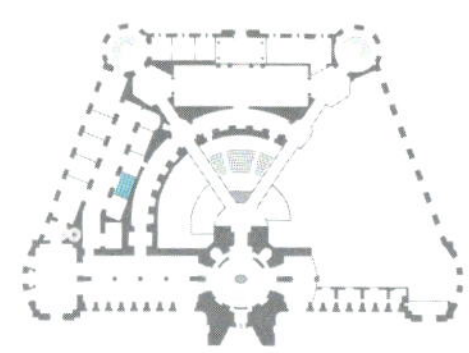

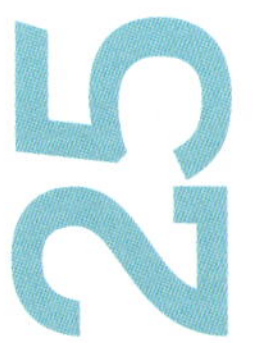

Dutch genre painting

Genre painting deals with everyday scenes in a highly realistic manner. Fitting neatly with Dutch tradition and the tastes of a basically middle class clientele, it flourished in 17th-century Holland, with Steen as one of its principal exponents. His substantial and highly varied oeuvre testifies to a wide range of influences, notably from his presumed masters - his father-in-law Jan van Goyen (1596-1656) and Adriaen van Ostade (1610-1685) - and from friends like Frans van Mieris the Elder (1635-1681). In line with the practice of the time, his highly picturesque and often comic scenes are never without their moralistic side.

JAN STEEN (1626-1679) The Little Alms Collector

c. 1663-1665, oil on panel - signature bottom right "Jan Steen" - Dutuit Bequest, 1902 - Inv. PDUT00930

The subject of this picture was only recently identified as a Pentecost procession. The key to the painting is the potted *cardamine pratensis* or Cuckoo Flower, of which the baby seated on the wooden railing is offering a bloom to the alms collector. So common that its presence as an ornament is quite improbable, this plant is called in Dutch *pinksterbloem*, meaning "flower of May"; this is also the name given by Catholics to the little girl who leads this kind of procession.

The doubts as to the correct title for the work are due to Steen's parodic presentation of the traditional event: here, instead of the girl who goes seeking alms in the streets, dressed as a bride and crowned with flowers, the artist has pictured a boy with a paper flower pinned to his bonnet.

All Steen's virtuosity is to be found in this painting: the skilled rendering of the various textures, the subtlety of the bright, richly intense colours, and the geometrical complexity of the composition.

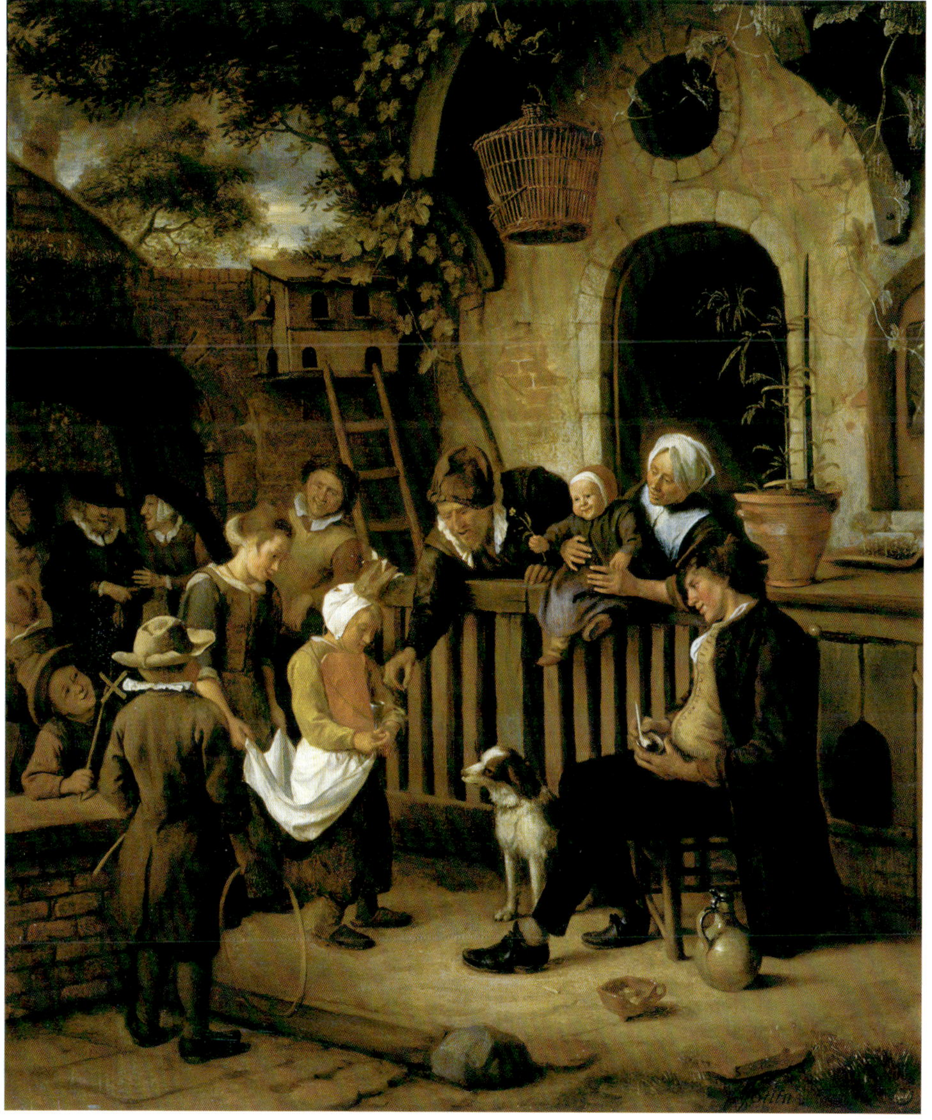

26 The Dutch portrait

For the portrait, emblematic of the relationship between the individual and the state, the 17th century was a golden age throughout Europe. In the monarchies - France, England and Spain - it was essentially a court affair, while in Holland, where it found its fullest flowering both as an individual and group genre, it pointed up the place of the middle classes on the social scale. The dominant figures are Frans Hals (1581/1585-1666) and Rembrandt, the latter producing portraits of unrivalled intensity and depth, vibrant with the inner life of their subjects. When Rembrandt moved to Amsterdam in 1631 he was immediately recognised as the city's most remarkable portraitist, a position he would hold until his death.

REMBRANDT HARMENSZ. VAN RIJN (1606-1669)

Self-Portrait in Oriental Attire

c. 1631-1633, oil on wood - signature bottom right "Rembrandt f. 1631" (later and perhaps apocryphal?) - Dutuit Bequest, 1902 - Inv. PDUT00925

Because of this painting's unusual character - it is the only one of Rembrandt's many self-portraits that shows him standing - its authenticity was long challenged. X-ray examination of the panel has revealed that the artist, dissatisfied with the position of the legs, first shortened them and then, at a later date, masked them with a dog. The hair was also modified.

He might have chosen a water spaniel to emphasise the subject's regal character. The thick coat which protected it from the cold made this dog ideal for hunting waterfowl, but the rear part of its body had to be shorn to keep it from drowning. The resemblance between the animal's head and the abundance of curly hair Rembrandt sports in all his early self-portraits adds a playful touch to the irony-tinged disparity between the hang-dog look of the animal and the dramatic pose of the subject, with his turban and finery.

There is, too, a striking contrast between the scarcely-defined space occupied by the artist and the subtle precision of the purplish brown of the costume; and between the satiny texture of the tunic and the furriness of the dog.

Greatest # of self portraits - 40 paintings 30 engravings 7 drawings without counting the numerous paintings in which he represented himself as a secondary figure. He was an inexpensive model - to practice the transformation

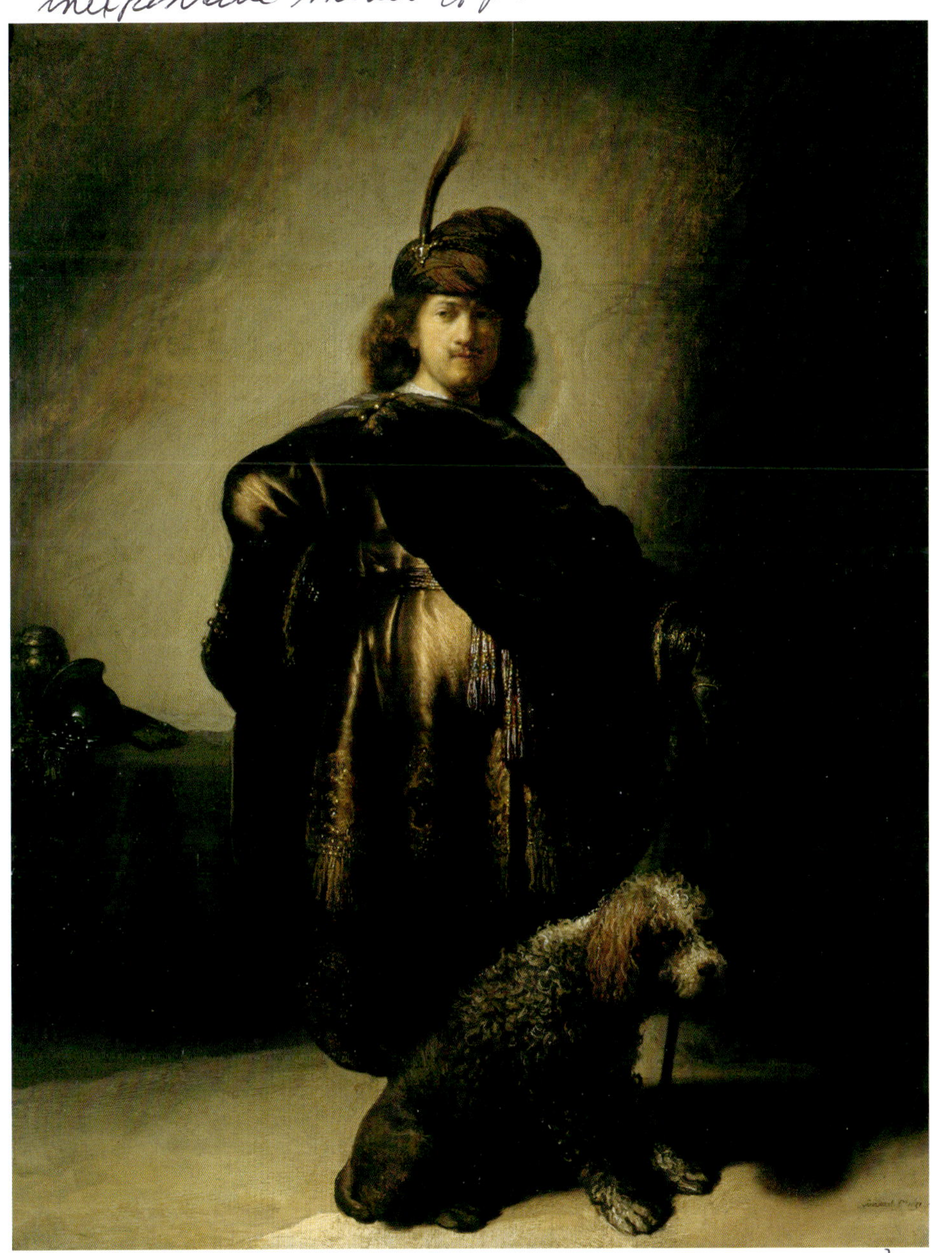

of his face under an emotion; or a character figure or his will to show himself as a portrait artist

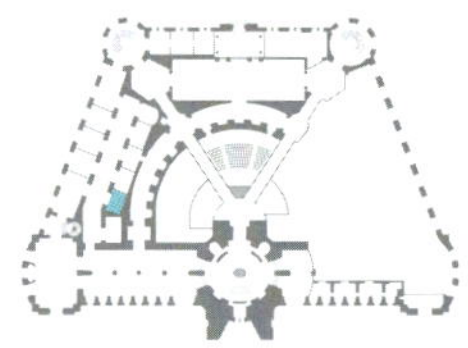

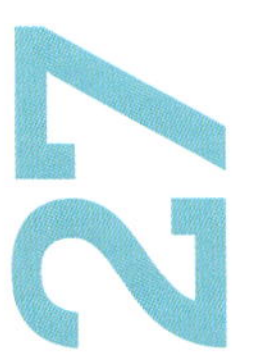

The Classical landscape

It was in the 17th century that the landscape, which had achieved autonomy in the preceding century, came to full flower in all the contemporary schools of painting. It found two main forms of expression: Franco-Italian Classicism and Dutch Naturalism.
The first of these styles, of whom the representative par excellence is Claude Gellée - born in Lorraine and also known as Claude Lorrain - is marked by a conscious poeticisation of landscape, obtained by the incorporation of idyllic scenes mostly borrowed from antiquity. Here nature is reshaped and elevated by the addition of ancient ruins.
Somewhere between 1612 and 1620 Claude left to study painting in Rome, where he would spend almost the rest of his life. It was in part due to him that Rome became the focal point for this approach to landscape. Fame and fortune came in 1630, bringing a flood of commissions from local and foreign dignitaries.

CLAUDE GELLÉE known as **CLAUDE LORRAIN (1600-1682)**
Landscape with the Port of Santa Marinella
c. 1637 - 1638, oil on octagonal copper panel - Dutuit Bequest, 1902 - Inv. PDUT00872

This picture is one of a pair commissioned from Claude by Urban VIII, pope from 1623 to 1644. *Pastoral landscape with Lake Albano and Castel Gandolfo* is now in the Fitzwilliam Museum at Cambridge University. Its pendant, which came to the Petit Palais as part of the Dutuit collection, shows the little port of Santa Marinella near Civitavecchia, not far from Rome. Urban had plans for extending the port, but the scheme never got beyond the laying of foundations.
Although Claude went to Santa Marinella to make drawings, this is no topographical view. The aim was, rather, to show a site in a whimsical setting, and curiously the role of the landscape - the point of the picture, after all - is minimised. Following Claude's traditional plan the scene is framed between two symmetrical stands of trees; and as in most of his small works, the figures in the foreground loom quite large, being set against a vague backdrop with no intervening middle ground.
The true subject, however, is light. The vivid orange of the sky lights up the background, is reflected in the water and unifies the picture space. The beauty of the actual picture surface, the density of touch in even the tiniest details and the richness of the pigments all converge in conveying the truth of nature in both its concrete and symbolic forms.

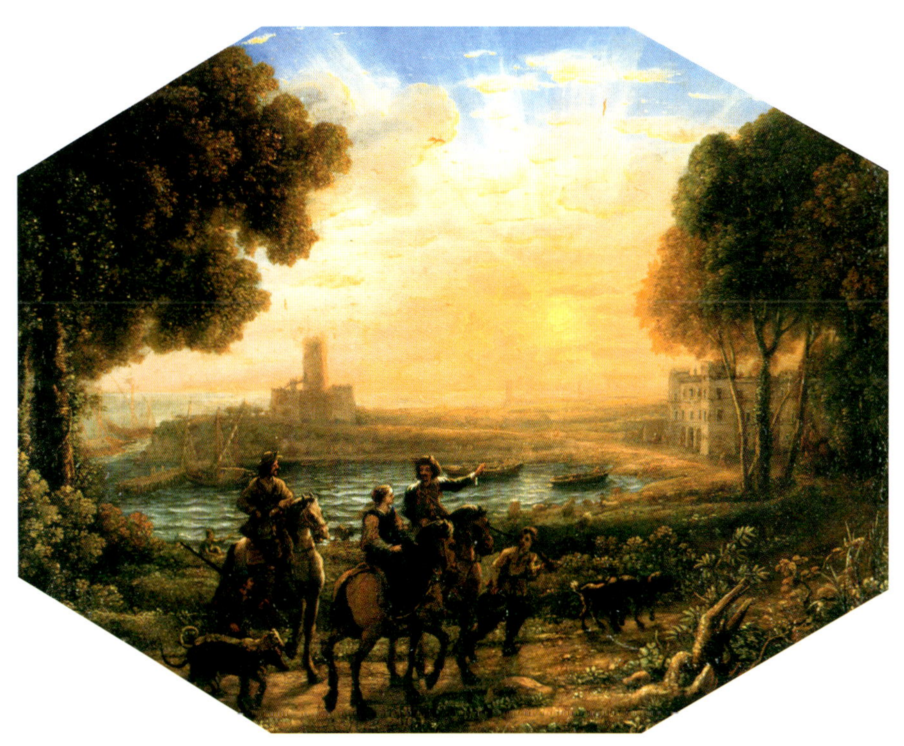

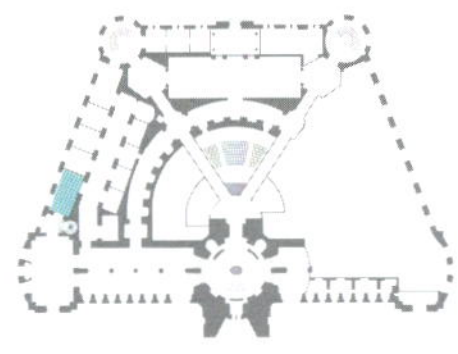

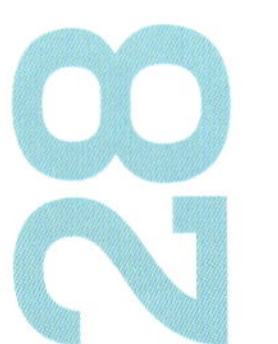

The Dutch landscape

A rare combination of sociological, religious and scientific factors led to a true revolution in the 17th-century Dutch landscape. The fresh eye the Dutch brought to nature was receptive even to its most humble aspects, while the human figure is either absent or merges totally with the landscape as it goes about its daily round.
With his master Jacob van Ruisdael (1628/1629-1682), Hobbema was one of the main moving forces in this movement devoted to portraying the Dutch countryside. His mature period covers the years 1664-1668, after which he worked as a wine-gauger for the Amsterdam customs and produced very few pictures.

MEINDERT HOBBEMA (1638-1709) The Water Mill

c. 1664-1668, oil on canvas - Dutuit Bequest, 1902 - Inv. PDUT00905

The water mill, symbolising for some both human destiny and 17th-century ingenuity, is a recurring motif in the Dutch painting of the time, and one in which Hobbema became something of a specialist. The one in the Dutuit picture has been identified as the Deventer mill on the banks of the Yjssel in a remote part of the Guelders region in northern Holland. The artist had seen it, it seems, in the course of a trip in the 1660s, and his many different paintings of the subject are evidence of the part played by personal interpretation: this was in fact an urban mill, in a setting quite different from the rural one he almost always provided. Dating from Hobbema's mature period of 1664-1668, this picture was extremely famous in the 19th century, often serving as a point of reference for the series as a whole. This spacious composition focuses on the mill itself, whose red roof stands out against a blue sky adorned with white clouds.

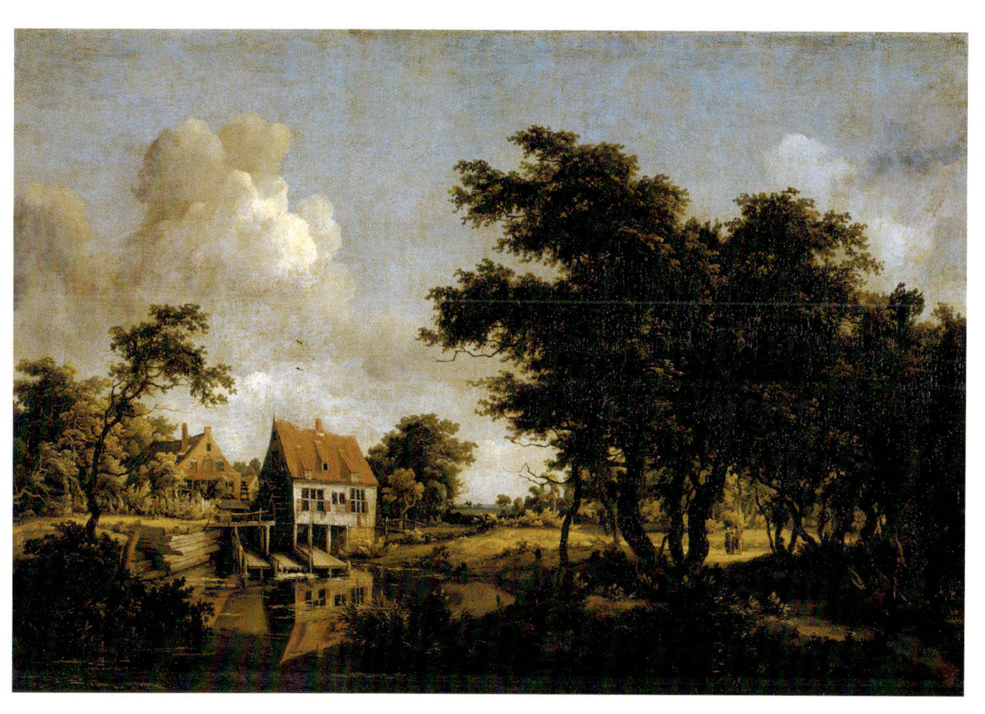

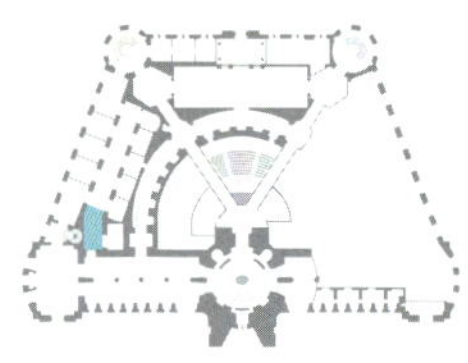

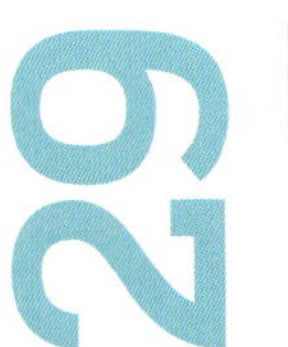

The still life

The paintings on show in Room 29 offer an insight into the evolution of the still life from the early 17th century, when it became an accepted genre, to the 18th century. *Still Life: Fruit and Flowers* by Isaac Soreau (1604 - c. 1644) is a good illustration of the early approach: a static, realistic description of juxtaposed motifs.
Nicolas de Largillierre, generally considered the greatest portraitist of his time, but a successful practitioner of all the other genres as well, is a perfect representative of the art of the still life in the late 17th and early 18th centuries. He began as a pupil in Antwerp, painting still lifes into compositions by his master Anton Goubau (1616-1698); in the course of a long career he would produce some fifty pictures of this kind. After spending the years 1675-1679 in London, where he worked with the great portraitist Peter Lely (1618-1680), he settled in Paris.

NICOLAS DE LARGILLIERRE (1656-1746) Partridge Hanging in a Niche
c. 1680-1685, oil on canvas - Gift of Georges Sortais, 1928 - Inv. PPP00833

This picture almost certainly dates from between Largillierre's arrival in Paris in 1679 and his reception into the Academy in 1686.
Largillierre borrowed the still-life-in-a-niche motif from the 17th-century Flemish and Dutch painting he knew so well. The paintings beside this one, by Dutchman Jan-Baptist Weenix (1621-1660) and his son Jan (1642-1719), are examples of the constant presence of animals hung by the feet in hunting pictures. As it happens, two very similar still lifes by Largillierre, now in the Grenoble Museum, were long attributed to Jan-Baptist Weenix.
This still life may have an allegorical significance. Hanging pitifully by one foot, the partridge may symbolise the ordeal of Christ, with the fruits around it also chosen for their symbolic character. The crack in one of the stones framing the niche, the dried-up grape in the very heart of the bunch and the tiny fallen feather by the bird are reminders of the temporal fragility of things and as such support this metaphorical interpretation.
The composition's use of undulating curves is extremely skilful. Concentrating on reflections and harmonies between close values, Largillierre works with a deliberately limited range of warm colours.

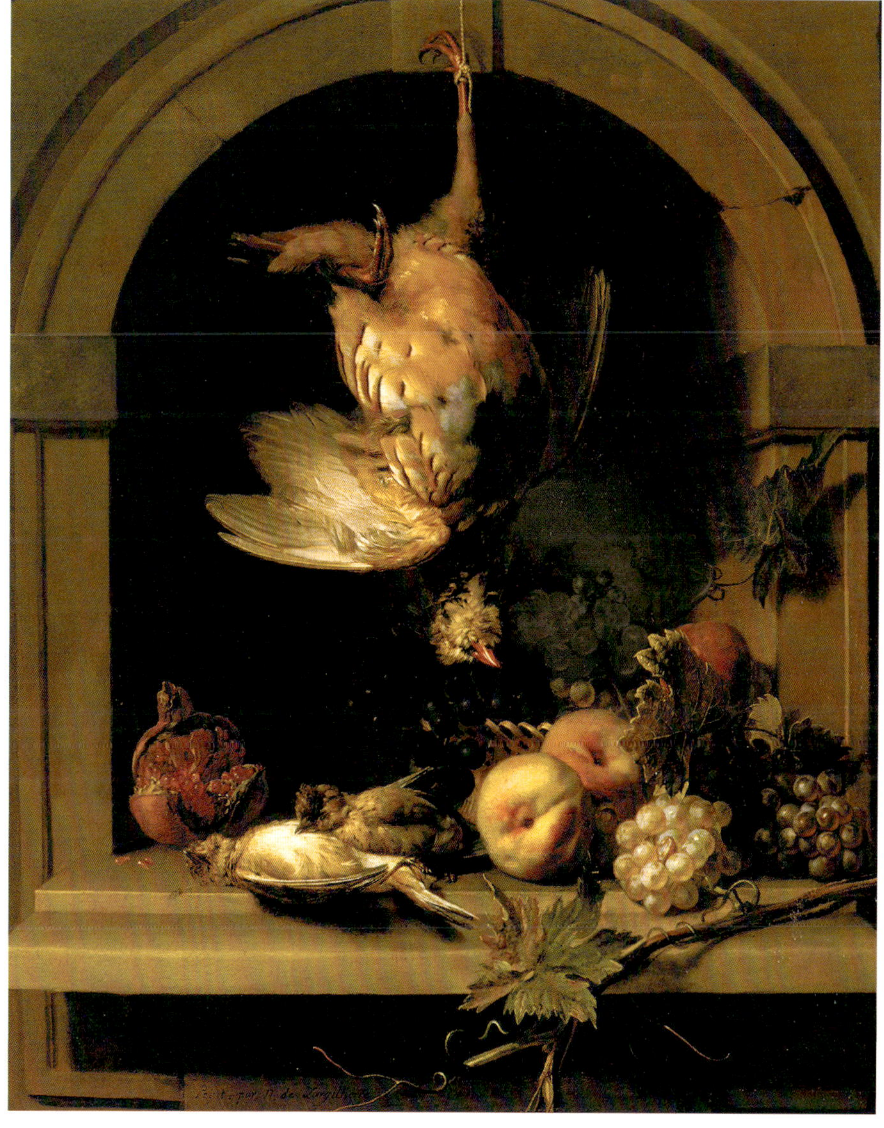

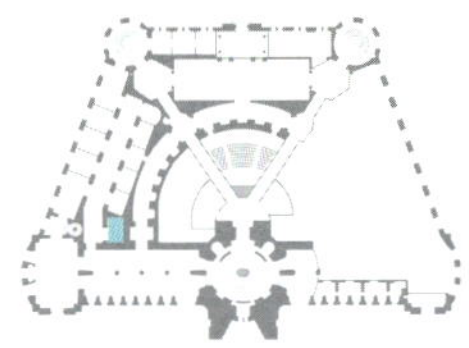

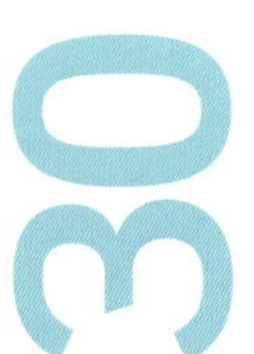

History painting

Rubens is undoubtedly the greatest Flemish artist of the 17th century and one of the foremost names in the entire history of painting. In his humanist training, knowledge of antiquity and literary tastes he is very much a Renaissance man. He worked in all genres, but history painting, the dominant mode of the time, naturally looms largest in his oeuvre. In his own lifetime his influence was enormous and artists following in his wake would be forced to take sides regarding the soaring use of colour and formal tensions he had already pushed to their limits.

SIR PETER PAUL RUBENS (1577-1640) The Rape of Proserpine

c . 1614-1615, oil on panel - Dutuit Bequest, 1902 - Inv. PDUT00954

Rubens was a master of the sketch, which he produced in great number: thrown onto the canvas in the heat of the creative moment, this primary vision combined all the power of his imagination with rapidity of execution. Intended to facilitate the work of his assistants and pupils, the Rubens sketch is above all a stunning lesson in conciseness and efficacy.

This sketch - for a large painting once part of the Duke of Marlborough's collection and destroyed when a wing of Blenheim Castle burnt down in 1861 - shows the rape of Proserpine. Caught up in a plot prepared by Venus, Pluto falls in love with Proserpine, daughter of Ceres and Jupiter, and carries her off. As presented by Rubens, the scene seems closer to the account given by the 4th-century Latin writer Claudian in his epic poem *De Raptu Proserpinae* than to the version in Book V of Ovid's *Metamorphoses*. Rubens captures splendidly the brutal rapidity of the event. Pluto's gesture as he crushes Proserpine's body against him unites their figures in a single, luminous diagonal running counter to the darker diagonal of Minerva's attempt to foil him. All of Rubens' technical mastery is put into conveying this violence. On a saffron base he draws fluently with the tip of the brush, succeeding in bringing to this work in oils the graphic qualities of watercolour and even of drawing.

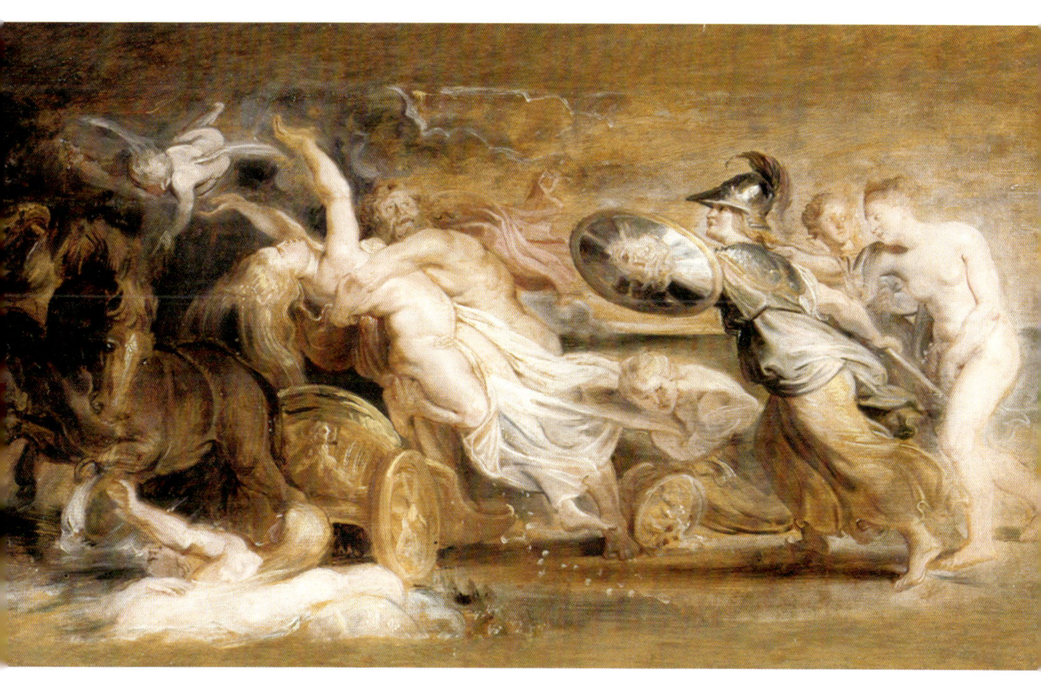

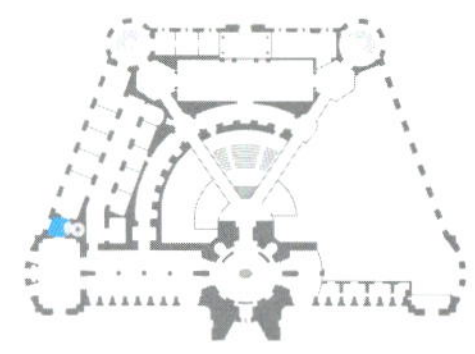

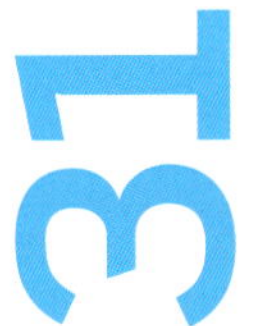

The measurement of time

The Renaissance was truly a golden age for clockmaking. The first mechanical clocks, functioning with a weight, made their appearance on public buildings in the 13th century. However, the real technical revolution came in the 15th century with the invention of the spring: by replacing the weight it made for smaller clocks the aristocracy could have in their homes.

Table clocks came in architecturally inspired designs: round or square towers ornamented with pilasters, colonnettes and arcades. The most valuable of them were also fitted with an astrolabe dial that allowed the owner to follow the movement of the heavenly bodies and delve into the mysteries of astrology (1).

Appearing in the second half of the 15th century, watches were the next step in the miniaturisation process, with 16th and 17th-century European models characterised by great formal inventiveness, delicate ornamentation and sumptuous materials: the watch had become a luxury item with the same status as a piece of jewellery (2, 3).

1 | Square tower clock with astrolabe dial
NICOLAS FÉAU
Gilt brass - Marseille, c. 1550 - Acquired with income accruing from the Dutuit bequest, 1925 - Inv. ODUT01604

This table clock possesses a delicately chased mechanism set below chimes hidden behind openwork arcatures. What makes it truly remarkable, however, is the astrolabe dial on top, whose complex functioning allows the study of, among other things, the movements of the sun and moon through the zodiac.

This piece is testimony to the enormous enthusiasm of the wealthy, scientifically curious humanists of the Renaissance for astronomy and astrology. Its owner could readily observe the movement of the heavenly bodies and thus read his own horoscope without reference to an astrologer.

Unlike their German counterparts, French clockmakers were little given to this kind of complexity. This explains the extreme rarity of such clocks in France, where only seven examples are to be found - two of them in the Petit Palais.

2 | Tulip watch
JOHANN JACOB RUGENDAS
Silver, brass - Augsburg, Germany, second quarter 17th century
Dutuit Bequest, 1902 - Inv. ODUT01416

3 | Oval hunter watch
Gilt copper, enamel fused into sunken gold-line cells in a medallion of translucent glass - Paris, first half 17th century - Acquired with income accruing from the Dutuit bequest, 1925 - Inv. ODUT01606

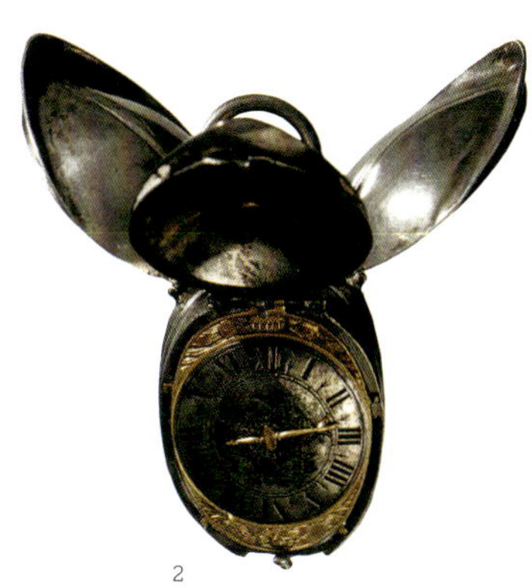

2

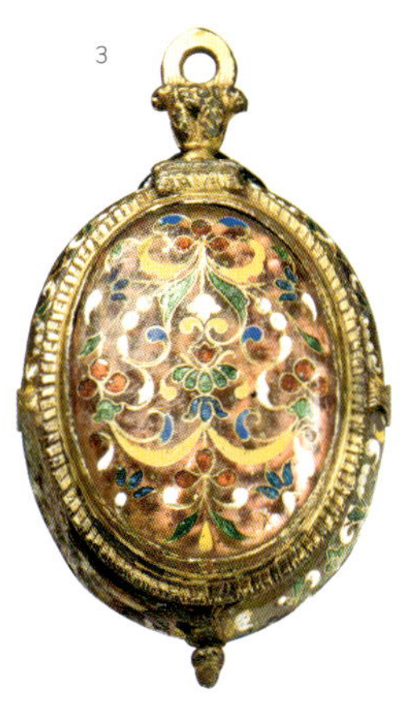

3

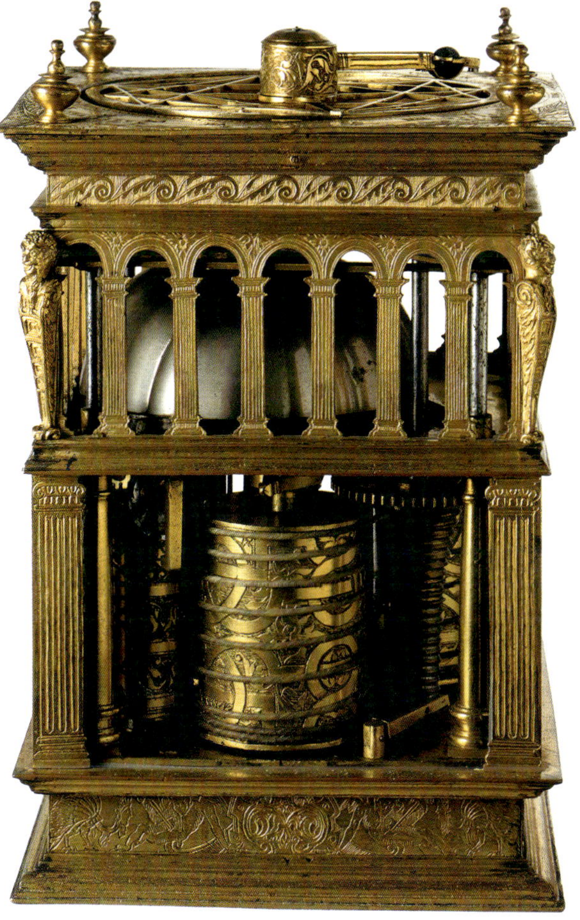

1

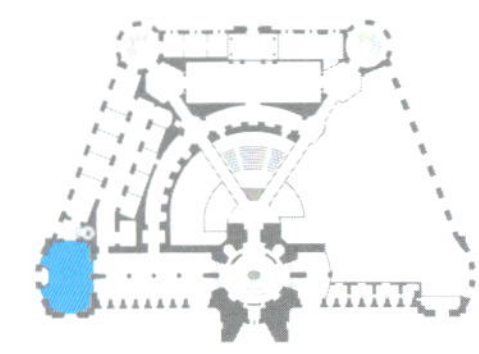

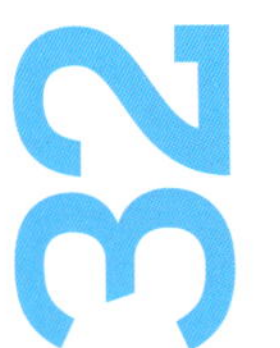

French ceramics

The pieces classified as "Saint-Porchaire pottery" (1) have a special place in the history of French ceramics, being renowned for the whiteness of the original clay and the fineness of the finished items. Too fragile to be used, these strictly decorative pieces made only between 1540 and 1560 were doubtless commissioned by royalty and the aristocracy.

The most typical of Renaissance French ceramic styles, however, is "terre vernissée", in which the clay is coated with a coloured, translucent lead glaze. Traditionally associated with the famous ceramicist Bernard Palissy (1510-1590), pieces ornamented with "rustic figulines" (2) - animals, and plants moulded from the life - or narrative scenes (3) were still being made in the 17th century, doubtless to be shown off on the dresser. They illustrate wonderfully well the taste of the aristocracy of the time for the combination of oddness and technical virtuosity.

1 | "Saint-Porchaire" pottery

France, mid-16th century - Dutuit Bequest, 1902 - Inv. ODUT01126, 1127 and 1128

The Petit Palais has the privilege of housing three examples of this remarkable type of ceramic ware, of which only some seventy pieces have survived in the entire world.

The candlestick and the two ewers - known as "baby bottles" because of their small mouth - present two types of highly sophisticated ornamentation: moulded elements applied to the body of the piece - figurines, coats of arms, masks, shells - and inlaid arabesques and tracery. The mystery of this latter technique was solved only recently: the ornamentation was stamped with relief and hollow matrices, either directly onto the piece or onto a thin sheet of clay which was then glued to the piece in question.

The Petit Palais candlestick bears the arms of France, the monogram of Henri II and the coat of arms of Anne de Montmorency, whose family owned land at Bressuire, not far from Saint-Porchaire, thought to be the source of this type of ceramic ware.

2 | Illustrated oval dish: Henri IV and his family

Terre vernissée - Fontainebleau workshop, known as Avon(?), first quarter 17th century - Dutuit Bequest, 1902
Inv. ODUT01141

3 | Large oval dish ornamented with "rustic figulines"

A SUCCESSOR OF BERNARD PALISSY

Terre vernissée - France, late 16th - first half 17th century
Dutuit Bequest, 1902 - Inv. ODUT01129

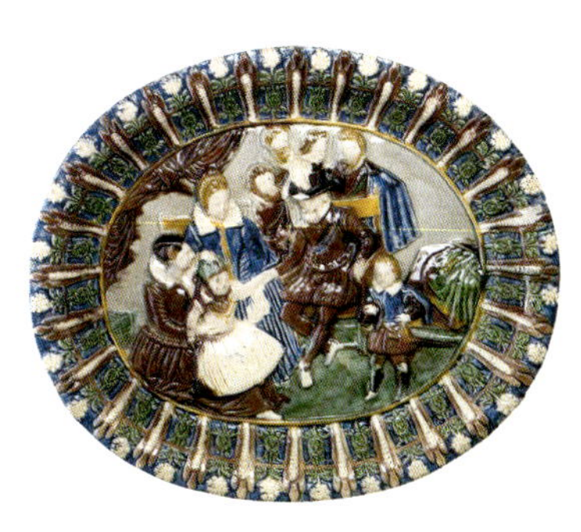

2 | 3

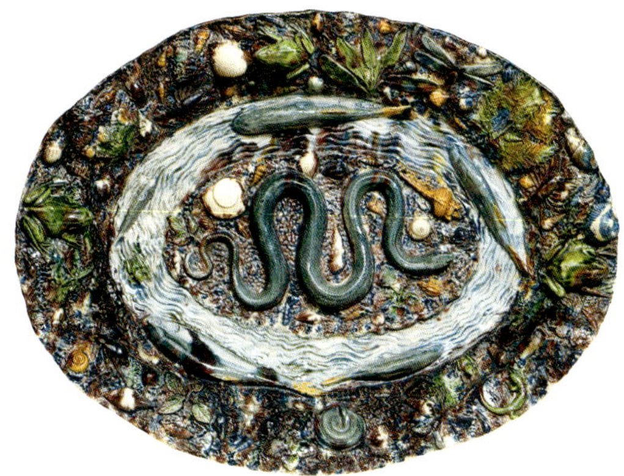

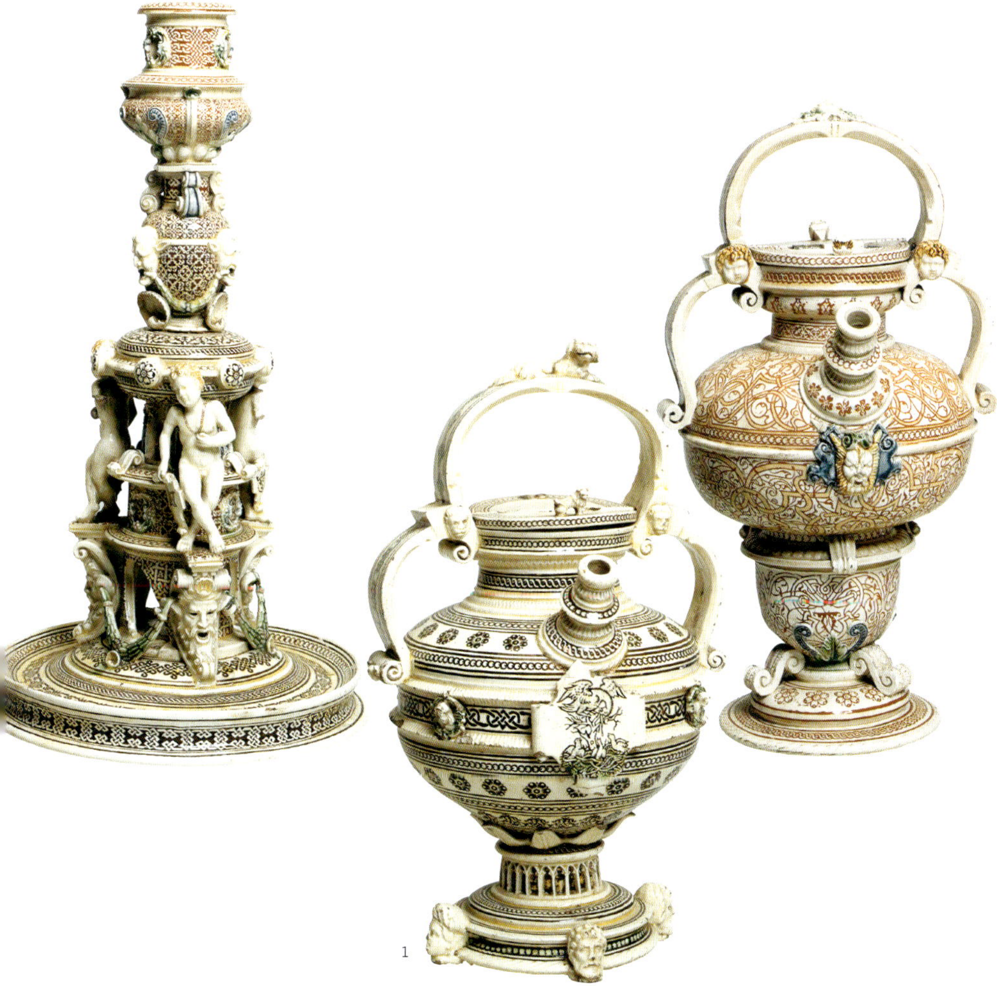

1

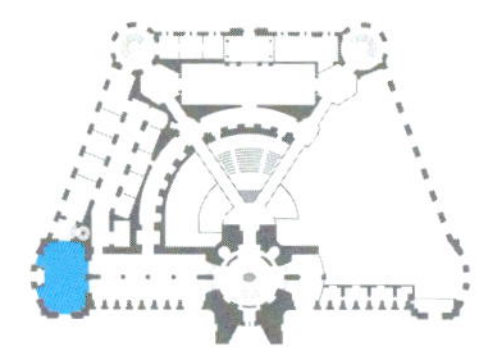

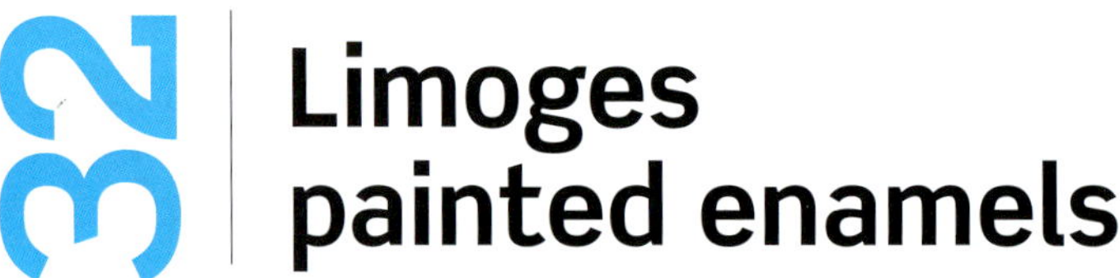

32 Limoges painted enamels

Born in Limoges in the late 15th century, enamel painting enjoyed a surge of popularity in the following century. The technique consists of applying layers of enamel - a silica-based product related to glass - to copper with a brush or spatula, and sometimes scratching the enamelled surface back with a needle to expose an underlying lighter or darker layer.

After concentrating on religious subjects early in the 16th century, in the 1530s enamellers began drawing on such tales and myths of antiquity as the Labours of Hercules, Jason and the Golden Fleece, and Virgil's Aeneid. The images were obtained from engravings of the works of the Italian, French and Northern masters, then circulating throughout a renascent Europe.

The most popular items were ceremonial pieces - ewers, basins, *tazze*, plates, salt cellars - of no practical use, some of them bearing the arms of a wealthy client whose taste and standing they existed to celebrate.

1 | Ewer. Scenes from the story of Jason and the Golden Fleece.
MAÎTRE I.C.
Painted enamel - Limoges, late 16th-early 17th century - Dutuit Bequest, 1902 - Inv. ODUT01245

The scenes on this ewer are based on illustrations in the *Livre de la Conqueste de la Toison d'or*, published in Paris in 1563 with engravings by René Boyvin after drawings by Léonard Thiry. When Jason, hero of classical antiquity, sets out in search of the Golden Fleece, he meets and falls in love - tragically - with the beauteous Medea.

This piece testifies to the rich palette used by the Limoges enamellers at the turn of the 17th century. Placed on silver foil, the translucent coloured enamels suggest the shine of gold and silver-gilt tableware.

2 | *Tazza*. The Banquet of Dido and Aeneas
PIERRE REYMOND
Painted enamel - Limoges, 1544
Dutuit Bequest, 1902 - Inv. ODUT01267

3 | Plaque. Thought to be the portrait of Jeanne d'Albret
ATTRIBUTED TO THE WORKSHOP OF LÉONARD LIMOSI
Painted enamel - Limoges, mid-16th century
Dutuit Bequest, 1902 - Inv. ODUT01253

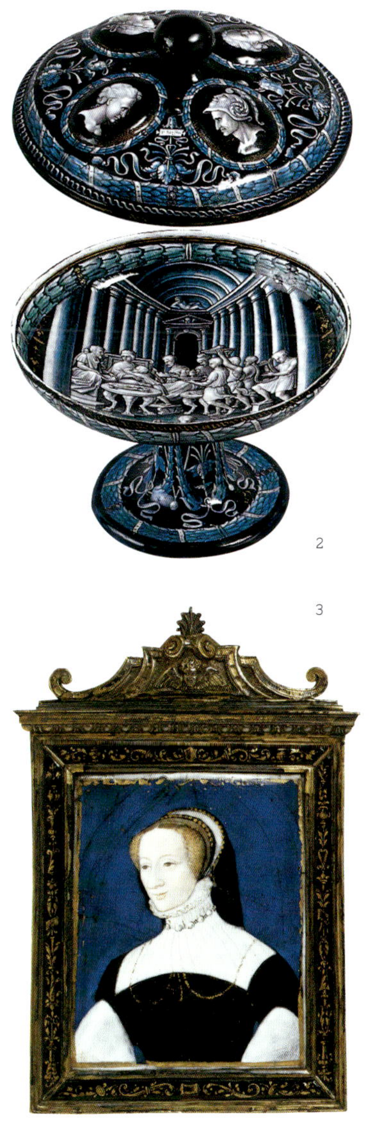

2

3

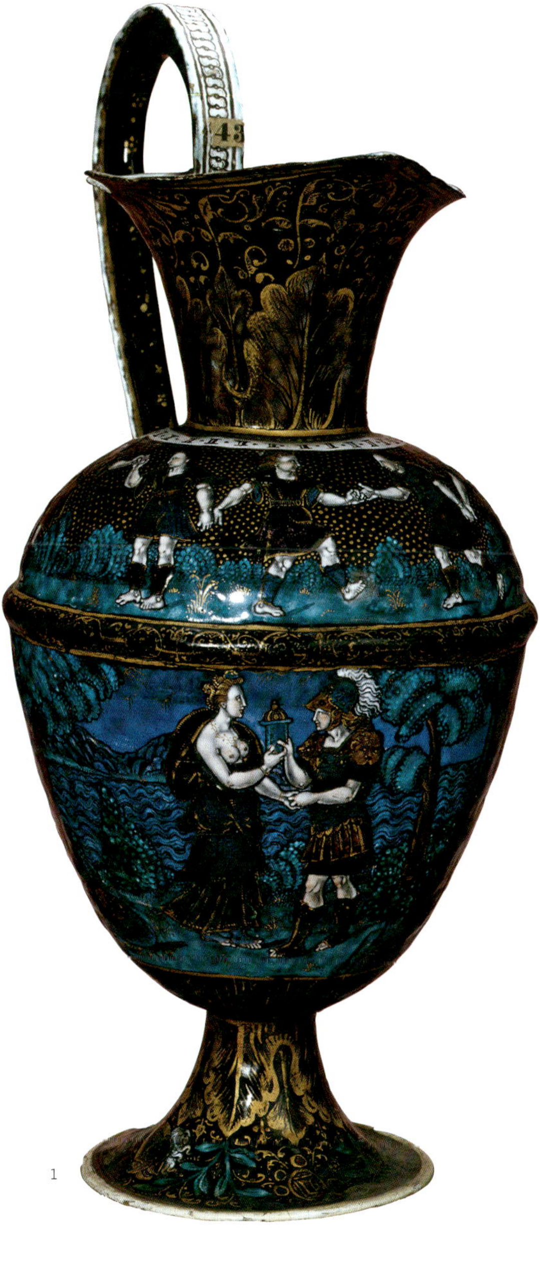

1

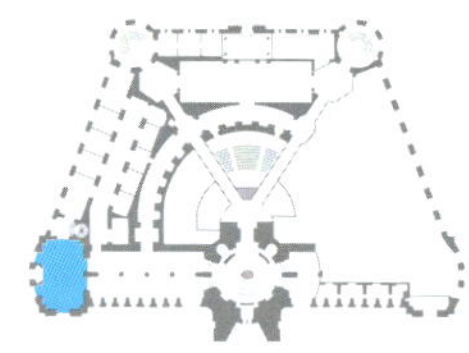

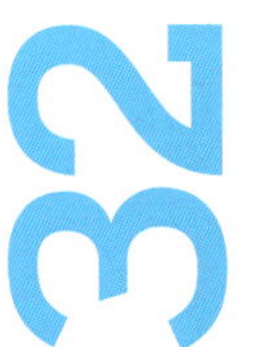

Italian majolica

Majolica is the Italian earthenware of the Renaissance and may owe its name to the island of Majorca, a port of call on the trade route between Spain and Italy. Initially influenced by Spanish earthenware with its iridescent metallic highlights (2), this subtly luxurious form underwent a distinctive evolution in Italy, reaching its high point in the 16th century.

Earthenware is clay covered with an opaque tin glaze that serves as a support for ornamental or figurative painted decoration. The taste for *istoriati* - historiated or narrative ornamentation - using mythological, Biblical or historical scenes often drawn from famous engravings, peaked in the early 16th century in such northern and central Italian cities as Faenza, Pesaro, Urbino, Casteldurante, Deruta and Cafaggiolo.

The handsomest majolica items were often purely decorative and intended for the *credenza* - a piece of furniture designed for the display of ceremonial tableware - as proof of the wealth, culture and taste of their owners.

1 | Dish. The Judgement of Paris

PAINTER OF THE JUDGEMENT OF PARIS, WORKSHOP OF MAESTRO GIORGIO

Lustred earthenware - Gubbio, Italy, 1520 - Dutuit Bequest, 1902 - Inv. ODUT01091

This dish is decorated with an episode from Greek mythology much appreciated in Renaissance times: Paris, called on by the gods to arbitrate a dispute between the goddesses Hera, Athena and Aphrodite, chose Aphrodite as the most beautiful of the three and awarded her the golden apple. The images take their inspiration from engravings after Raphael and Timoteo Viti.

The painted scene is highlighted with iridescent yellows and reds, this lustred effect being obtained by the application of salts of silver or copper onto a once-fired glaze, followed by a final low-temperature, oxygen-free reduction firing. First used in a number of pottery centres in the late 15th century, the technique was further developed in the 16th century in Gubbio - where it made the reputation of Maestro Giorgio's workshop - and in Deruta, another major centre in Umbria.

2 | Large basin. Two women in profile, one on each side of a tree of life
Lustred earthenware
Manises, Spain, first half 16th century
Dutuit Bequest, 1902 - Inv. ODUT01039

3 | Ewer basin. The Wedding of Alexander and Roxana
GIACOMO MANCINI, known as **EL FRATE**
Lustred earthenware
Deruta, Italy, c. 1540-1545
Dutuit Bequest, 1902 - Inv. ODUT01115

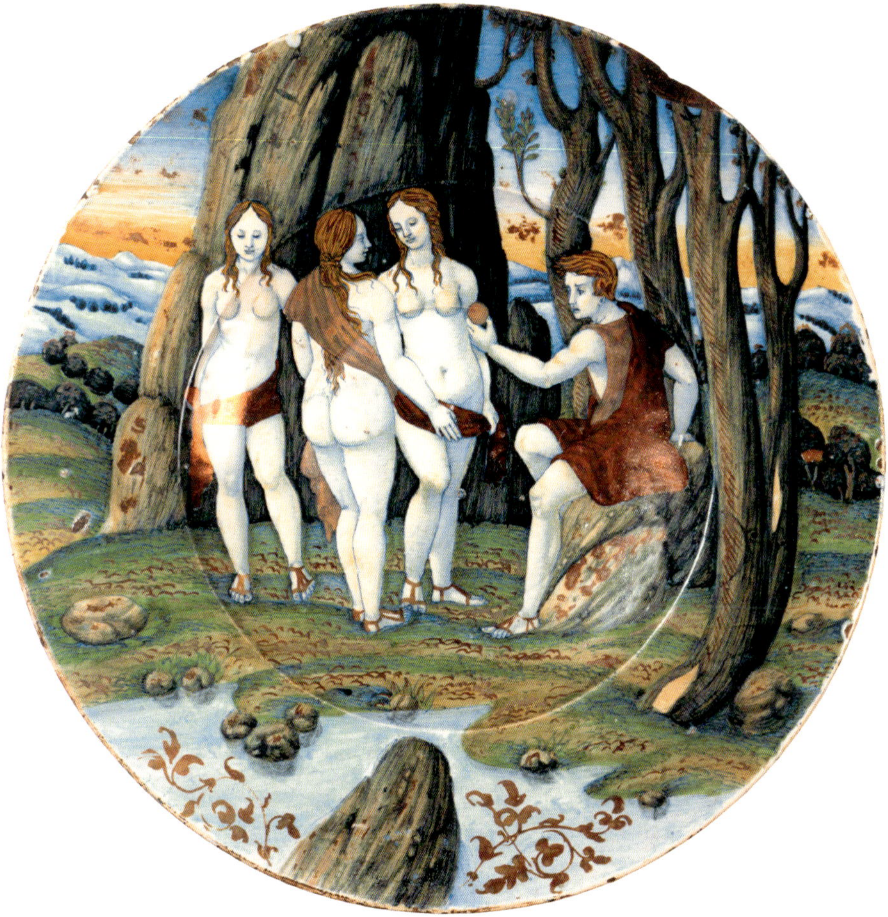

1

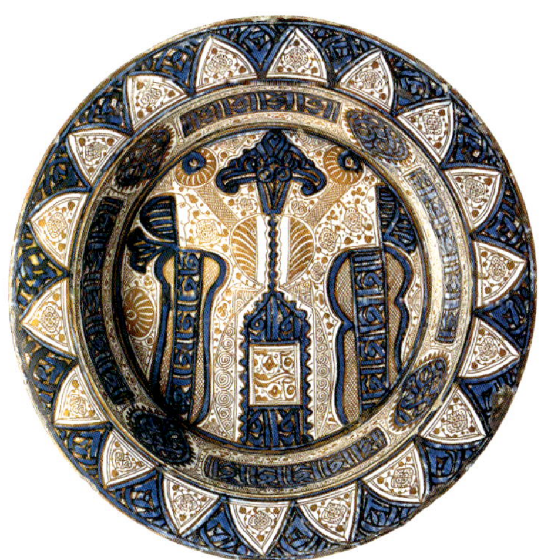

2

3

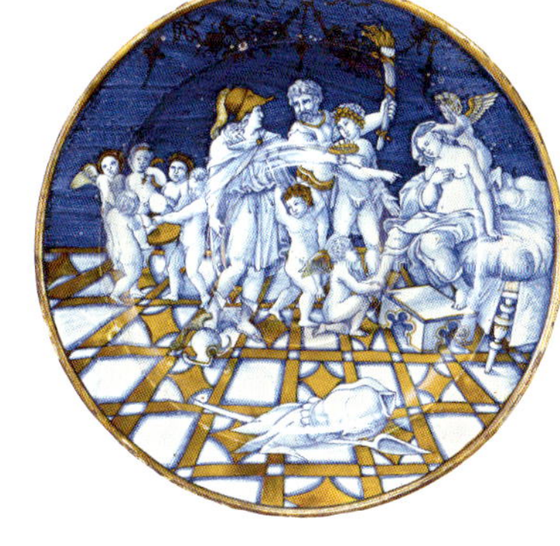

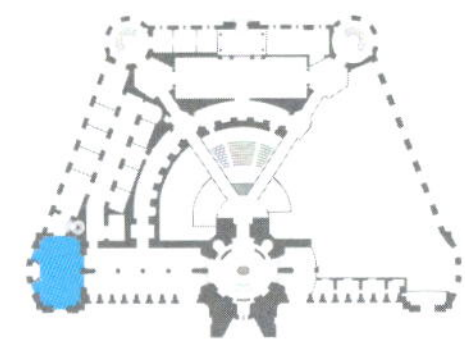

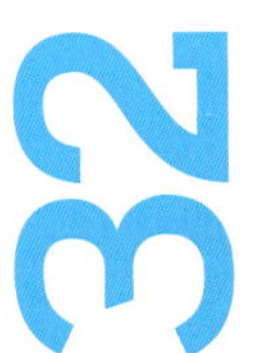

Venetian glassware

Venice was the birthplace of Renaissance glassware. Glass had been made and worked since ancient times, but in the mid-15th century the invention of a very pure, colourless substance – *cristallo* – triggered a boom. Blown with or without the aid of moulds, crystal became a luxury product much prized by Europe's elites.

In the late 15th century glassware shapes often imitated the work of goldsmiths, with gilt and enamel decoration inspired by Oriental models: coloured glass powder was placed on the piece, then given a low-temperature firing. Venetian glass reached its highest point of perfection in the 16th century, when unprecedented formal subtlety and elegance made every item a masterpiece. Dazzling technical mastery and the invention of *lattimo*, a milky-coloured glass, led to the creation of filigree ornamentation, in which opaque white threads were incorporated into the body of the glass to create interweaving spirals. The workshops also excelled in painted decoration applied to the back of the completed piece.

Widely exported to other European countries, Venetian glassware gave rise to massive production of "Venice-style" pieces, notably in Bohemia, Germany and Holland from the 16th to the 18th century.

1 | Glass. Dance of the Cupids.

Clear glass, cold-painted polychrome decoration, gold - Venice, mid-16th century - Dutuit Bequest, 1902 - Inv. ODUT01289

This large crystal piece offers a delightful cold-painted scene on its inside. The subject, visible through perfectly colourless glass, draws on an engraving by Marcantonio Raimondi after Raphael: two cupids leading a children's dance in a landscape setting.

The delicate gilt foliated patterns along the rim add to the rich distinction of the ornamentation, which is in a remarkable state of preservation. Designed for show, this luxury item was certainly never used.

2 | Lidded vase with filigree ornamentation

Glass - Venice, second half 16th century - Dutuit Bequest, 1902 - Inv. ODUT01304

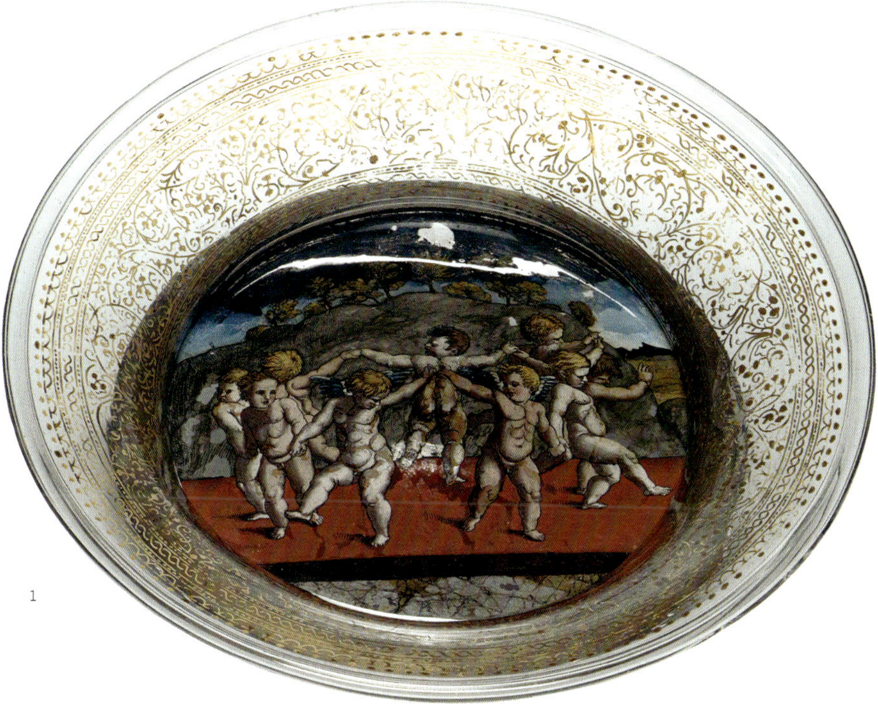

1

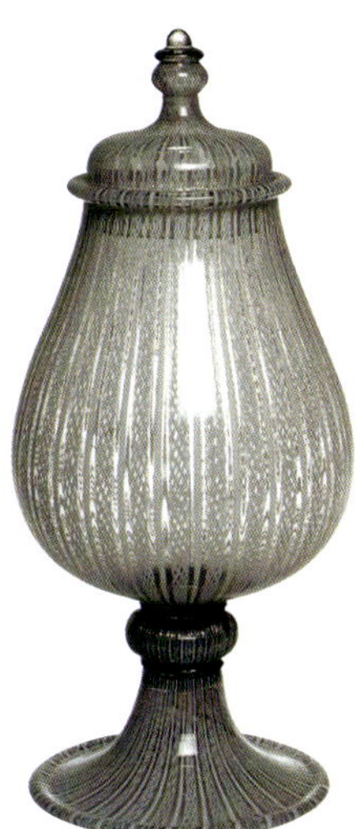

2

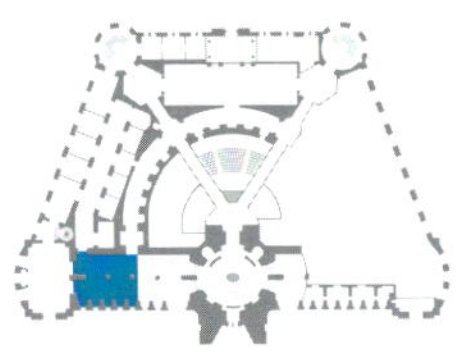

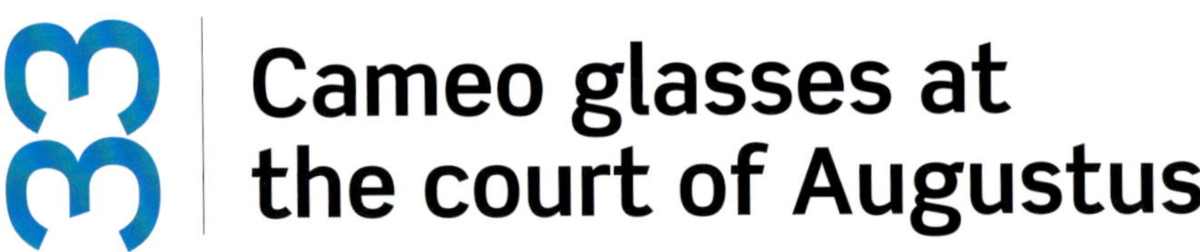

33 Cameo glasses at the court of Augustus

The few cameo glasses preserved nowadays constitute one of the highest artistic achievements of glassmaking in the Roman world. The delicate carving of the scenes points towards the techniques used by the artists who created large cameo plaques of layered semi-precious stones for the Hellenistic kings. When Ptolemaic Egypt was conquered by the Romans in 30 B.C., Augustan Rome became the sole patron of the arts. Given the historical circumstances, it is not unlikely that the technique originated in Alexandria and further developed in Italy. The earliest known cameo glass dates from the 1st century BC. Apparently cameo vessels and panels remained the privilege of an elite.

The four cameo panels that have come down to us all illustrate Dionysian rites.

The *Carpegna Cameo* in the Louvre, from the Catacomb of Priscilla in Rome, shows Bacchus and Ariadne in glory. The two cameo glasses found amid the ruins of the living room, or *triclinium* in the house of Fabius Rufus in Pompeii, portray the Appearance of Dionysus to Ariadne and the Initiation of Ariadne into the Dionysian Mysteries. They can be seen in the National Museum of Archaeology in Naples.

SATYR HOLDING OUT A BUNCH OF GRAPES TO THE INFANT DIONYSOS

Cameo glass - Italy, late 1st century BC - Dutuit Bequest, 1902 - ADUT00240

The subject of the Dutuit panel is part of the same repertoire, much in vogue during the last years of the Republic, then during the Augustan era. In a rural setting a young satyr seated on a rocky outcrop offers a bunch of grapes to the infant Dionysos, in the shade of the pine tree traditionally associated with the god of wine. Perched on a column, a statue of the god Pan surveys the scene.

The purpose of these small, square plaques is not certain. We know of the *quadraturae vitrae*, costly plates of glass fixed to the walls of Roman houses, but the backs of the panels show no sign of such use. The Romans did, however, have a marked taste for inlaid furniture: the inlays were mostly ivory, but may also have been glass.

We can be sure of one thing: the repairs made to such pieces in ancient times - the *Initiation of Ariadne* is an example - indicate that they were treasured by their owners.

Symbols of technical perfection, cameo glasses vanished with the Julio-Claudian dynasty of 27 BC - 68 AD.

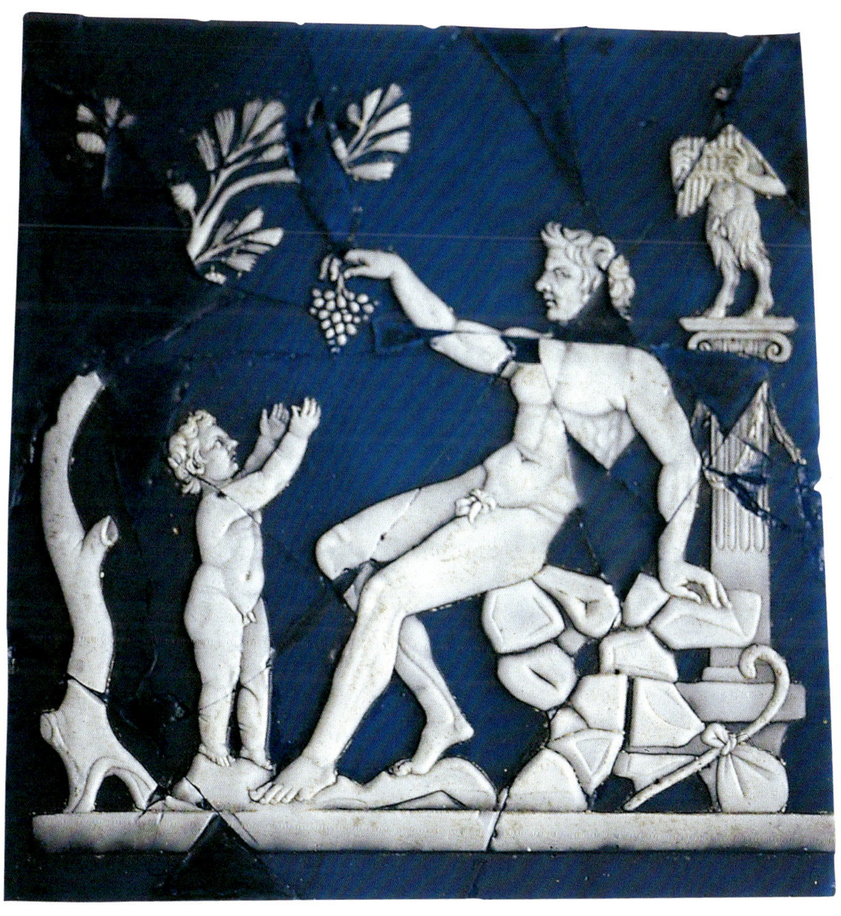

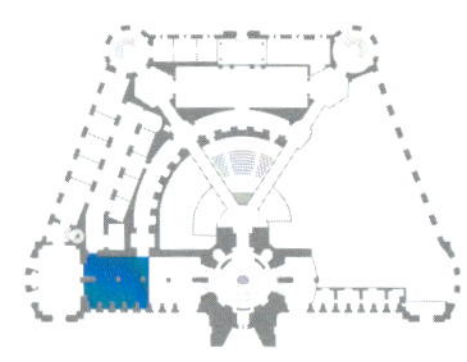

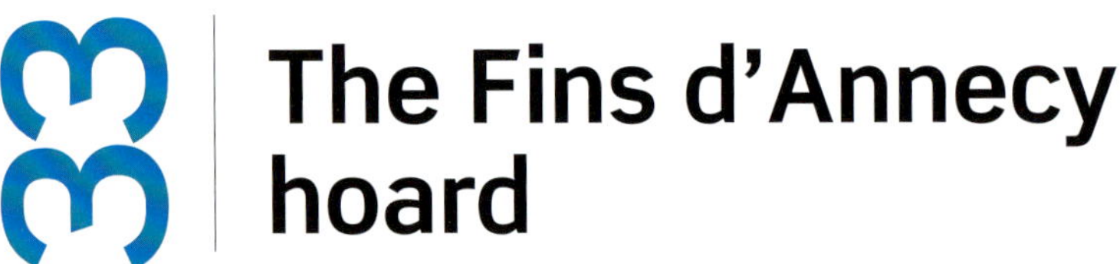

33 The Fins d'Annecy hoard

After a half-century of civil war resulting in the death or banishment of all his opponents, Octavian set about a fictive restoration of the Republic in 27 BC. Given the title of Augustus by the senate, he ruled Rome and its empire until his death in 14 AD. When he came to power Rome was already the largest and wealthiest city in the Mediterranean world. It was also a museum, home to works plundered from southern Italy and Greece, then from the Hellenistic kingdoms of the Eastern Mediterranean and, ultimately, Egypt.

Augustus launched an ambitious building programme intended to transform the ancient brick city into one made of marble. Bent on creating a new Athens, he established the model that would be followed, on a local scale, by the cities of Rome's provinces.

Such was the case of Boutae (now Annecy), a Gallo-Roman town dependent on the city of Vienne. A stopping-place on the imperial way Augustus had created between Milan and Strasbourg, Boutae adopted the Roman planning model early in the 1st century AD. Under the Flavians and Antonines, stability and prosperity brought a host of new public buildings, while the subsequent reign of the Severans saw a period of stagnation followed by troubled times. In the second half of the 3rd century Boutae was twice destroyed by fire.

The bronzes discovered at Les Fins d'Annecy in 1867 provide a striking summary of local history. In a carefully prepared hiding place were found a statuette broken into several pieces and three portraits, all of which had clearly played a part in the public life of the city.

1 | The Fins d'Annecy Ephebe Bronze – Rome, c. 30 BC

Provenance: Les Fins d'Annecy (formerly Boutae) - Dutuit Bequest, 1902 - Inv. ADUT00001

The late 2nd century BC saw the appearance of a Neo-Attic school in Greece and Italy, providing this new market with "classical-style" works inspired by the Greek masterpieces of the 5th and 4th centuries BC. Countless copies - mostly marble, but occasionally bronze - were turned out. Dating from 50-30 BC and derived from a bronze by Polykleitos, the *Fins d'Annecy Ephebe* is a perfect illustration of this late Republican artistic trend. How did this statuette find its way to Gaul? In the luggage of some state official? Or brought from Rome by a member of the local Romanised elite?

It may initially have been intended as a cult object. The divine attribute, originally in the statuette's hand but now broken, had been added at a later date. What was the identity then assumed by the bronze statuette? Perhaps as Hermes bearing the caduceus, the staff with intertwined serpents. Or as Bonus Eventus, the god of rural prosperity, with his cornucopia, promise of ripe harvests.

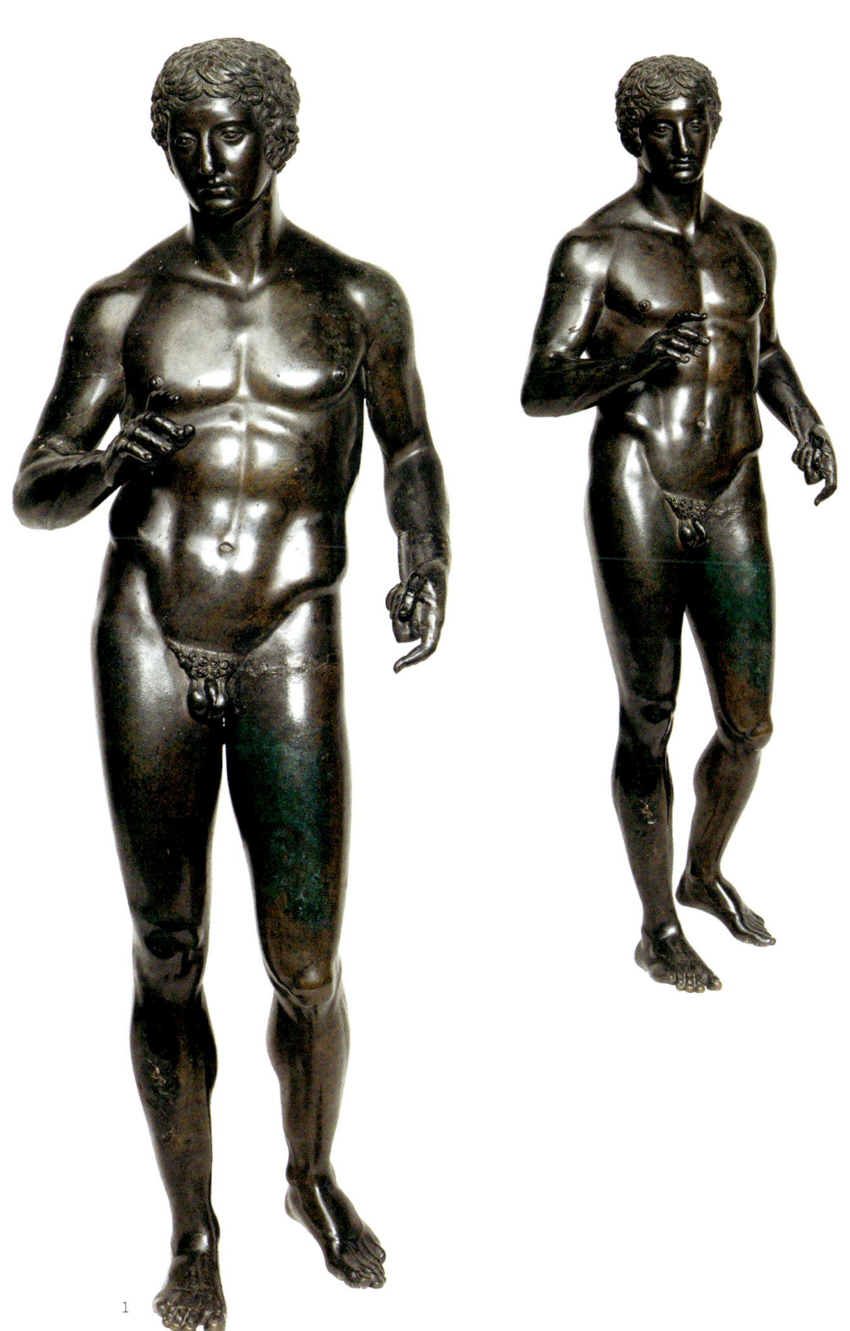

1

2 | Antoninus Pius (Roman emperor 138-161 AD) Hollow bronze casting – Northern Italy, 2nd century AD
Discovered at Les Fins d'Annecy (formerly Boutae) in 1867 - Dutuit Bequest, 1902 - Inv. ADUT00002

Beginning with Augustus, who laid down the official model, the portrait of Rome's ruling emperor was displayed in all public places throughout the Empire.
This head of Antoninus, whose reign was one of great prosperity for Boutae, was originally a bust intended to be set atop a square hermaic pillar.
The style suggests it was made, not in Rome, but in a workshop in northern Italy.

3 | Magistrate Hollow bronze casting – Roman Gaul, 2nd century AD
Discovered at Les Fins d'Annecy (formerly Boutae) in 1867 - Dutuit Bequest, 1902 - Inv. ADUT00003

The break at shoulder level indicates that this larger-than-life head was part of a standing statue. When the hoard was buried, only the head was included. The impressive dimensions of the statue make it clear that the subject was an official, but his identity has not been established.
The raising of statues to public figures was a custom borrowed from Rome, but the execution of this head belongs to a totally different manner. The decoratively stylised beard and hair emphasise the powerful planes of the face.

4 | Magistrate Hollow bronze casting – Roman Gaul, 2nd century AD
Discovered at Les Fins d'Annecy (formerly Boutae) in 1867 - Dutuit Bequest, 1902 - Inv. ADUT00004

Smaller than the preceding one, this head is also from an official, life-size statue. The resemblance between the two reflects a similar stylistic approach, although there are more realistic touches here. This portrait was made in the same region, and perhaps in the same workshop and at the same period, as the other one.
The urge to preserve that led to the burying of these three heads points to the Roman conception of the image as something sacred, as a guarantee of eternal survival in historical memory.

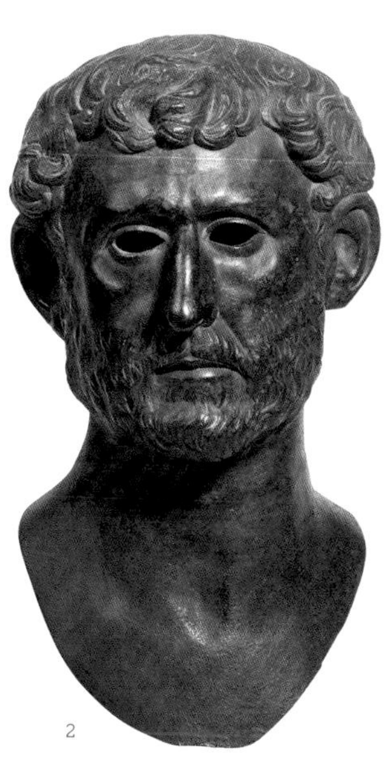
2

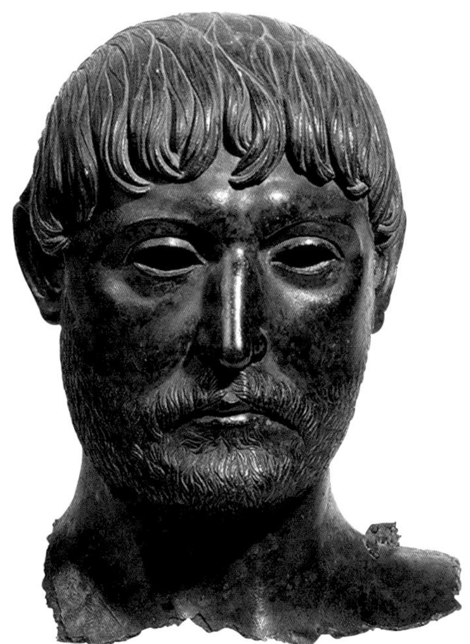
3 | 4

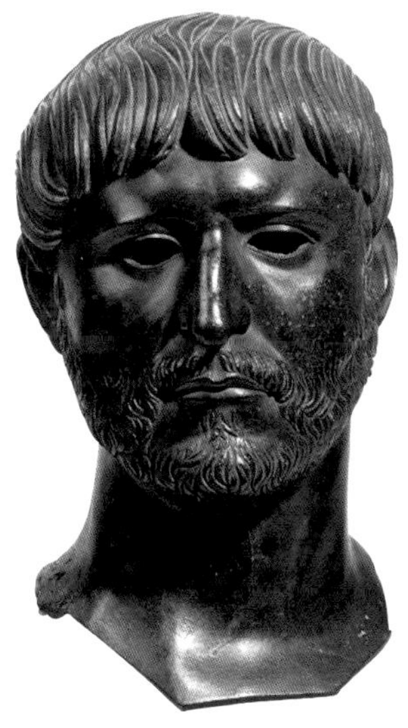

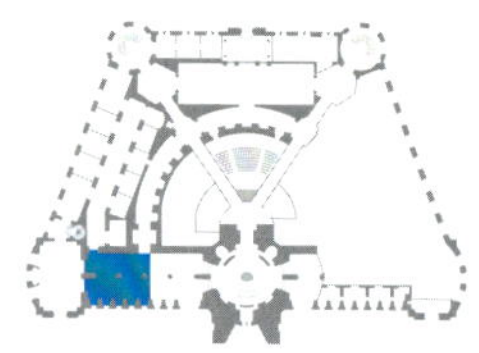

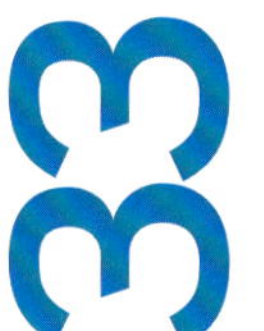

Late Antiquity and sumptuary art

Archaeological strokes of luck have brought us major "silver hoards" dating from Late Antiquity - the 4th and 5th centuries AD. Among the most impressive of these finds art those of Mildenhall, Chaource, Kaiseraugst, Carthage and Esquilinus - all in the western part of the empire and subject to the barbarian invasions that only reached the Eastern regions in the 7th century.
Discovered in 1793, the inaccurately named Esquiline Treasure comprises twenty-seven pieces of silverware. Technically speaking, "treasure" designates an ensemble of pieces of varying provenance and from different periods, some of them inherited, representing for their owner a financial reserve, and hastily buried at a time of imminent danger. The Esquiline objects, however, were made within a fairly short period, twenty-two of them in the same workshop. As indicated by the monograms and inscriptions on a number of them, they belonged to various members of the Turcia family. Four silver statuettes for use in public ceremonies - they represent the goddesses of the four great cities of the Empire: Rome, Constantinople (founded by Constantine in 330 AD), Alexandria and Antioch - allow the treasure to be dated to the second half of the fourth centuries. Their presence is a sign that their owner was a prominent figure in terms of wealth or rank.

THE ESQUILINE PATERA Silver – c. 380 AD – Venus at her toilet. On the handle: Adonis
Dutuit Bequest, 1902 - ADUT00171

Like the Projecta Casket in the British Museum - the best-known item from the Esquiline Treasure - this silver patera belonged to the private sphere. The facade of the casket produced by the Esquiline Workshop shows Venus at her toilet, and while not from the same workshop, the patera offers a similar treatment of the same subject. The vessel takes the form of a seashell from which the goddess of beauty is seen emerging. Thus the young hunter on the handle, with his spear and dog, is clearly identifiable as Adonis, the goddess's handsome beloved; killed by a boar when hunting, Adonis was revived by Jupiter for part of every year, and so embodies the life force. Long given a religious interpretation, the subject here no longer has any more than decorative, or at best symbolic value.

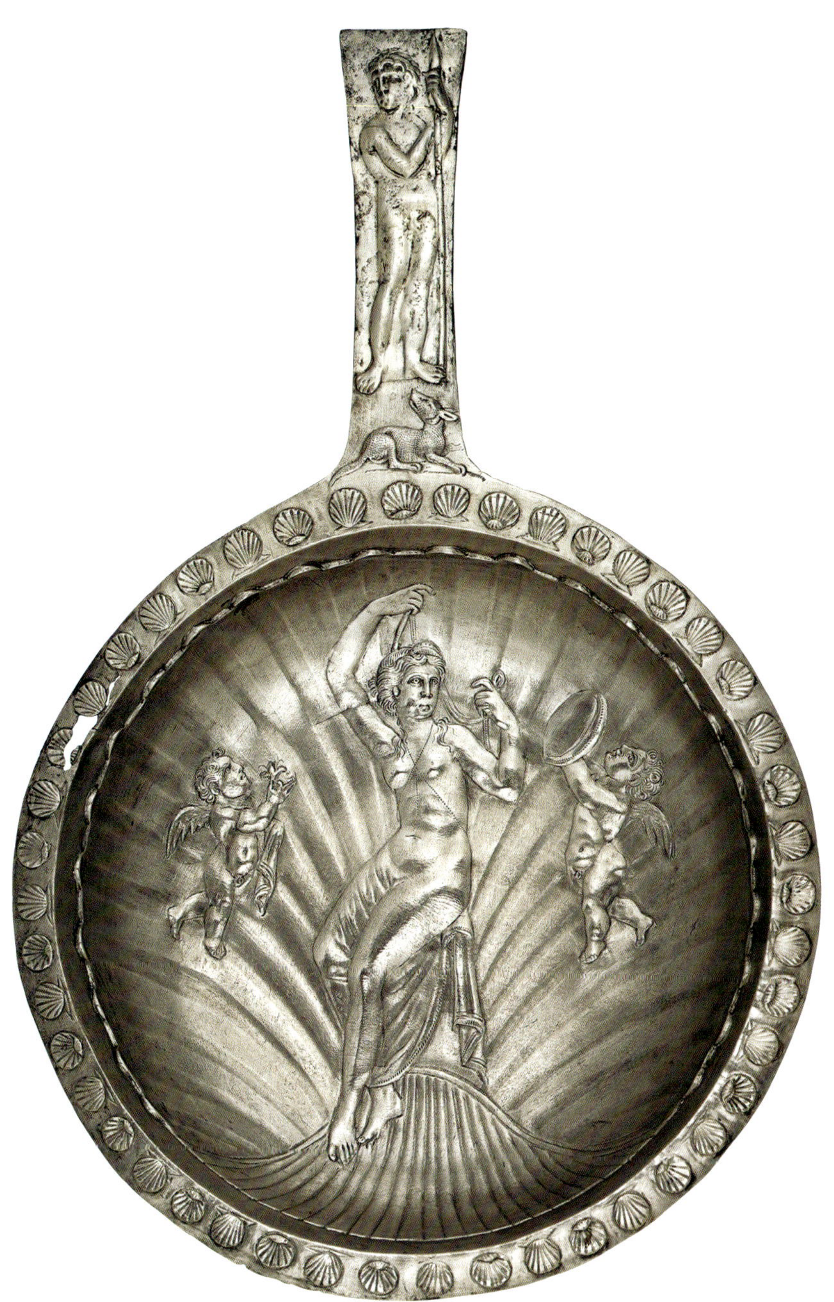

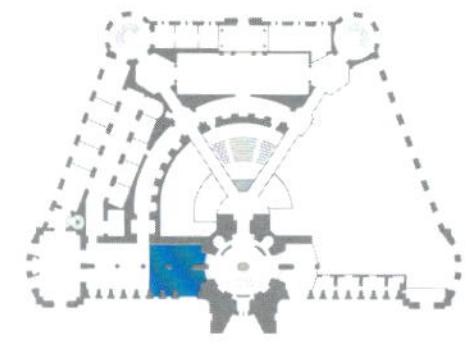

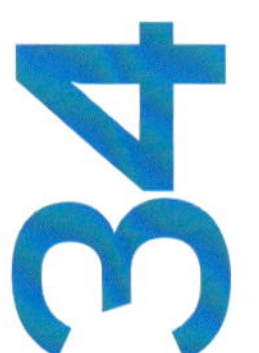

Psiax and the artistic revolutions in Athens

Although developed in Corinth, black-figure reached its apogee in Athens under the Pisistratides (561-510 BC). While representing only a tiny part of the total output, this figuratively decorated pottery came to supplant all others on Greece's international markets. It was especially appreciated by the Etruscans, witness the rich finds made in such burial grounds as the one at Vulci. Even so, black-figure painters were aware of its limitations and towards 530 BC their search for new modes of pictorial expression resulted in the red-figure technique, which reversed the figure-ground relationship of its predecessor. Henceforth the figures in reserve let the colour of the clay show through, the details being added with a brush and diluted varnish.
During this innovatory period, Psiax was the head of a major workshop, and the colleague of the Lysippides and Andokides painters. He was a "bilingual" painter, one of the last great black-figure masters and among the initiators of the new technique. Active between approximately 530 and 515, he also practised subtler, more fragile modes of decoration like "coral red", Six's technique and white ground.
For the last-mentioned, a layer of fine primary clay, which turns white on firing, is laid on the surface of the piece as a ground. The decoration is then painted in black figure or in contour, sometimes with polychrome highlights. Psiax was one of the pioneers of this technique, practised in the workshops of two great potters, Nicosthenes and Andokides. This kind of ornamentation was extremely fragile and restricted to vases used only for decorative and funeral purposes.

White ground hydria
Potter: **PSIAX?** Decoration attributed to **PSIAX** – Made: Athens – c. 525 BC
Provenance: Vulci, excavations by Lucien Bonaparte, prince of Canino - Dutuit Bequest, 1902 - Inv. ADUT00322
Hermes and his mother, Maia. Ram, lion and goat
The exceptional nature of this piece is matched by the originality of the painted composition. In the absence of the traditional framework, the image unfolds along the circumference of the hydria, thus gaining in sober monumentality. At the centre of the main side, two figures in profile stand facing each other on a simple ground line: shown in black figure, they occupy the full height of the belly, with the female skin tone painted in white on the black varnish. Visually isolated, they are flanked, beneath the horizontal handles, by a goat to the left and a ram to the right. Under the vertical handle is a roaring lion. The meticulously incised drawing is complemented by a host of white, black and red highlights.

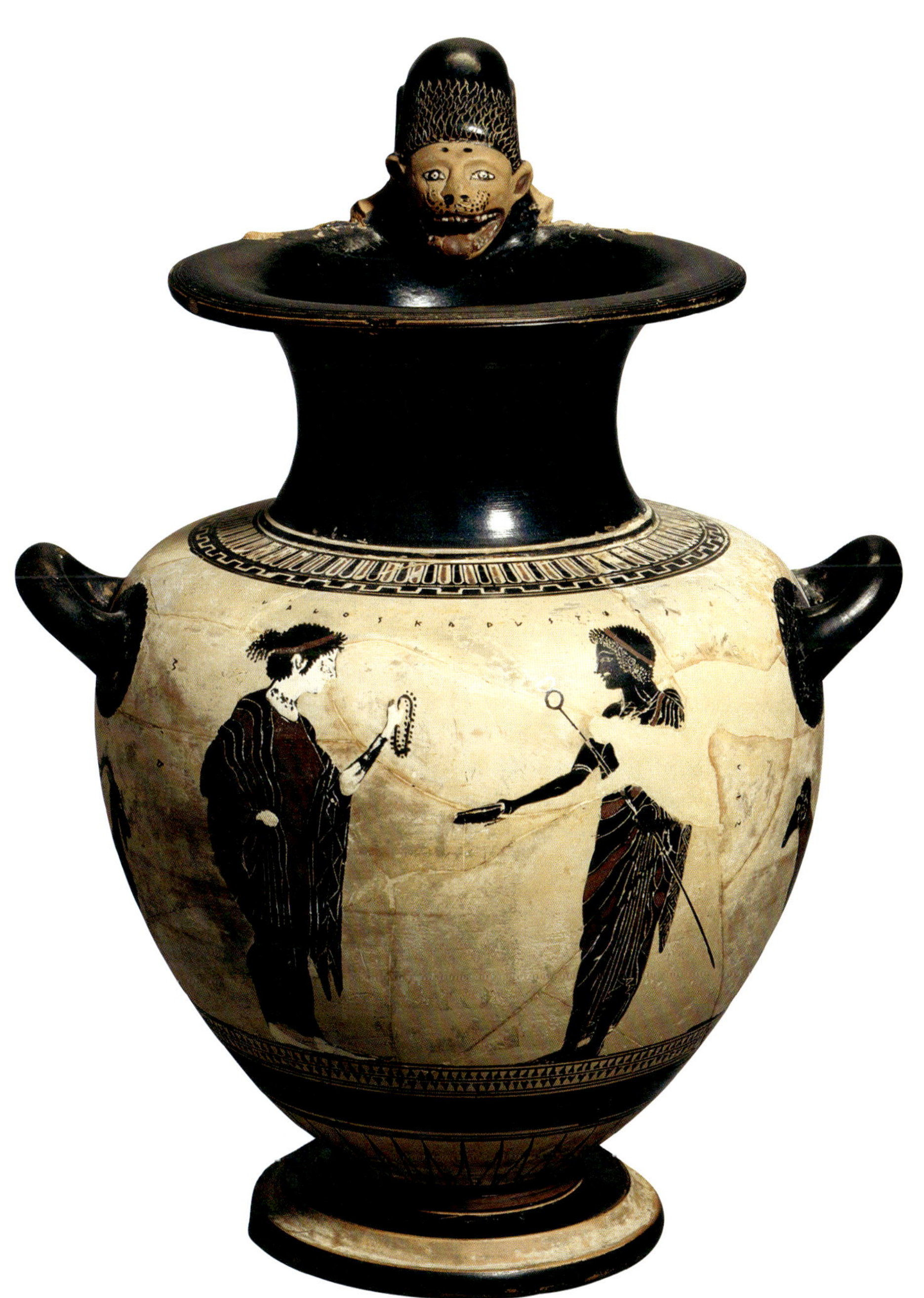

The partially conserved painted inscriptions name the figures - Hermes and Maia - in small, neat script, together with the mention "KARUSTIOS KALOS" ("Karystios is beautiful").
Clear as the identity of the figures may be, the interpretation of the scene - the only one of its kind - is problematical. The rendering of Hermes - young and beardless, with short, curly hair, and facing his mother Maia - is most unusual: as a rule he is shown as a child or a bearded adult. The choice of animals - goat, ram, lion - seems to suggest Hermes' role as a divine conductor of souls to the afterworld. The youthful portrayal of someone usually shown in his maturity is a gambit this artist used on a number of occasions.
The applied ornamentation on the vertical handle is equally rare, especially the lion's head at the top, a three-dimensional echo of the roaring lion drawn underneath. The affinities between the style of the painter and that of the potter have been noted on two white ground pieces decorated by Psiax, and the same is true here. Such is the imbrication of form, technique and ornamentation that the hypothesis of a painter/potter cannot be excluded. Indeed, given Psiax's debt to his master, the Amasis Painter - very probably a painter/potter himself - and the part Psiax played in training Euphronios, his most brilliant pupil and an accomplished painter/potter, the assumption seems justifiable.
As is often the case, the piece bears no signature. Of all the works attributed to Psiax, only two alabasters are signed: one from Athens, now in Karlsruhe, the other in Odessa.

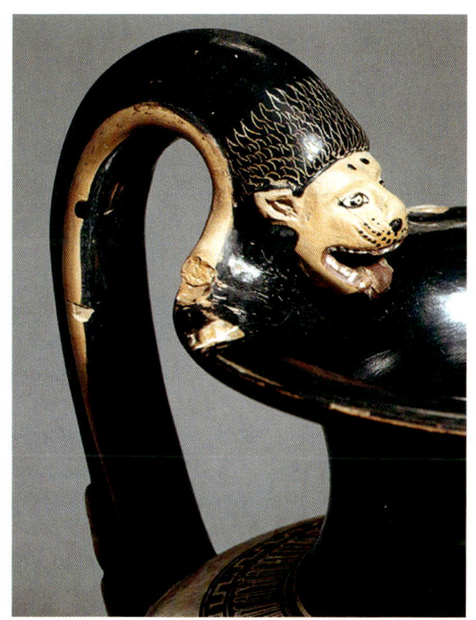

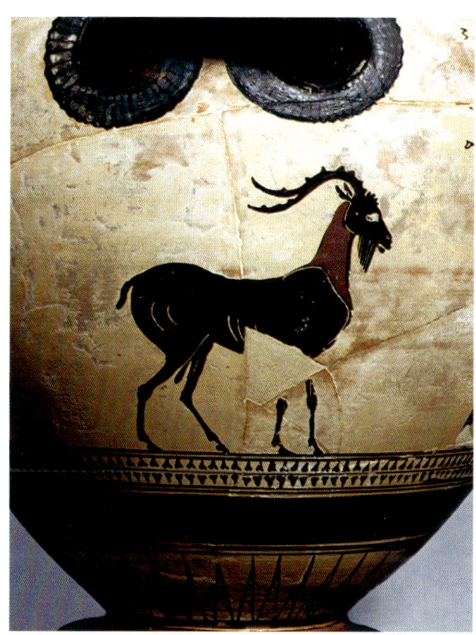

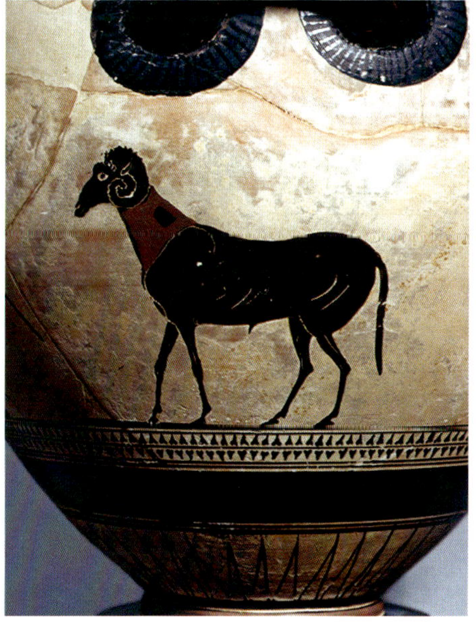

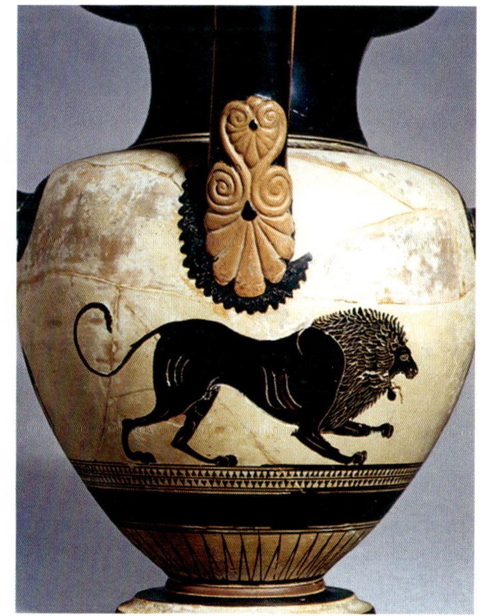

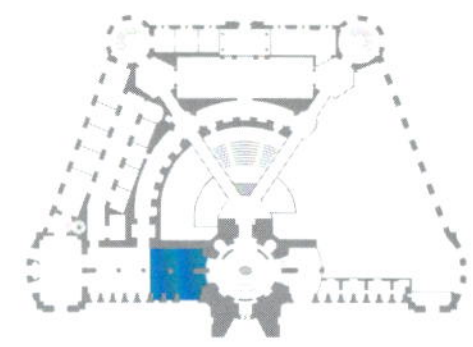

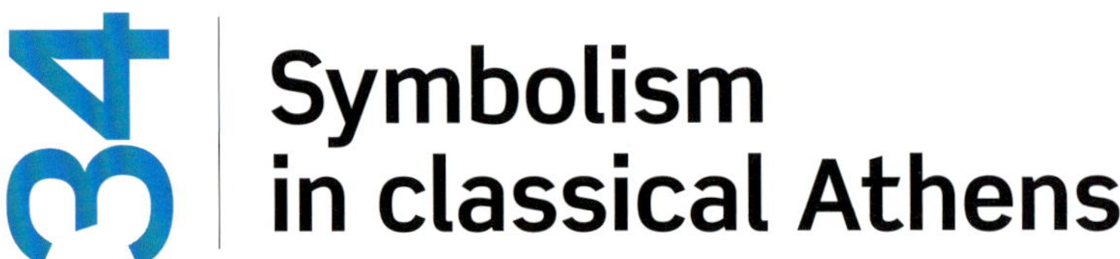

34 Symbolism in classical Athens

A rhyton by Sotades. An Ethiopian attacked by a crocodile.

Potter: **SOTADES**. Decoration attributed to the **SOTADES PAINTER** - Made: Athens, c. 470 BC - Dutuit Bequest, 1902 - Inv. ADUT0360

The rhyton was originally Dionysos' drinking cup. The prerogative of the god himself and the heroes, it was made of precious metal and combined the drinking horn with an animal's head. At the banquets held for heroes, Dionysian rituals or funerals, the head of a bull or ram held high was a reference to the animal sacrificed. For funeral rites and in shrines, a terracotta rhyton replaced those made of gold or silver. Here the sheen of the dark blue varnish is reminiscent of that of the silver from the mines of Laurion, one of Athens' great assets. This exceptionally pure metal led the philosopher Thrasyalces to observe that "silver is black".

A recurrent element in the work of the potter Sotades, the ram was the most prized, most sexually potent of the domestic animals, and the most highly esteemed of sacrificial victims since early antiquity. This explains the undeviating Athenian predilection for its head as a rhyton: the unrivalled royal ram was identified with the doomed tragic hero, himself seen as a sacrificial victim, and was thus associated with Dionysos.

In Sotades' bestiary, the crocodile devouring an African provides the most deliciously striking contrast with the heroic ram's head. Fallen on one knee, the Ethiopian struggles against the upright crocodile, which has seized him by the arm and whose upcurled tail forms the handle of the piece.

The victim's facial features point up the familiarity of Greek modellers with African subjects - hardly surprising given the close relationship between Greece and Egypt in the 6th century BC. On the other hand, the unconventional treatment of the crocodile indicates an artist who has never had the chance to study a living example.

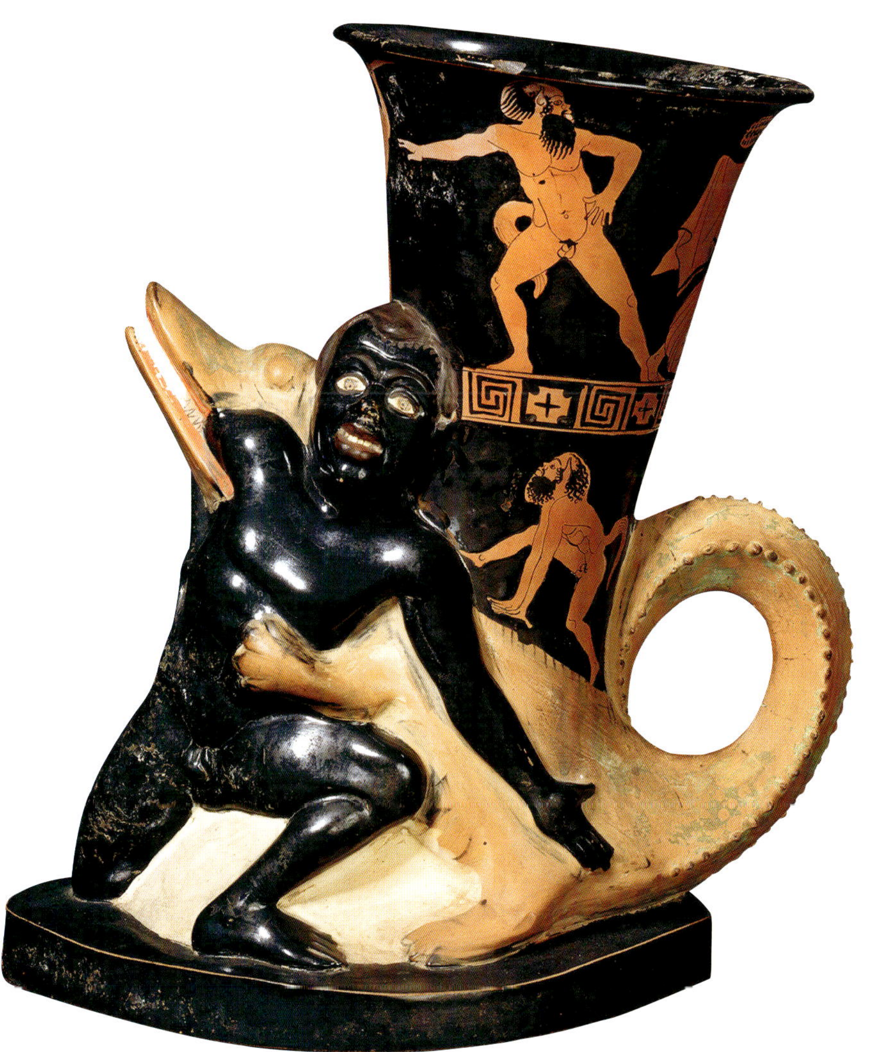

The subject would seem to be at the opposite extreme from the heroic values of the Athenian elite, sole authorised users of the rhyton. Yet this remains one of Sotades' most popular works, for it immediately takes us "through the looking glass" into the Dionysian world where nothing is what it seems: a topsy-turvy world in which the Greek concept of heroism has been stood on its head.

Governed by self-control and moderation (*sophrosune*), the 5th-century Athenian refused all expressions of fear or suffering (*pathe*). A scene such as this would thus have given rise not to pity, but to ridicule and contempt. The craven attitude to death portrayed is the parodic antithesis of *thanatos kalos*, the noble, glorious death of the hero.

One typically Greek way of asserting a social ideal is to deride its opposite. As Thales puts it, man has three reasons for thanking the gods: for being born a human being rather than an animal; man rather than woman; and Greek rather than barbarian.

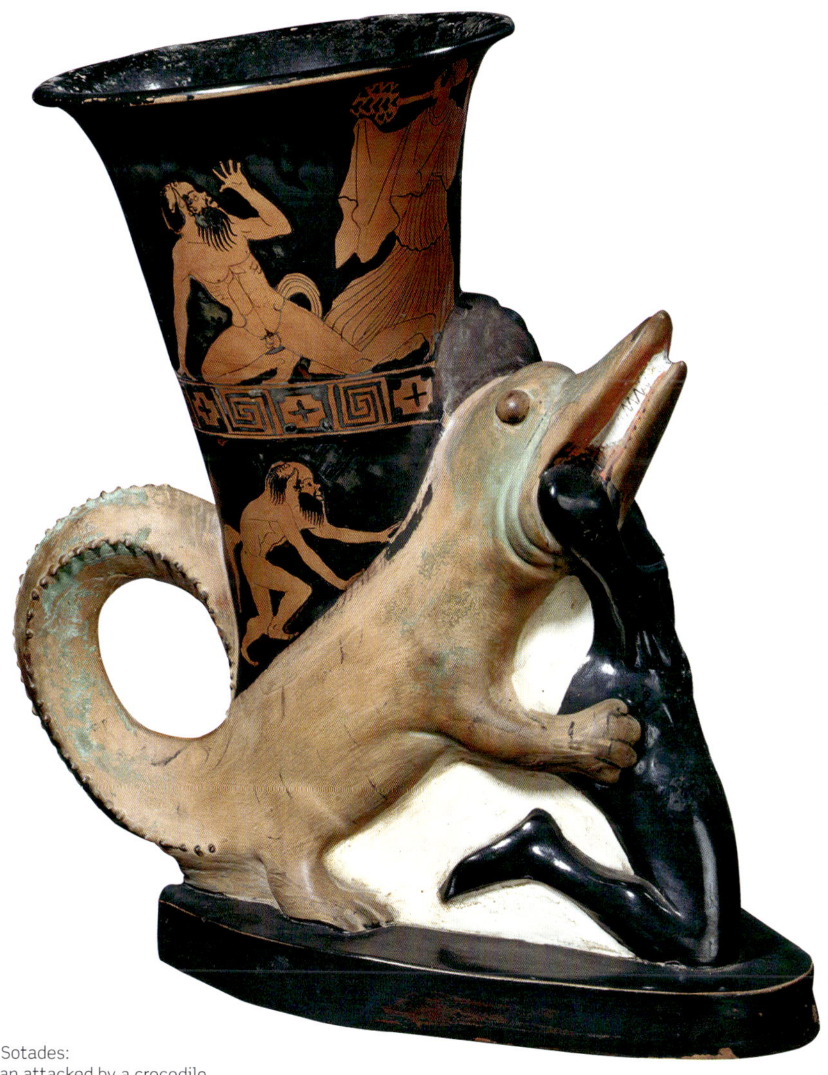

Rhyton by Sotades:
An Ethiopian attacked by a crocodile

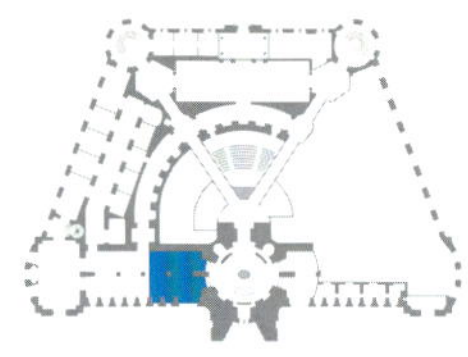

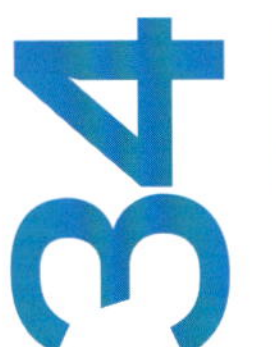

The Erotes of Myrina

In Greece there were two major sources for the subject matter taken up and disseminated by the Hellenistic workshops. Athens was a creative hub, with its output of vessels remaining much higher than that of terracotta figures. For the latter, the workshops in Boeotia - at Tanagra and Thebes - were much more productive. Between c. 330-200 BC Tanagra was a major production and export centre.

In Eastern Greece artisans arriving from Boeotia in the second half of the 3rd century BC began producing Tanagra-type pieces in the workshops in Myrina, a small port city near Kyme, halfway between Smyrna and Pergamum on the Anatolian Coast. In the early second century BC the influence of the major "Ionian" schools of sculpture - Pergamum and Rhodes - was very marked, over a range including winged Erotes and Victories. Myrina was destroyed by an earthquake at the end of the 2nd century AD.

North of Izmir (ancient Smyrna) on the western coast of what is now Turkey, the interiors of tombs in a necropolis dating from the second half of the 3rd century BC were hung with graceful, gleamingly polychrome terracotta figures: Erotes and Winged Victories accompanying the dead. Here the god of love Eros, the eternally young, ambiguously appealing son of Aphrodite, is portrayed as an adolescent or a winged child. Redoubtably seductive, for mortals he simultaneously embodies torment and consolation, with powers deriving from the four elements. Fickle, elusive and always in movement, he glides through the air; yet on his mother's side, he belongs to the marine world. His arrows wound, his flaming torch fires the senses.

1 | Winged Eros holding a bunch of grapes.

Moulded terracotta, traces of slip and coloured paint - Myrina - First half 2nd century BC

Provenance: Myrina(?) - Acquired with income accruing from the Dutuit bequest, 1992 - ADUT01778

Closely linked to the mysteries of life, Eros also watches over the world of the dead. Thus it would be superficial and reductive to consider the gradually developing relationship between the world of Aphrodite and that of Dionysos as no more than a natural alliance between euphoria and carnal delights. Facing the unknown, the initiates share the hope that the forces governing the universe can guarantee them a renewal of their pleasures and joys in the hereafter.

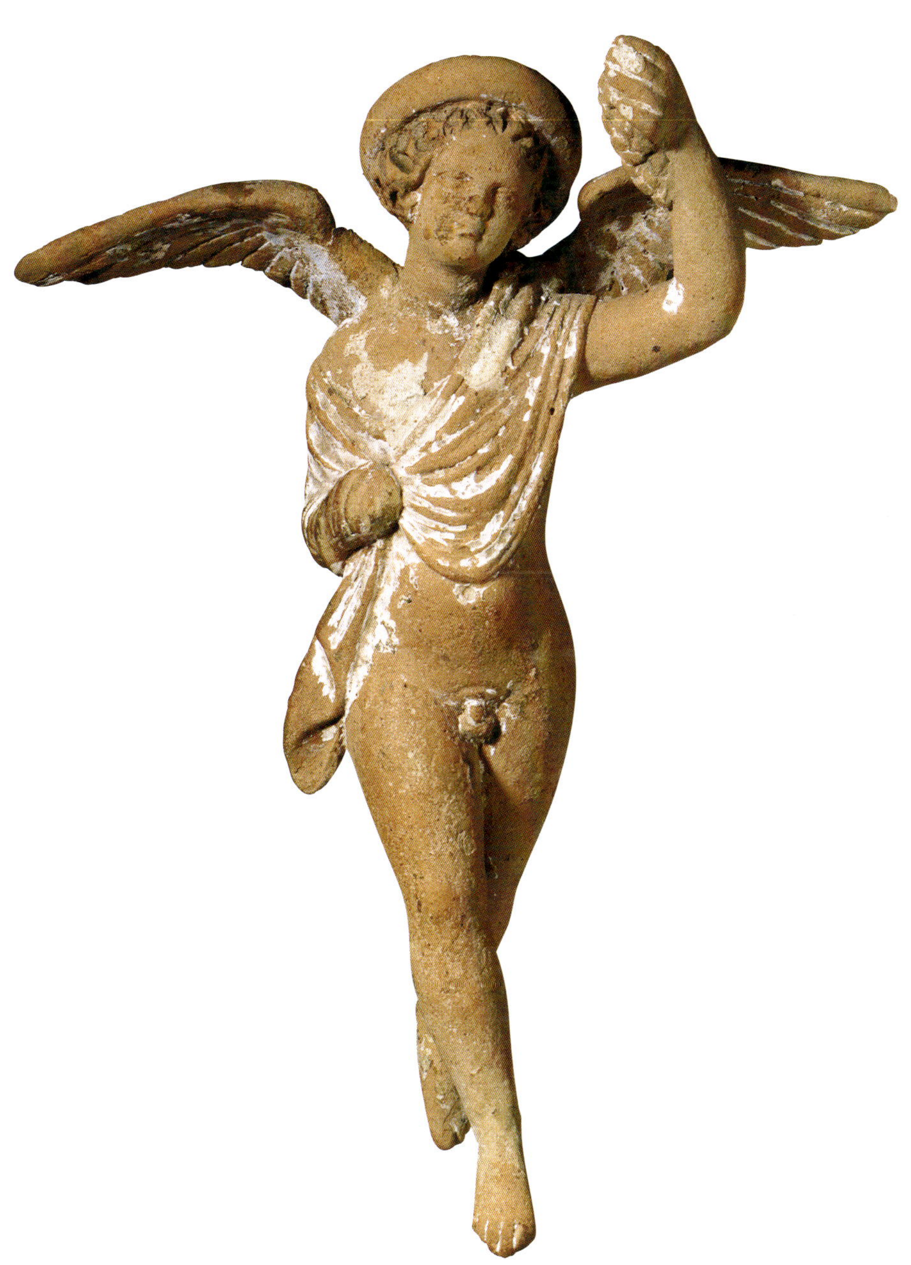

This belief gave rise to a clear shift in the representation of Eros, the handsome ephebe of the archaic and classical periods being supplanted by the androgynous adolescent or the plump baby of the Hellenistic burial grounds. The banquet crown on his curls and the bunch of grapes held high return him to the Dionysian setting, in a vision that still retains all the grace of the Tanagra models. In the 2nd century BC this tradition covered the cherubs, game-players and musicians - equally prized in Asia Minor and Italy - who would become Cupid and the putti of Roman art.

2 | Eros as a funerary torchbearer

Moulded terracotta - Myrina - Second half 2nd century BC

Provenance: Myrina(?) - Acquired with income accruing from the Dutuit bequest, 2001 - ADUT01891

This Eros Lampadephoros (torchbearer) made in Myrina in the second half of the 2nd century BC also belongs to the world of Dionysos and the dead, as is proclaimed by the extinguished torch he is holding and the crown of ivy and corymbs set on his long curls. Yet the creator of this piece offers a new vision of the god, one going counter to the ambiguous appeal of the classical Erotes as children or adolescents. A new genius animates Eros here, perceptible both in the sweep of his movements and the pathos of his expression. The tragic fate of mortals, symbolised by the funerary spirit's extinguished torch, can be read in the expressive features of the Psychopomp, or conductor of souls.

The treatment here harks back to the great Ionian schools of sculpture, notably Pergamum and Rhodes, whose growing influence filtered all the way down to the coroplaths, or clay modellers.

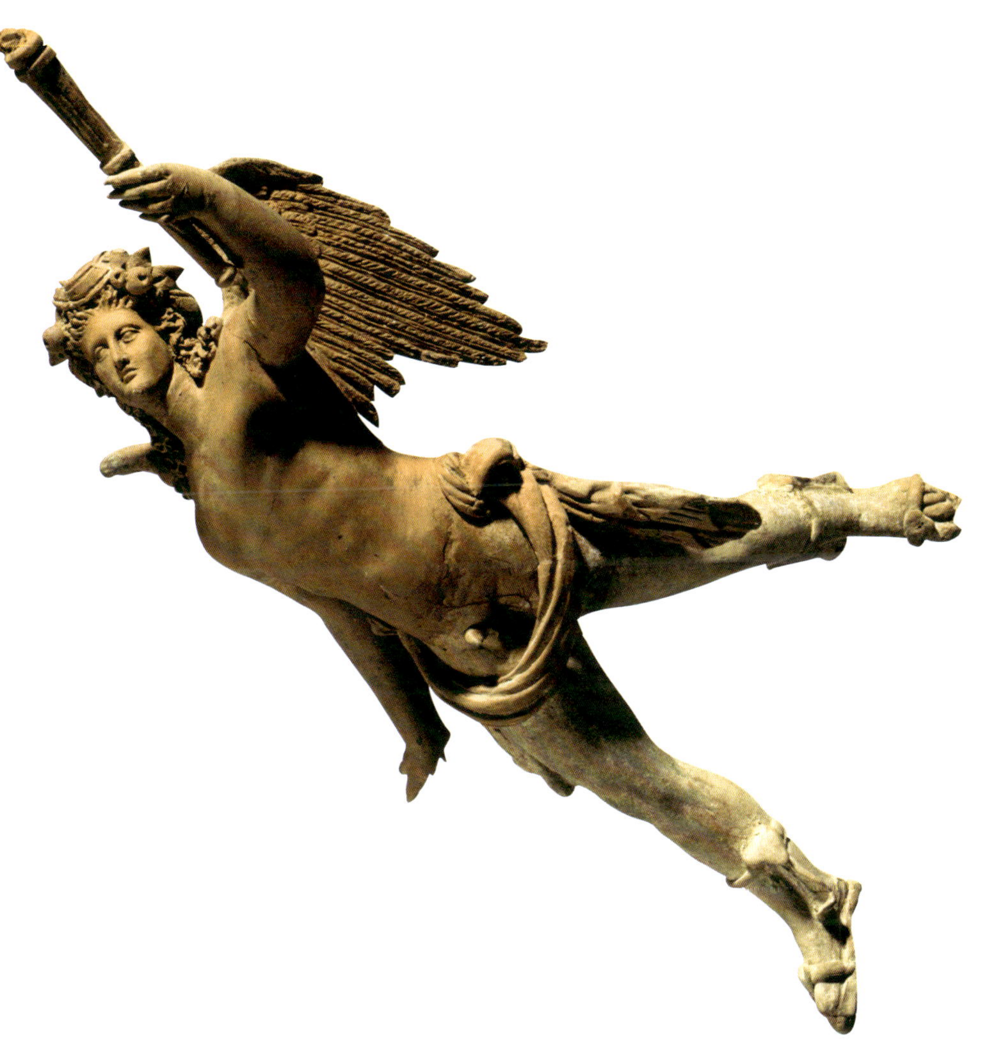

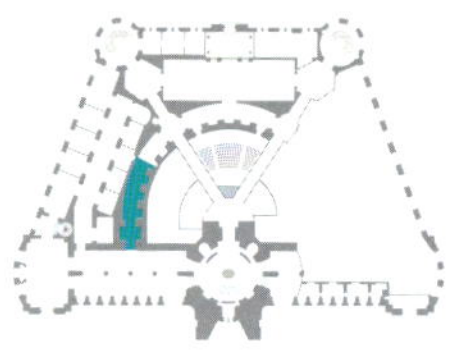

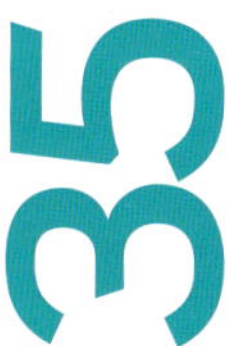

Champlevé enamel

The term "enamelware" covers a number of techniques - mainly cloisonné, champlevé and painted - which have the common feature of using firing to fix a vitreous substance called enamel onto a metal support. Initially a colourless, transparent powder, enamel is coloured by the addition of metal oxides.

Heirs to techniques going back to classical times, the artisans of the Rheno-Mosan and Limousin regions built their reputation in the 12th and 13th centuries on champlevé enamelware. The technique consists of digging into a relatively thick sheet of copper and creating cavities to receive enamels of various colours. In the Middle Ages champlevé enamel was a much appreciated means of embellishing such precious religious objects as altarpieces, reliquaries, chalices, book covers and croziers, as well as more everyday items like candlesticks and censers.

1 | Altar plaques. Saint Paul and Saint Thomas

Repoussé copper, champlevé enamel - Limoges, c. 1220-1230 - Dutuit Bequest, 1902 - Inv. ODUT01239 (1-2)

Each of these plaques bears a low-relief image: Paul and Thomas. They are part of a set, now dispersed, showing the apostles, and probably adorned the high altar of the church at Grandmont, in France's Haute-Vienne département.

The figures are shown against an enamelled backdrop decorated with twining vegetal motifs, flowers, a throne with a cushion and an inscription including their names. Nobly monumental, they are outstanding examples of the 1200 Style that blossomed in the early 13th century, especially in northeastern France. Their frontal posture and the fluidly clinging lines of their clothing point to the "return to antiquity" movement, whose influence extended as far as Limoges. Technically and aesthetically striking, these pieces illustrate the mastery of metalworking and champlevé enamel techniques achieved by Limoges craftsmen in the 13th century.

The Petit Palais is fortunate to possess two of the six surviving plaques from this remarkable set.

2 | Reliquary for the True Cross

Repoussé copper, champlevé enamel, silver, semiprecious stones - Mosan region, c. 1170-1180
Dutuit Bequest, 1902 - Inv. ODUT01237

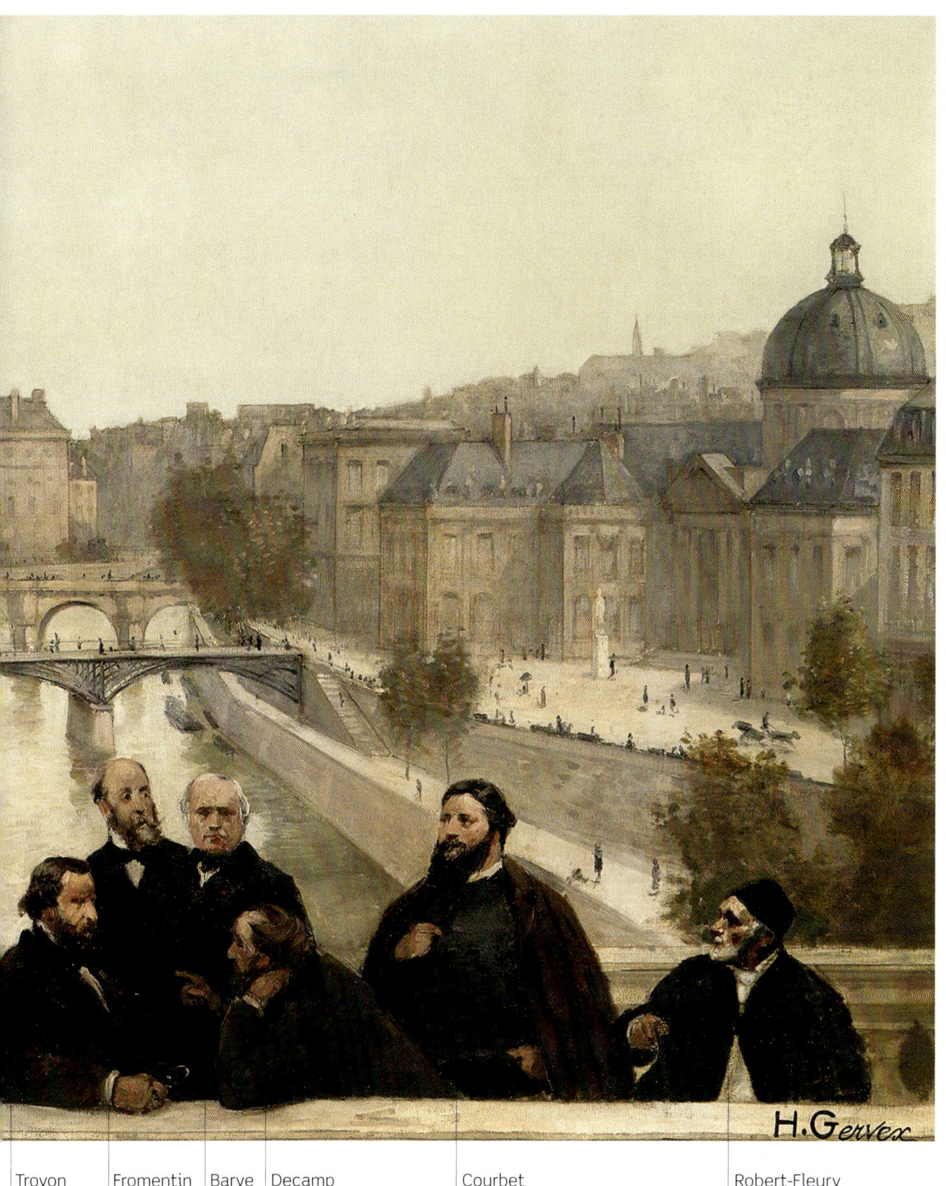

Troyon | Fromentin | Barye | Decamp | Courbet | Robert-Fleury

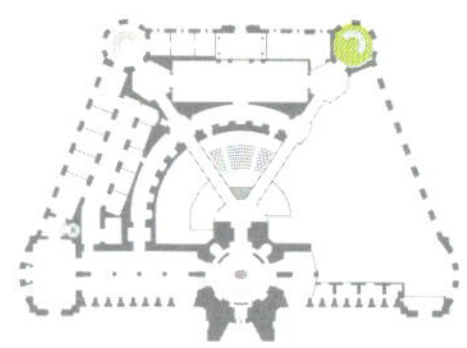

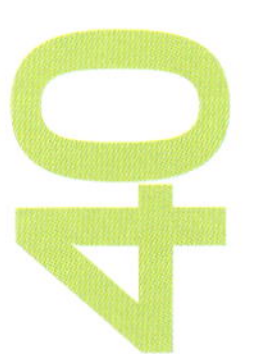

The Dalou studio

Aimé-Jules Dalou's skill as a modeller gained him early recognition from his teachers, Carpeaux among them, but the war of 1870 interrupted a promising career: a dedicated socialist, Dalou, like Courbet, sided with the Communards and had to go into exile in England in 1871, remaining there until he was pardoned in 1879. In London he taught, sculpted, exhibited and successfully sold elegant busts and genre scenes drawing on 18th-century French models.
His goal on returning to France was to become the sculptor of the new Third Republic. In 1879 his *Monument to the Republic* was chosen for the Place de la Nation in Paris and two large reliefs received the medal of honour at the 1883 Salon. Without ever becoming a major figure, Dalou had achieved recognition as a master before his fellow student at the Petit Ecole, Auguste Rodin.
When he died in 1902, his studio yielded a marvellous hoard of sculpture sketches - over three hundred works in all - completely unknown to the public. The collection was sold to the City of Paris and given its own Dalou Room at the Petit Palais in 1905. Room 40 is an evocation of that exhibit.

1 | **JULES DALOU (1838-1902)** Sower on a Pedestal
1894, terracotta - Purchased from Georgette Dalou, the artist's daughter, 1905 - Inv. PPS00117
A hundred or so of these sketches bear on a project dear to Dalou's heart: a monument to the workers to whom this socialist and man of the people felt himself so close. A small terracotta sketch, the *Sower on a Pedestal* was the initial idea for a *Monument to the Peasantry*. The statue and its pedestal are based on a series of portraits of workers, drawn and modelled from the life or from memory.
Since the 1880s - a generation after the realist painters and novelists - sculpture had also turned to the portrayal of everyday life. Dalou remains the leading representative of this new current. At a far remove from the picturesque and the trivial, he captures, with the simplest of gestures, the very essence of work.

2 | **JULES DALOU (1838-1902)** Fraternity
Sketch for the plaster high relief *Fraternity*, shown at the Salon in 1883 - c. 1878-1882, terracotta - Purchased from Georgette Dalou, daughter of the artist, 1905 - Inv. PPS00341

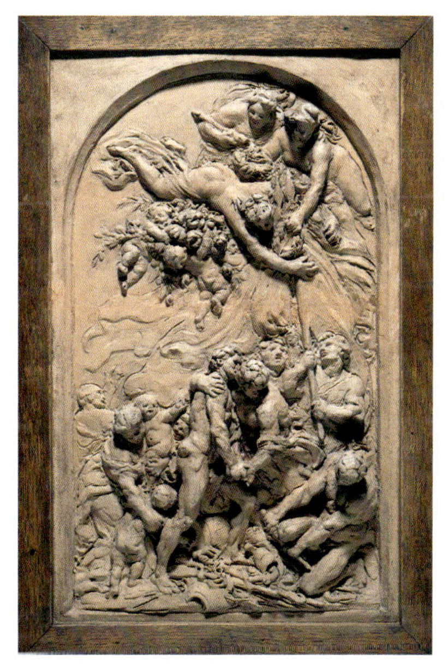

2

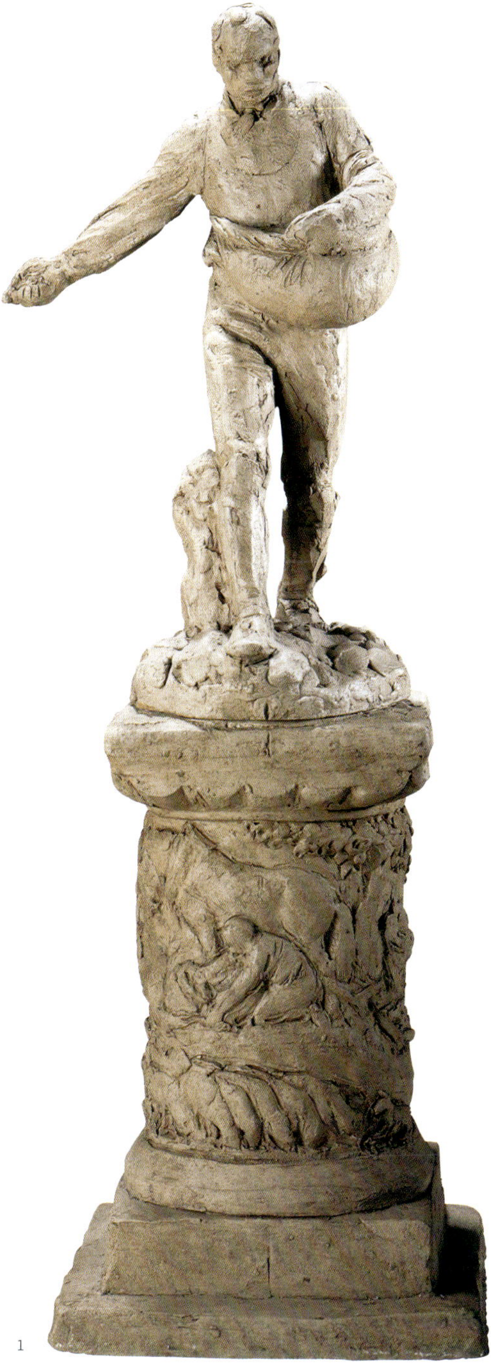

1

Chronological index
of the illustrations in the Petit Palais collection

Date	Artist, work	Materials, media	Room	Page
Antiquity				
c. 525 BC	Psiax, *White Ground Hydria*	Ceramic	34. The Greek World	143, 145
c. 470 BC	A rhyton by Sotades: An Ethiopian attacked by a crocodile	Ceramic	34. The Greek World	147, 149
First half 2nd century BC	Winged Eros holding a bunch of grapes	Terracotta	34. The Greek World	151
Second half 2nd century BC	Eros as a funerary torchbearer	Terracotta	34. The Greek World	153
Late 1st century BC	Satyr holding out a bunch of grapes to the child Bacchus	Glass cameo	33. Rome and its empire	135
c. 30 BC	Ephebe (Fins d'Annecy)	Bronze	33. Rome and its empire	137
Second century AD	Antoninus Pius (Fins d'Annecy)	Bronze	33. Rome and its empire	139
Second century AD	Magistrate (Fins d'Annecy)	Bronze	33. Rome and its empire	139
Second century AD	Magistrate (Fins d'Annecy)	Bronze	33. Rome and its empire	139
c. 380 AD	The Esquiline patera	Silver	33. Rome and its empire	141
Middle Ages				
Paintings				
c. 1480	The Master of Saint Bartholomew: *The Nativity*	Oil on panel	35. Middle Ages and Renaissance	163
c. 1480-1500	*The Nativity*	Icon, tempera on panel	36. The art of the icon	167
Sculptures				
Late 15th century	Saint Barbara(?)	Wood	35. Middle Ages and Renaissance	165
Objets d'art				
Second half 10th century	Book cover: Virgin and Child in Glory	Ivory	35. Middle Ages and Renaissance	161
c. 1170-1180	Reliquary for the True Cross	Champlevé enamel	35. Middle Ages and Renaissance	155
c. 1220-1230	Altar plaques: Saint Paul and Saint Thomas	Champlevé enamel	35. Middle Ages and Renaissance	155

c. 1220-1230	Virgin and Child	Ivory	35. Middle Ages and Renaissance	161
c. 1370-1380	Diptych: Scenes from the Life and Passion of Christ	Ivory	35. Middle Ages and Renaissance	161
Renaissance				
Paintings				
Late 16th century	School of Moscow, *Head of St John the Baptist on a dish*	Icon, tempera on wood	36. The art of the icon	11
Sculptures				
c. 1525	Workshop of Niklaus Weckmann, *The Nativity*	Wood	35. Middle Ages and Renaissance	165
Objets d'art				
First third 16th century	Attributed to the workshop of the "Master of the Large Foreheads", *Altarpiece: Scenes from the Passion of Christ*	Painted enamel	35. Middle Ages and Renaissance	157-159
First half 16th century	Large basin: Two women in profile, one on each side of a tree of life	Earthenware	32. Italy	131
1520	Painter of the Judgement of Paris, workshop of Maestro Giorgio, Dish: *The Judgement of Paris*	Earthenware	32. Italy	131
c. 1540-1545	Giacomo Mancini, known as El Frate, Ewer basin: *The Wedding of Alexander and Roxana*	Earthenware	32. Italy	131
1544	Pierre Reymond, Tazza: *The Banquet of Dido and Aeneas*	Painted enamel	32. France	129
Mid-16th century	"Saint-Porchaire" pottery	Ceramic	32. France	127
Mid-16th century	Attributed to the workshop of Léonard Limosin, Plaque, thought to be *the portrait of Jeanne d'Albret*	Painted enamel	32. France	129
Mid-16th century	Glass: *Dance of the Cupids*	Glassware	32. Italy	133
c. 1550	Nicolas Féau: Square tower clock with astrolabe dial	Clockmaking	31. The precious arts	125
Second half 16th century	Lidded vase with filigree ornamentation	Glassware	32. Italy	133
Late 16th century	A successor of Bernard Palissy: Large oval dish ornamented with "rustic figulines"	Ceramic	32. France	127
Late 16th-early 17th century	Maître IC, Ewer: *Scenes from the story of Jason and the Golden Fleece.*	Painted enamel	32. France	129
17th-18th centuries				
Paintings				
c. 1614-1615	Sir Peter Paul Rubens, *The Rape of Proserpine*	Oil on panel	30. History painting	123
c. 1631-1633	Rembrandt van Rijn, *Self-portrait in Oriental Attire*	Oil on panel	26. Portraits and figures	115
c. 1637-1638	Claude Gellée, *Landscape with the Port of Santa Marinella*	Oil on copper	27. Landscapes	117
c. 1663-1665	Jan Steen, *The Little Alms Collector*	Oil on panel	25. Portraits and figures	113

Chronological index

c. 1664-1668	Meindert Hobbema, *The Water Mill*	Oil on panel	28. Landscapes	119
c. 1680-1685	Nicolas de Largillierre, *Partridge Hanging in a Niche*	Oil on canvas	29. Still lifes	121
Second half 17th century	The Archangel Michael - The Archangel Gabriel	Tempera on panel	36. The art of the icon	169
Between 1765-1767	Jean Pillement, *Chinoiserie*	Oil on canvas	13. Large-scale decoration	71
c. 1775	Hubert Robert, *Washerwomen in the Grounds of a Château*	Oil on canvas	12. Art under Louis XIV	69
Print				
c. 1649	Rembrandt van Rijn, *Christ Healing the Sick ("The Hundred Guilder Print")*	Etching	Graphic Arts Room	13
Objets d'art				
First quarter 17th century	Illustrated oval dish: *Henri IV and his family*	Ceramic	32. France	127
First half 17th century	Oval hunter watch	Clockmaking	31. The precious arts	125
Second quarter 17th century	Johann Jacob Rugendas, *Tulip watch*	Clockmaking	31. The precious arts	125
c. 1700	Tapestry: *The Return from the Hunt*	Tapestry	11. Art under Louis XV	59
First half 18th century	Dish	Earthenware	9. Portraits	55
c. 1700-1715	Sedan chair	Furniture	9. Portraits	55
c. 1700-1720	Nicolas Sageot, "Mazarin" office table	Furniture	9. Portraits	55
After 1741	Tapestry from the *Story of Psyche* set, after Boucher	Tapestry	11. Art under Louis XV	60-61
c. 1750	Pierre IV Migeon, Bed Table	Furniture	10. Art under Louis XV	57
c. 1738-1750	Group: *The Merchant of Hearts*	Hard-paste porcelain	11. Art under Louis XV	65
c. 1744-1750	Figurine: *Lady with Pug-dogs*	Hard-paste porcelain	11. Art under Louis XV	65
c. 1740-1760	Attributed to Jacques Dubois, Desk	Furniture	10. Art under Louis XV	57
c. 1755-1760	Organ clock: *The Monkey Concert*	Horlogerie	11. Art under Louis XV	65
1760	Cuvette Verdun	Soft-paste porcelain	11. Art under Louis XV	63
c. 1760	Attributed to La Croix, Secretaire: drawers behind sliding doors, writing table in drawer, cupboard	Furniture	10. Art under Louis XV	57
c. 1757-1765	"Broc Roussel" ewer and basin	Soft-paste porcelain	11. Art under Louis XV	63
c. 1765-1770	Pierre I Roussel: Chest of drawers	Wood marquetry, bronze	12. Art under Louis XVI	67
1771	Attributed to Jean-Louis Morin, Rope festoon vase	Soft-paste porcelain	11. Art under Louis XV	63
c. 1780	Tapestry: *The Dance*	Tapestry	11. Art under Louis XV	59
c. 1770-1780	Attributed to the workshop of René Dubois, Secretaire "à abattant", low cupboard	Furniture	12. Art under Louis XVI	67
c 1775-1785	Attributed to the workshop of René Dubois, Bureau: "Bonheur du jour", writing table in drawer, dressing table	Wood, bronze	12. Art under Louis XVI	67

19th-early 20th century

Paintings

1804	Jean-Antoine Gros, *Portrait of Jacques Amalric*	Oil on canvas	17. Neoclassical and Romantic portraits	83
1807	Louis-Léopold Boilly, *Portrait of Miss Athénaïs d'Albenas*	Oil on canvas	17. Neoclassical and Romantic portraits	83
1818	Jean-Auguste-Dominique Ingres, *Death of Leonardo da Vinci*	Oil on canvas	24. Ingres and the Troubadour style	111
1835	Eugène Delacroix, *Combat of the Giaour and the Pasha*	Oil on canvas	23. Delacroix and Romanticism	109
1842	Victor-Louis Mottez, *Portrait of Julie Mottez*	Oil on canvas	17. Neoclassical and Romantic portraits	83
1843	Camille Corot: *Marietta*	Oil on canvas	16. Realist portraits	81
1848	Félix Philippoteaux, *Alphonse de Lamartine Rejecting the Red Flag of the Socialists, 25 February 1848*	Oil on canvas	5. Dalou and the celebration of the Republic	39
1848	Alfred De Dreux, *The Mosselman Family*	Oil on canvas	15. Carpeaux and the portrait	77
1851	Gustave Courbet, *Firemen Going to a Fire*	Oil on canvas	4. Courbet and Realism	37
1857	Gustave Courbet, *Young Ladies on the Banks of the Seine (Summer)*	Oil on canvas	4. Courbet and Realism	35
c. 1860	Félix Ziem, *Gust of Wind at Fontainebleau*	Oil on canvas-backed paper	7. Monet and landscape painting	45
1863	James Tissot, *The Prodigal Son: the Departure*	Oil on canvas	22. Historicism	106-107
1866	Gustave Courbet, *Sleep*	Oil on canvas	4. Courbet and Realism	37
1868	Édouard Manet, *Portrait of Théodore Duret*	Oil on canvas	16. Realist portraits	79
c. 1860-1870	Honoré Daumier, *The Etching Amateur*	Oil on canvas	16. Realist portraits	8
1874	Jean-Baptiste Carpeaux, *Self-portrait*	Oil on canvas	15. Carpeaux and the portrait	75
1880	Claude Monet, *Sunset on the Seine at Lavacourt (Winter Effect)*	Oil on canvas	7. Monet and landscape painting	45
1879-1882	Paul Cézanne, *Three Bathers*	Oil on canvas	8. Cézanne and modernity	53
1883	Gustave Doré, *Valley of Tears*	Oil on canvas	6. Doré and the Christian tradition	41
1883	Charles-Alexandre Giron, *Woman Wearing Gloves*	Oil on canvas	3. Roll and Naturalism	29
1885	Albert Carrier-Belleuse, *Flour Carriers: Paris scene*	Oil on canvas	3. Roll and Naturalism	27
1888	Fernand Pelez, *Grimaces and Misery (Circus Performers)*	Oil on canvas	3. Roll and Naturalism	31-33
1888	Alfred Roll, *Portrait of Adolphe Alphand*	Oil on canvas	3. Roll and Naturalism	27
1889	Carolus-Duran, *Portrait of Mrs Edgar Stern*	Oil on canvas	3. Roll and Naturalism	29
1889	Henri Gervex and Alfred Stevens, *The Painters and the Ile de la Cité*	Oil on canvas	39. The Universal Exhibitions in Paris	172-173

Chronological index

Objets d'art				
1820	Jacob-Desmalter, *Chairs from the "cabinet gothique" of the Countess of Osmond*		24. Ingres and the Troubadour style	111
1867	Léon-Joseph-Thomas Alessandri and son, *Vitrine*	Furniture	39. The Universal Exhibitions in Paris	171
1866-1875	Félix Bracquemond, *Fruit bowl: Rousseau dinner service*	Earthenware	21. Vuillard and the new approach to decoration	103
Last quarter 19th century	Paintbox, easel, etc	Outdoor painting equipment	7. Monet and landscape painting	45
After 1876	Auguste Rodin and Albert Carrier-Belleuse, *Vase of the Titans*	Ceramic	1. The decorative arts in 1900	23
1886-1887	Paul Gauguin, *Jardinière*	Stoneware	8. Cézanne and modernity	51
1889-1894	Jean Carriès, *Large Vase with Ornamental Base*	Glazed stoneware	19. Carriès, sculptor and potter	93
1895	François-Rupert Carabin, *Vitrine*	Furniture	18. Moreau and Symbolism	89
c. 1895	Henry Cros, *Bust of Marie Cros*	Glass paste	18. Moreau and Symbolism	87
1897	Paul Grandhomme, , *Europa* (after Gustave Moreau)	Painted enamel	18. Moreau and Symbolism	85
1898	Émile Gallé, *Vase*	Crystal	1. The decorative arts in 1900	21
1899	Armand Point, *Peacock Casket*	Casket	1. The decorative arts in 1900	21
c. 1900	Georges Fouquet, *Waterfall Pendant*, mount based on a model by Mucha, décor after Desrosiers	Jewel	20. Guimard and Art Nouveau	97
c. 1905	Georges Fouquet, *Byzantine Comb*, after a model by Mucha	Jewel	20. Guimard and Art Nouveau	97
c. 1905-1908	Mary Cassatt, André Metthey, *Children's Dance*	Glazed earthenware	8. Cézanne and modernity	53
c. 1909	Hector Guimard, *Dining room suite*	Furniture	20. Guimard and Art Nouveau	95
c. 1909	Paul Philippon, *Vase*, after a model by Hector Guimard	Bronze	20. Guimard and Art Nouveau	95
c. 1905-1910	Georges Fouquet, *Sycamore Pendant*	Jewel	20. Guimard and Art Nouveau	97

Photo credits

© **Bibliothèque Forney:** p. 171

© **Étude de Maître Binoche:** p. 65 (bottom)

© **Galerie Elstir:** p. 87 (left)

© **P. Nadalini:** p. 135

© **Neurdein Frères:** pp. 14-15

© **Paris-Musées/ Karin Maucotel, 2005:** cover, pp. 17, 19, 73

© **Photothèque des musées de la Ville de Paris/ Cliché Irène Andréani:** pp. 21 (top), 55 (bottom right), 57 (left, bottom), 63 (bottom left), 95 (bottom right), 125 (left, bottom right), 127 (top left), 131 (bottom); **René Briant:** pp. 9, 75 (bottom), 91, 155 (top); **Philippe Joffre:** pp. 23 (right), 29 (bottom right), 53 (bottom left), 63 (top left, right), 78, 79, 85, 93 (right), 161 (left, bottom right), 165, 175 (right); **Joffre/Lifermann:** p. 59 (bottom); **Philippe Ladet:** pp. 13, 45 (bottom left), 47 (top), 88, 103 (bottom), 111 (bottom), 153, 175 (left); **Daniel Lifermann:** p. 23 (left), 75 (top), 80, 81, 83 (bottom right), 113; **Patrick Pierrain:** pp. 8, 10, 11, 21 (bottom), 24, 25, 27, 29 (left, top right), 31, 32-33, 35, 37, 39, 41, 43, 45 (top, bottom right), 47 (bottom), 49, 51 (bottom), 53 (top, bottom right), 55 (top, bottom left), 57 (top), 59 (top), 60-61, 65 (top), 67, 69, 71, 77, 83 (top, bottom left), 87 (right), 89, 93 (left), 95 (bottom left), 97, 99, 100, 101, 103 (top), 105, 106-107, 109, 111 (top), 115, 117, 119, 121, 123, 125 (top), 127 (except top left), 129, 131 (top), 133, 137, 139, 141, 143, 145, 147, 149, 151, 155 (bottom), 157, 158, 159, 161 (top), 163, 167, 169, 172-173; **Claire Pignol:** p. 51 (top)

© **StanRies.com:** p. 95 (top)

Patrimonial rights

Pierre Bonnard, Georges Fouquet, Aristide Maillol, Édouard Vuillard
© Adagp, Paris 2005

Charles Jacqueau
© Donation Jacqueau, Petit Palais

Reserved rights:
Paul Grandhomme; Hector Guimard

Design and layout:
Nicolas Hubert
Flaps: © Doc. Levin
Editorial secretary:
Stéphanie Grégoire
Translation:
John Tittensor
Executive editor:
Catherine Ojalvo
Illustration rights:
Laurence Goupille
Production: Audrey Chenu,
Saint-Véron Pompée

Photoengraving:
IGS, Angoulème
Printing/binding:
Eurografica, Vicenze (Italie)

Printed by Eurografica, Italy,
October 2005

Set in Scene, New Caledonia
Paper: Garda matt 150g

Distribution
Actes Sud Distribution
UD-Union Distribution
AS 2021

ISBN 2-87900-910-3
Copyright deposit:
November 2005

Les musées de la Ville de Paris
28, rue Notre-Dame-
des-Victoires
75002 Paris

www.parismusees.com

Petit Palais
Coordinating editor
Maryline Assante di Panzillo
Publications director
Laurence Delécluse

Petit Palais
Musée des Beaux-Arts de la Ville de Paris
Avenue Winston-Churchill
75008 Paris

Access:
- Metro: Lines 1 and 13, get off at Champs-Elysées Clemenceau
- Bus: 42, 72, 73, 80, 83

Entry:
- General public: Main staircase, Avenue Winston-Churchill
- Handicapped persons (♿) and groups: Ground floor, Avenue Winston-Churchill

Opening hours:
Open daily except Mondays
and public holidays.

Admission:
- Permanent collection: free
- Temporary exhibitions: admission details from the ticket office

Visitor services:
- Free access to the interior garden, **the Jardin du Petit Palais Café** and the bookshop/boutique during museum opening hours
- Audioguides for hire
- Auditorium
- Graphic Arts Room:
consultation by appointment only

Individual and group activities
Adults: guided tours, stories, art/stories, focus visits
Young people and families: discovery visits, workshops, stories
Handicapped people: sign language, lip-reading and tactile visits
Teachers: training, documentation
Programme details, bookings: 01 53 43 40 36
(10:00–12:00 and 14:00–16:00)

Postal address
Petit Palais
1 Avenue Dutuit
75008 Paris
Tel: 01 53 43 40 00
www.petitpalais.paris.fr

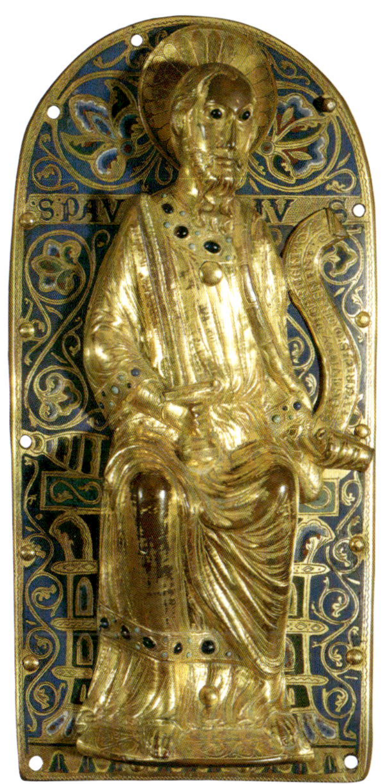

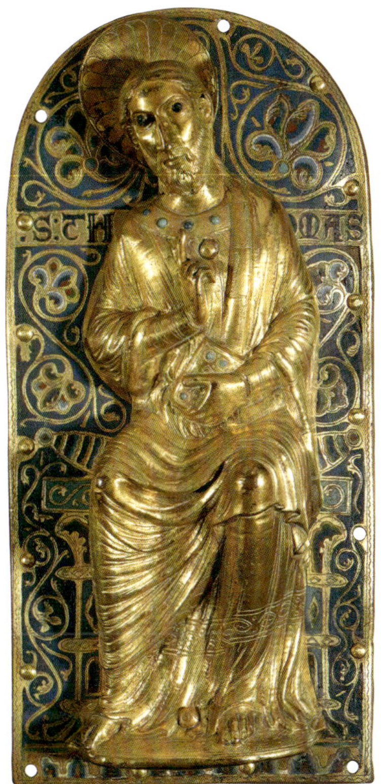

1

2

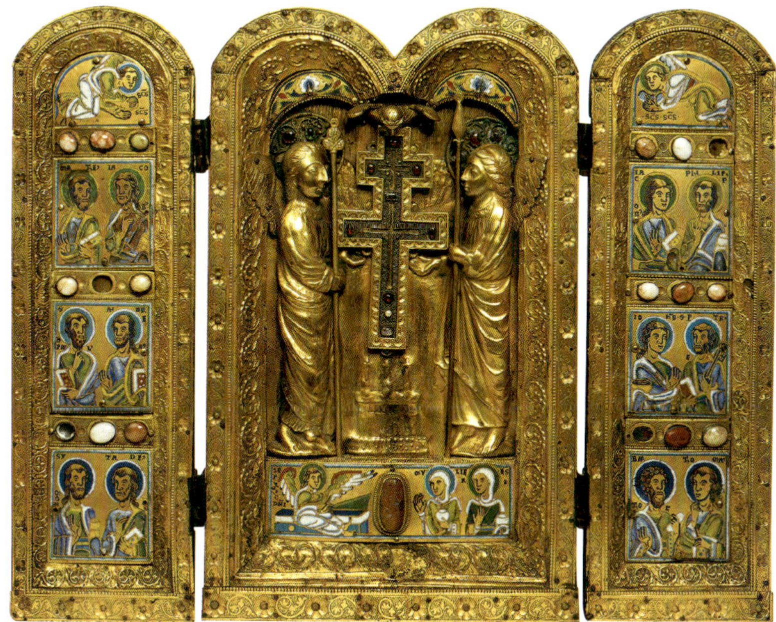

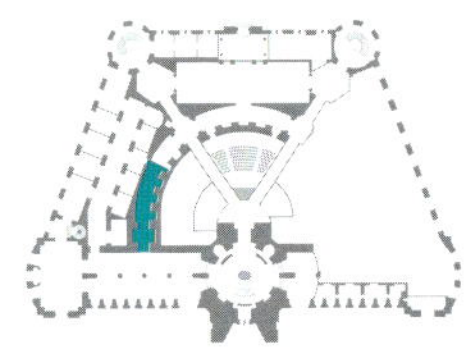

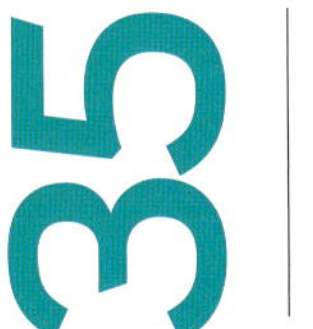

The first painted enamels

The success of champlevé enamel in the 13th and 14th centuries was followed by a decline in enamelling techniques, and it was not until the 1480s that workshops in Limoges found a fresh flowering with the arrival of painted enamels. Now thin and flat, the copper sheet was directly coated with enamel applied with a brush, spatula or needle. The painter-enameller worked in successive layers. As a rule, an initial coat of white would receive a dark-toned drawing which was then covered with successive, individually fired layers. The gold, which brought out all the object's luminosity, was added and fired last.

The earliest painted enamels are almost exclusively devoted to religious subjects. The plaques, either singly or assembled to form polyptychs - altarpieces in several sections - portrayed the Nativity or scenes from the life of Christ. The enamellers took their inspiration from existing illustrated sources: the illuminated manuscripts, printed books of hours and engravings that were the main vectors for images at the time. The painted enamel technique continued to develop throughout the 16th century: secular pieces decorated with mythological scenes enjoyed enormous success, although religious subjects continued to hold their own.

Altarpiece. Scenes from the Passion of Christ (ill. following pages)
Attributed to the **WORKSHOP OF THE "MASTER OF THE LARGE FOREHEADS"**
Painted enamel - Limoges, first third 16th century - Acquired with income accruing from the Dutuit bequest, 2000 - Inv. ODUT01828

The twelve plaques, descendents of the traditional triptych, are to be read from left to right and from bottom to top: *Christ in the Garden of Olives* (detail), *The Arrest of Christ, Christ before Annas* (or *Caiaphas*), *The Flagellation of Christ, The Crowning with Thorns, Christ before Pilate, Christ Carrying the Cross, The Crucifixion, The Burial of Christ, The Descent into Limbo* and *the Resurrection*.

All these scenes are inspired by the cycle of the Passion of Christ as portrayed in the engravings made in 1475-1480 by Martin Schongauer (Colmar, c. 1450 - Breisach, 1491). Looking beyond mere fidelity to the model, we see the painter-enameller's creativity emerge in a personal style marked by smoothness of contour, high foreheads, and specific decorative choices often involving an approach to colour - notably the use of *paillons*, fragments of silver foil bearing drops of translucent coloured enamel reminiscent of the sparkle of precious stones. In combination with this chromatic freshness, the graceful poses and harmonious forms give this work a place among the enamelware masterpieces of the early 16th century.

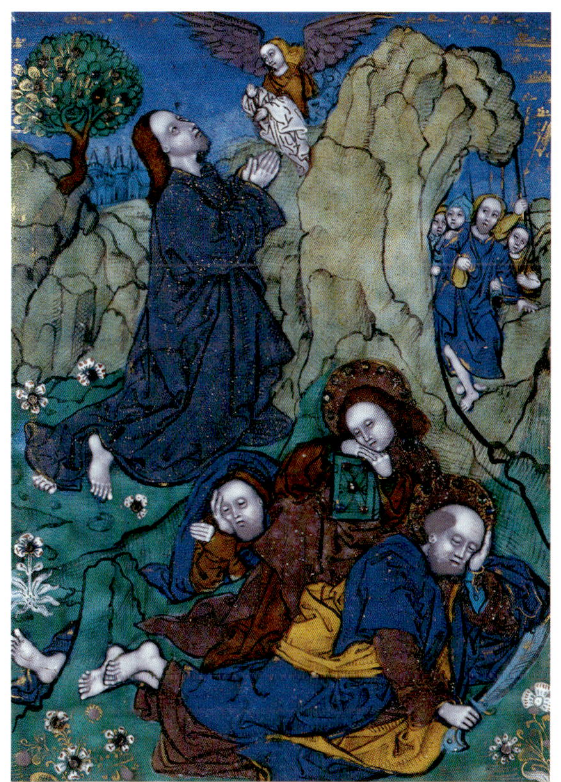

Christ in the Garden of Olives (detail)

Altarpiece. Scenes from the Passion of Christ

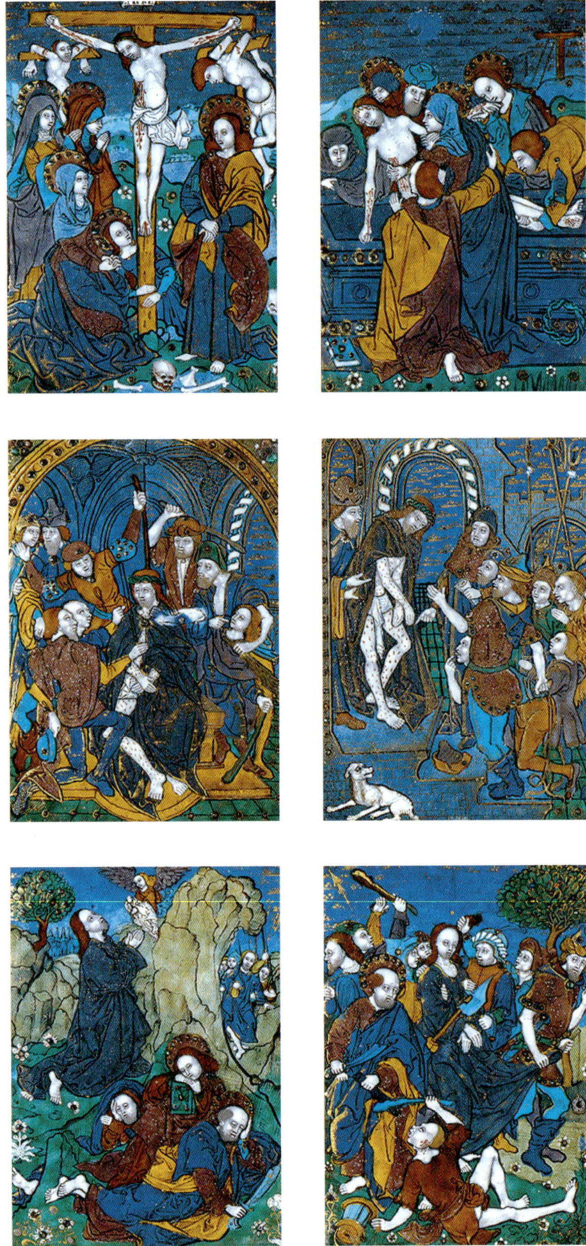

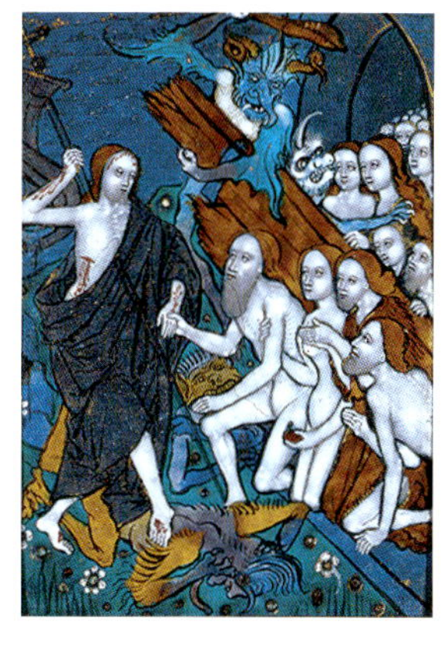
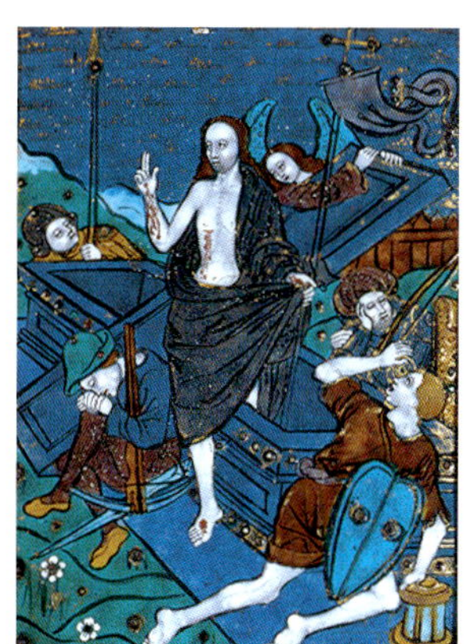
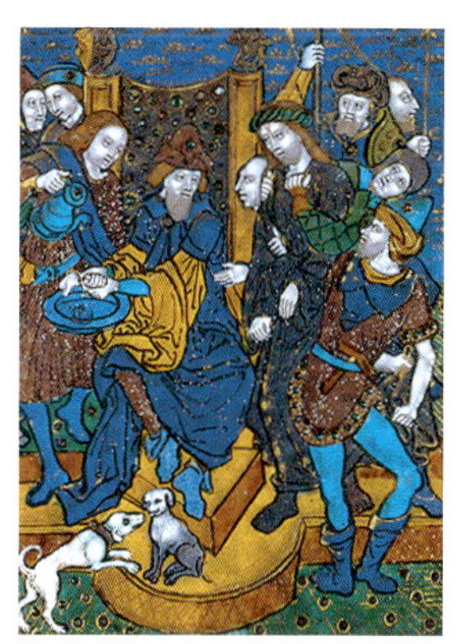
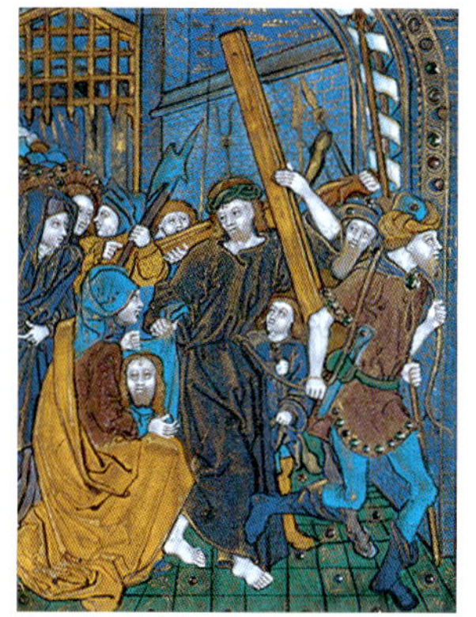
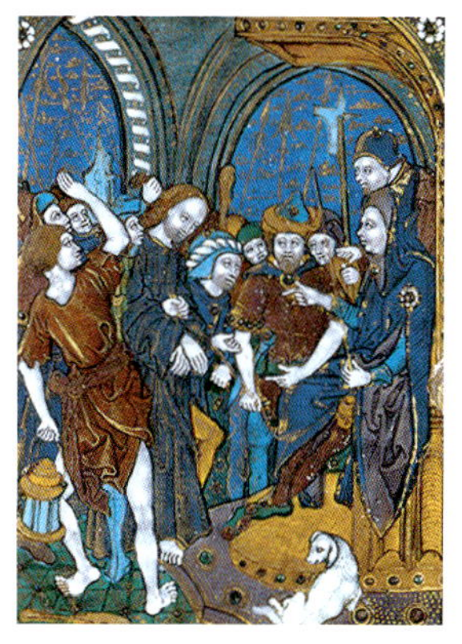
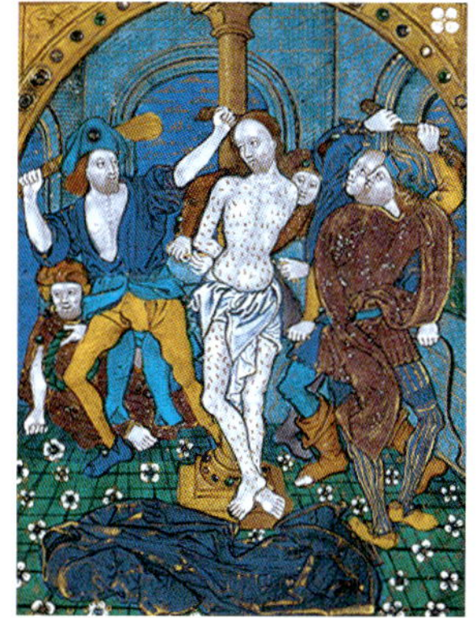

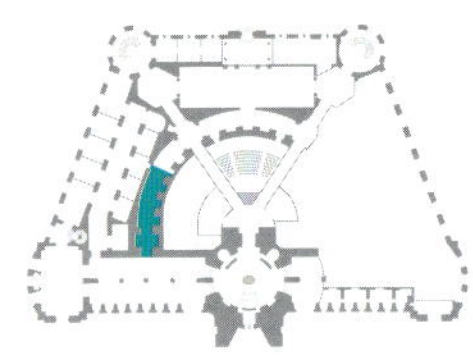

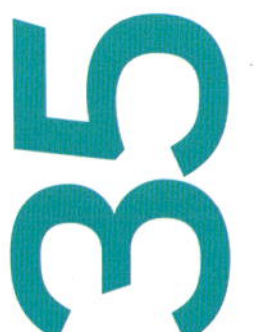

Medieval ivories

Ivory, a rare material deriving mainly from the tusks of elephants but also from those of such marine animals as the walrus, played an important part in the precious arts of the Middle Ages. Still following the tradition of ancient times, ivorywork flourished particularly in the eastern Christian world of Byzantium, capital of the Eastern Roman Empire from the 4th century until 1453 and a distinctive, independent art centre. A product of the movement known as the "Macedonian Renaissance", the *Virgin and Child in Glory* plaque (1) is in many respects heir to the visual repertoire of antiquity.
Ivory was, however, equally appreciated in the West, from Late Antiquity through to the Romance (9th-12th century) and Gothic (13th-15th century) periods. By the 13th century Paris had become the focal point for ivorywork, producing a proliferation of religious and other objects: diptychs (3) and triptychs forming small altarpieces for private devotion, caskets, mirror boxes, knife handles and above all statuettes. Following the curve of an elephant's tusk, the images of the Virgin and Child (2) or other holy figures have a leaning posture whose elegance is emphasised by the folds of their clothing. Unfortunately time has deprived us of the elaborate painting and gilding of pieces as finely worked as items in gold.

1 | Ivory book cover: Virgin and Child in Glory
Elephant ivory - Constantinople, second half 10th century - Dutuit Bequest, 1902 - Inv. ODUT01272

Seated on a monumental throne beneath a canopy, the Virgin is holding the Infant Jesus on her knee. To each side of her face is a medallion: the busts may represent the apostles John and Paul or the prophets Isaiah and Ezekiel.
This superbly sculpted plaque was probably part of the cover of a manuscript, and is an example of a major current in 10th-century Byzantine art in the way it reinterprets an ancient model. Its style makes it part of the "Nicephore group", named after Nicephore Phocas, emperor of Byzantium from 963-969: typical are the simplification of the folds of the clothing, the monumental character of the Virgin and the gentleness of the faces.

2 | Virgin and Child
Ivory, traces of gilding and paint
Paris region or northern France, c. 1220-1230
Dutuit Bequest, 1902 - Inv. ODUT01274

3 | Diptych: Scenes from the Life and Passion of Christ
Ivory
Paris, c. 1370-1380
Dutuit Bequest, 1902 - Inv. ODUT01277

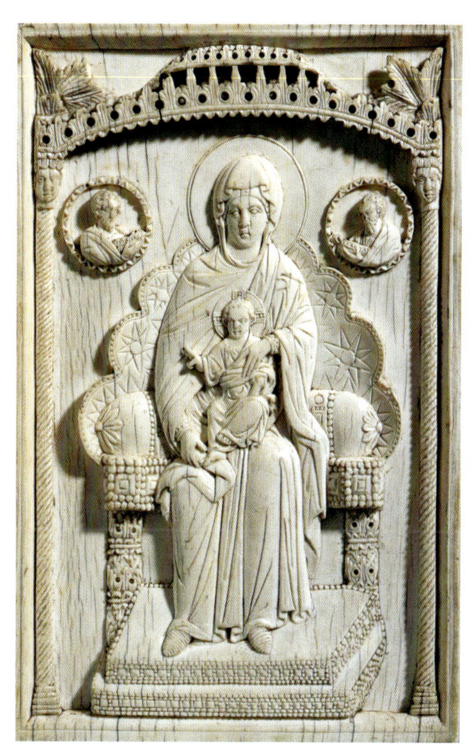
1

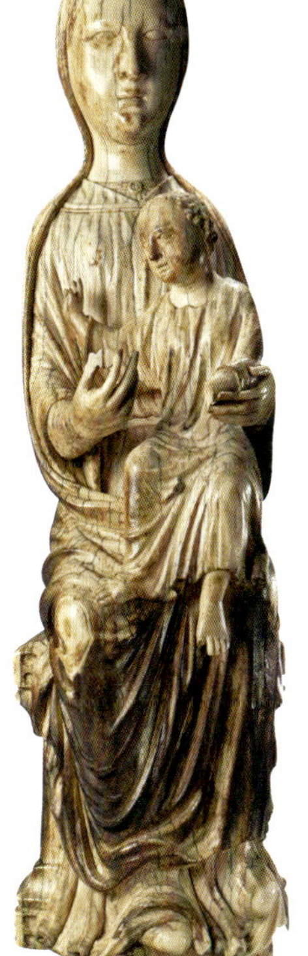
2

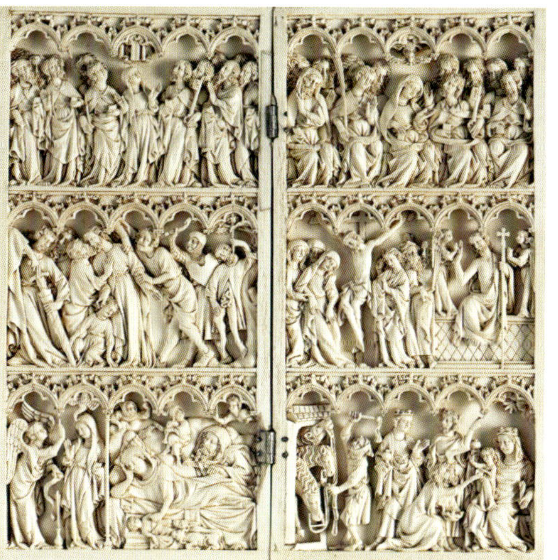
3

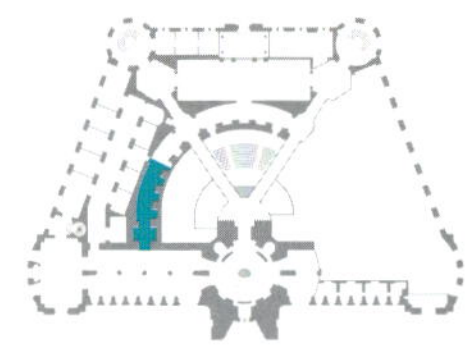

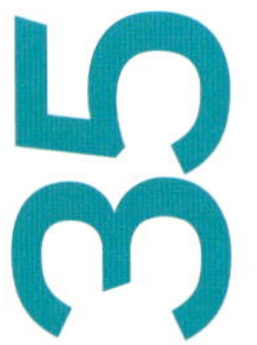

Western painting in the 15th century

Rooms 32 and 35 house paintings dated to the 15th century and coming from the two great art centres of the time: Italy and Holland.

From the first years of the 15th century Italy was swept by a new movement that would later be called the Renaissance (see Room 32 for examples from the workshops of Botticelli and Mantegna). In the 15th century this thoroughgoing artistic revolution remained very largely limited to Italy, and even in that country a substantial part of pictorial output was still Gothic (see Room 35 for the Florentine School *Virgin and Child*). The Renaissance moved out into Europe only gradually, and Dutch painting, then in full flower, remained untouched by it: the Van Eyck brothers, for example, who broke with the Gothic tradition and brought profound change with their sense of wonder and their mastery of the new technique of working in oils, were not part of the Renaissance world.

This was the school that gave us the Master of Saint Bartholomew, one of the greatest European artists of the late 15th century, whose precise identity still remains a mystery. Independent and innovative, he had neither pupils nor imitators. Doubtless from northern Holland and active between 1475-1510, he was a member of the Cologne School, having apparently settled in that city around 1480. Up until the early 16th century this school maintained a vibrantly medieval approach to painting, in a spirit of representational idealism and technical perfection.

THE MASTER OF SAINT BARTHOLOMEW (C. 1440/1450 - C. 1510/1520) The Nativity

c. 1480, wood - Tuck Donation, 1921; entered the collection 1930 - Inv. PTUCK00001

Permeated by the Dutch influence, this picture from the early part of the artist's career is characterised by angular drawing, stiff, separated figures, clothes with broken folds and faces with heavily accentuated features.

This would seem to be a section of an altarpiece devoted to the life of the Virgin Mary of which other panels are known. In keeping with the visual repertoire that began to spread through the West in the 15th century, the birth of Christ is shown in the form known as Adoration of the Christ Child, inspired by a vision recounted by the 14th-century mystic St Brigitte of Sweden.

Over the centuries some of the colours used here have lost their opacity. As a result the artist's preliminary underdrawing, usually visible only with the help of infra-red reflectography, shows through at many points.

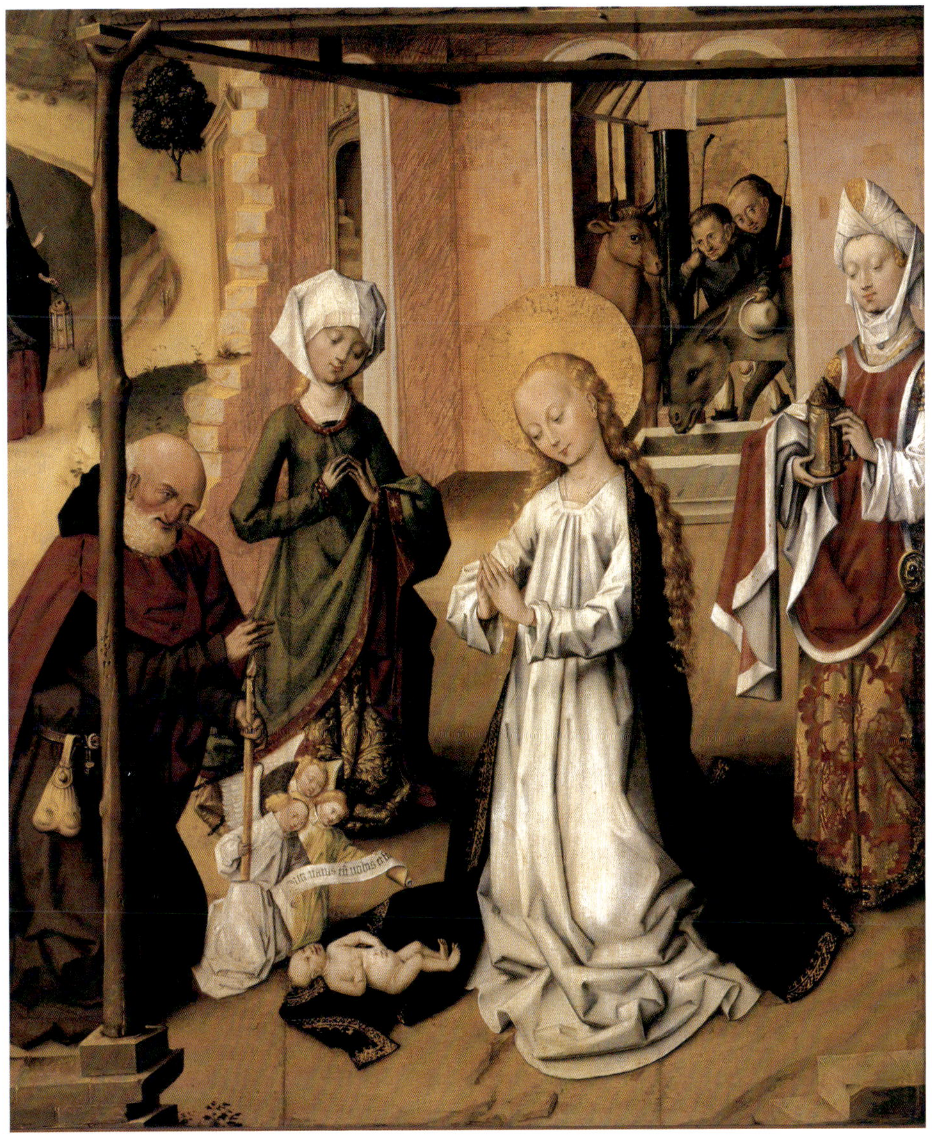

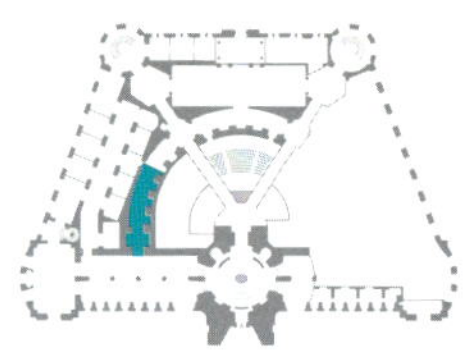

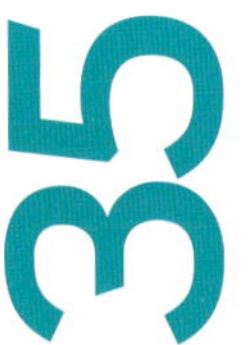

Germanic sculpture

Testimony to the Christian faith of the Middle Ages, the sculptures to be found in today's museums initially had a religious function. In most cases they were part of large-scale ensembles: the painted and gilded altarpieces sculpted in wood that stood at the time in a host of cathedrals and churches. It was during the 15th century that the altarpiece flourished in the Germanic countries: the central section with its large sculpted figures is protected by two folding wings - thus making a triptych - whose outside is often painted and whose inside is carved with low-reliefs.
The artists or craftsmen - in the Late Middle Ages the dividing line was often uncertain - worked for rich clients who commissioned illustrations of such profoundly sacred scenes as the Nativity, the Adoration of the Magi, the Crucifixion and the Dormition of the Virgin, or for an image of the patron saint of their church.
The Petit Palais sculptures come from southern Germany and Austria. Mostly of limewood, whose lightness and softness made it perfect for virtuoso sculpting, they illustrate the evolution of the Late Gothic style from the mid-15th century - dynamic, formally complex and featuring massive folds - until the early 16th century, when it began to incorporate the innovations of the Italian Renaissance.

1 | **WORKSHOP OF NIKLAUS WECKMANN** The Nativity
Polychrome limewood - Ulm (southern Germany), c. 1525 - Pierre Marie Donation, 1929 - Inv. PPS02075

The visual repertoire used in this low-relief Nativity was extremely common in the Late Middle Ages: in a stable with a partly collapsed roof, Mary kneels hands joined before the Christ Child. With her are Joseph, holding a candle and protecting the flame with one hand, the donkey and the ox. The decorative vocabulary is of Italian origin: the clumsy perspective, the palace-style architecture with its pilasters laden with candelabra and leaf-patterns, cherubs looking like *putti*, and the medallion showing the bust of a warrior in profile all point up the fresh interest in the Antique that characterised the Renaissance.
This panel was in all probability part of a wing of a monumental altarpiece.

2 | Saint Barbara(?)
Wood (lime?) stripped of its polychromy - Southern Germany (Ulm?), late 15th century
Pierre Marie Donation, 1929 - Inv. PPS02560

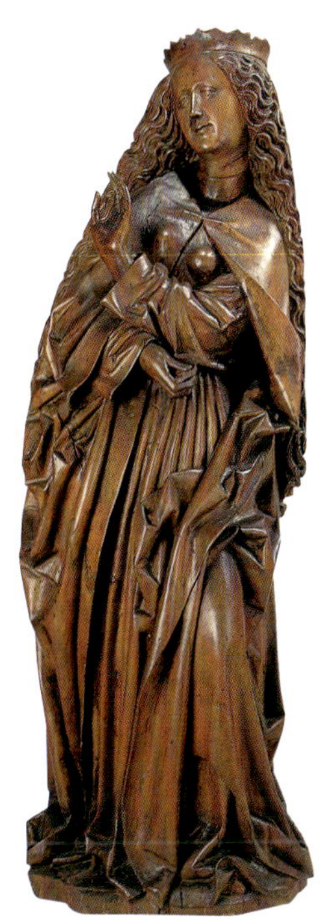

2

1

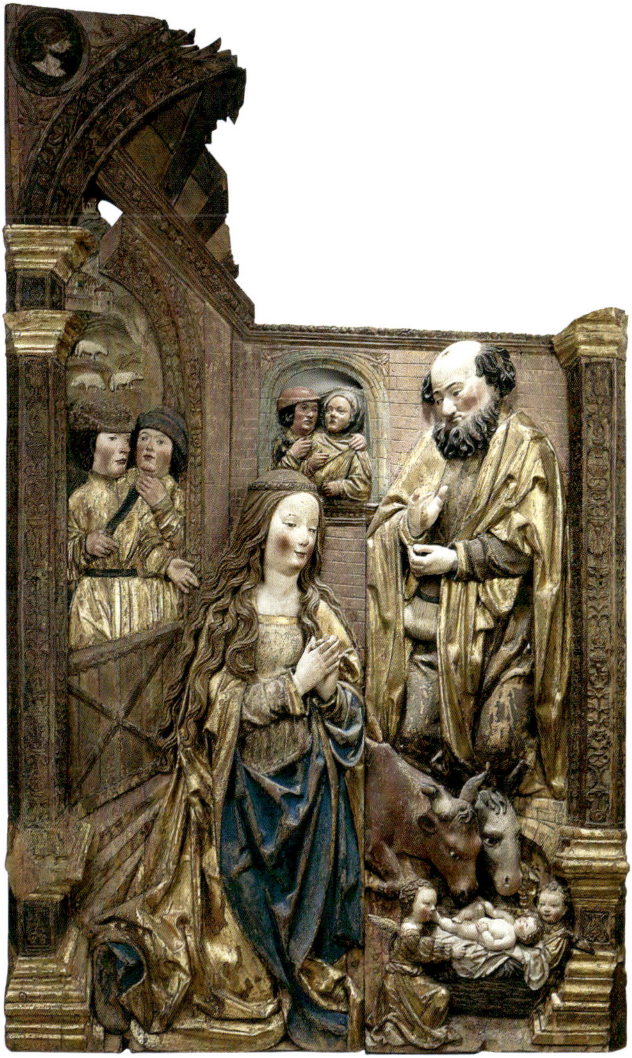

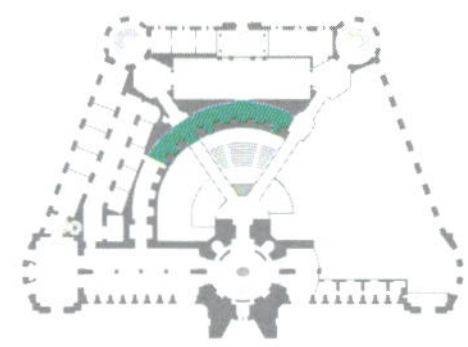

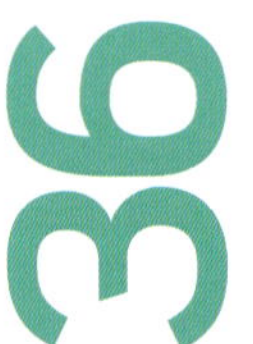

Cretan icons

Occupied by the Venetians after the taking of Constantinople by the Crusaders in 1204, Crete became a busy art centre trading with both Venice and Constantinople.

With the end of the Byzantine Empire when Constantinople fell to the Turks in 1453, Crete became the main refuge for icon painters and the leading source of icons in the Greek world. This supremacy lasted until the Turkish conquest in 1669. Coming in the wake of the Byzantine painting of the dynasty of the Palaeologus Emperors, the icons were both visually and technically magnificent. Created in a spirit of simplicity and restraint, they are characterised by exactness of outline, compositional balance, geometrical treatment of fabrics and a handling of flesh tints using a dark brown background overlaid with a delicate network of increasingly light-coloured lines. Cretan art also shows signs of borrowings from Italian and Flemish artists, whose innovations were remarkably well suited to the Byzantine tradition.

The Nativity

Crete - c. 1480-1500 - Tempera on plastered panel - Acquired with income accruing from the Dutuit bequest, 1997 - Inv. PDUT01975

Rather than directly incorporating Western motifs, this painting takes the singular approach of juxtaposing the Italian and Byzantine styles along a diagonal running from bottom left to top right. May we suppose, as some commentators have done, that this is in fact the work of two different artists, one operating in the Western tradition and the other in the Byzantine?

The curious thing about the panoramic landscape - a reflection of the Italo-Flemish tradition of the time - is not only its extremely odd spatial deployment, but also its use of perspective: the succession of little valleys helps to increase the depth of field, while a blue sky scattered with clouds replaces the usual gold backdrop.

This icon relates the birth of Christ on Christmas Day, 25 December. On that day the Orthodox Church celebrates the "Nativity in the Flesh of our Lord God and Saviour Jesus Christ" and recalls "the Shepherds who saw the Lord" and "the adoration of the Magi". Described in the gospels, these events are complemented by traditional elements allowing for visual expression of the theological description of the Incarnation as "real and not illusory".

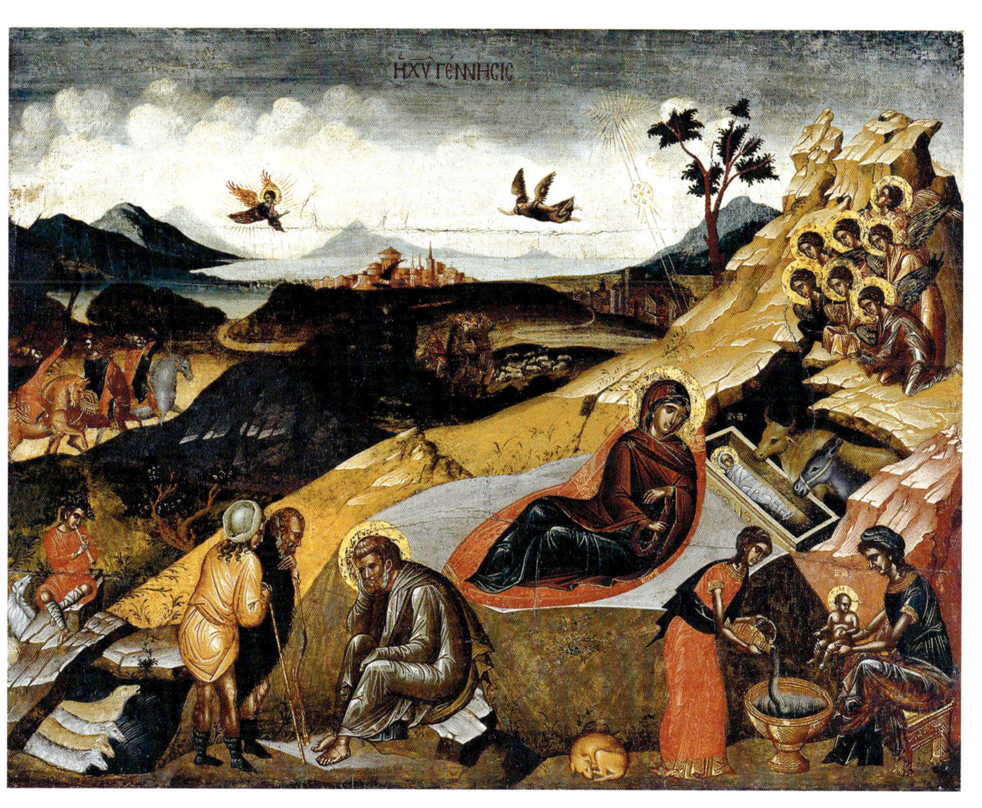
Η ΧΥ ΓΕΝΝΗCΙC

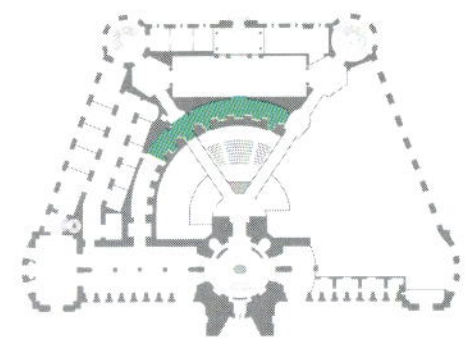

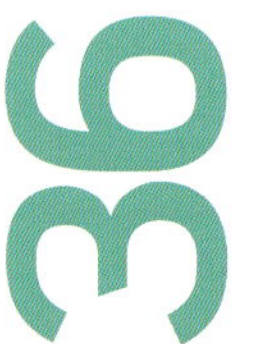

Russian icons

Officially, Russia converted to Christianity in 988 when Prince Vladimir, having been baptised himself, had all his subjects baptised in the Dneiper. The evangelists concerned having come from Constantinople, Russia inherited the Byzantine notion of the icon as developed within the Eastern Church after the disruption of the iconoclastic crisis of 726-843. As a reflection of Church dogma, liturgical images obeyed such strict formal principles as reverse perspective, the gold backdrop and the absence of cast shadows.

Russia, however, developed a religious art that was both technically and visually distinctive. More frequently than in the Byzantine equivalent, the central part of the side to be painted is hollowed out to receive the principal image, while the untouched surrounding area is decorated with portraits of saints, scenes or a goldsmithed covering. The primer is generally chalk-based. The Russian iconographer works with the support horizontal: this allows use of extremely diluted paint and thus great smoothness of texture. Shapes are stylised, luminosity is played down and the colours are stronger.

The visual repertoire reveals an interpretation of the classic subjects adapted to local sensibilities and is extended to include local saints.

Regional and national styles also developed - in Pskov, Novgorod and Moscow, for example - and continued to evolve over time.

The Archangel Michael; The Archangel Gabriel

Northern Russia, second half 17th century - Tempera on panel - Roger Cabal Bequest, 1998 - Inv. PPP04921 and 04922

These two icons come from the Deisis tier of an iconostasis, the screen that separates the sanctuary from the body of the church and is covered with icons arranged in a traditional order. Set at the centre, the Deisis comprises Christ Pantocrator flanked by the Mother of God and St John the Baptist; around it are the archangels Michael and Gabriel, representing the celestial powers mounting guard around Our Lord.

These icons were probably painted in northern Russia, the clues being the large faces of the archangels, their relatively thick-set bodies and the limited range of colours used: white, black, ochre, green and red.

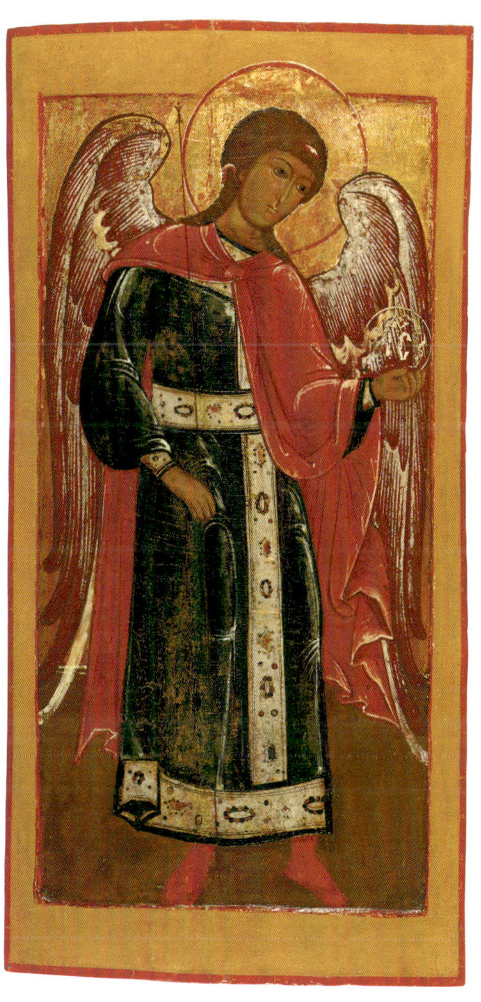

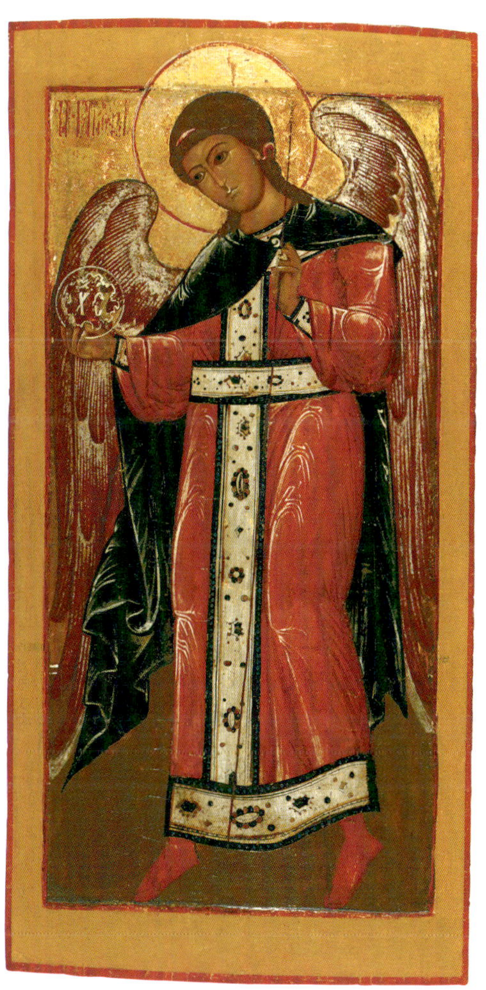

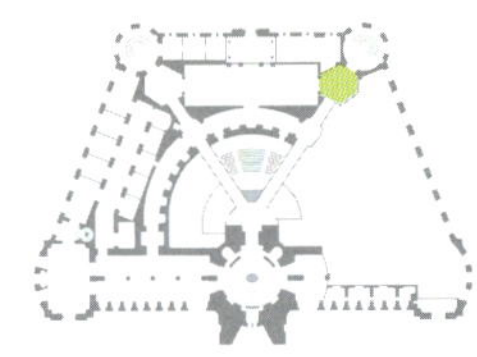

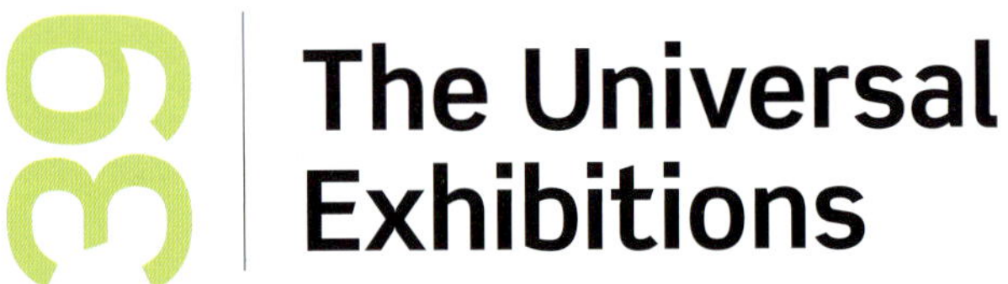

39 The Universal Exhibitions

From London in 1851 to Paris in 1900, the Universal Exhibitions covered the technical, industrial and artistic history of the 19th century. Veritable international showcases, these enormous state-organised events drew millions of visitors; participants from a host of different fields displayed their output and prizes were awarded to the most deserving exhibitors. In all Paris hosted five Exhibitions - in 1855, 1867, 1878, 1889 and 1900 - and a number of the city's most remarkable buildings were the direct result. Some of them, like the Palais de l'Industrie (1855) and the Palais du Trocadéro (1878) have disappeared; but the Eiffel Tower (1889) and the Petit Palais, Grand Palais and Alexandre III bridge (1900) live on as testimony to the sumptuousness of buildings created to celebrate "the alliance of art and industry".

1 | **LÉON-JOSEPH-THOMAS ALESSANDRI AND SON (1803 - ?)** Vitrine

1867, blackened pear wood, ivory and gilt bronze - Original Petit Palais collection - Inv. WPPO00097

An ivorywork specialist, Alessandri took out a gold medal at the Universal Exhibition of 1867 with this Renaissance-style vitrine in the shape of a little circular temple. For its creation he surrounded himself with the top craftsmen of the time: the designer of ornaments and interiors Eugène Prignot and the sculptors Carrier-Belleuse and Bernard. Prignot is said to have provided the overall design and overseen the execution of the work. Albert-Ernest Carrier-Belleuse made the models for the four low reliefs decorating the base - *Architecture, Sculpture, Commerce, Work* - and Victor Bernard sculpted the *Victory* that crowns the dome.

2 | **HENRI GERVEX (1852-1929)** and **ALFRED STEVENS (1828-1906)**
The Painters and the Ile de la Cité (ill. following pages)

Fragment of the "History of the Century" panorama created for the 1889 Universal Exhibition, oil on canvas - Acquired with income accruing from the Dutuit bequest, 1986 - Inv. PDUT01491

The nineteenth century panorama was a painting running round the interior of a circular building and looked at from a central observation platform. The Universal Exhibitions were the ideal venue for this kind of venture. For the 1889 Exhibition the painters Henri Gervex and Alfred Stevens, French and Belgian respectively, worked together to create a "History of the Century" panorama covering history and the arts in France in 1789-1889. After remaining on show for seven years in the Tuileries gardens, the painting was taken down and cut into sections, some of which have been brought together in this room.

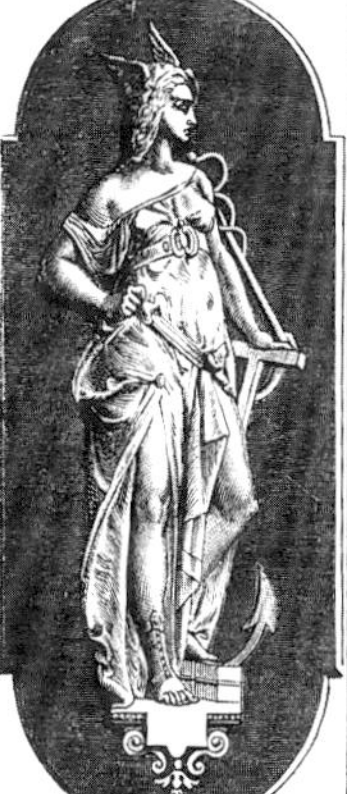

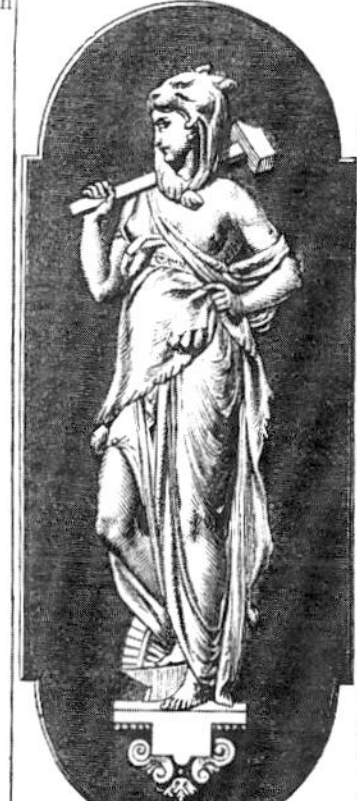

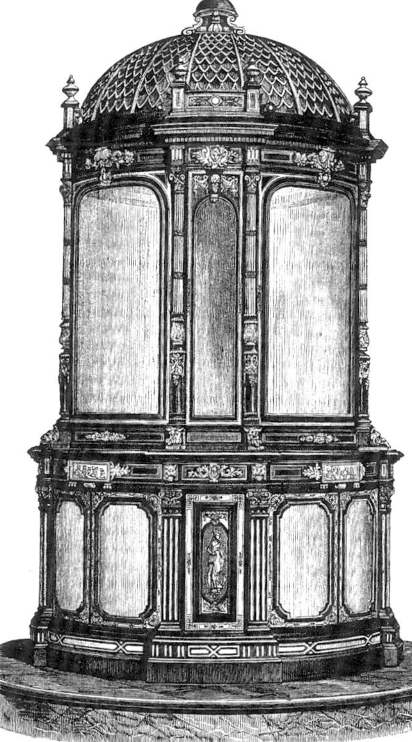

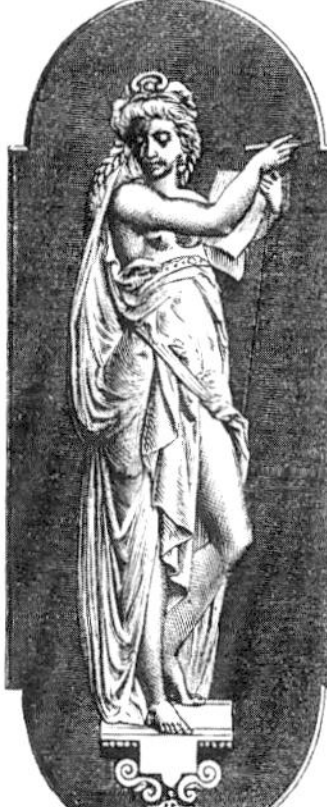

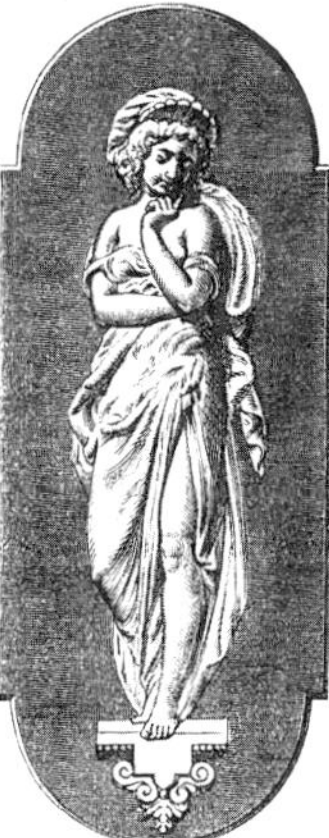

Der Prachtschrank von ALESSANDRI UND SOHN in GENUA kann eins der besten Kunstmöbel der Neuzeit genannt werden, fand daher auch zahlreiche Bewunderer. Er ist blos aus Ebenholz und Elfenbein angefertigt; alle Ornamente sind aus letzterm und sind mit seltener künstlerischer Bravour geschnitten. Die vier Figuren im Hochrelief, welche die Nischen des Untersatzes ausfüllen, sind wahre Meisterwerke der Bildschnitzerkunst. Nicht minderes Lob verdienen auch die kleineren Verzierungen, wie denn überhaupt das Ganze mit so viel Urtheil und Geschmack componirt ist, dass es mit Recht ein Anziehungspunkt geworden war.

hält der Kritik besser stand, während ein Ebenholzcabinet von Gobart den Werth eines wirklichen Kunstwerkes beanspruchen konnte. Mit wenigen Ausnahmen erscheinen übrigens die belgischen Möbel mehr dauerhaft als zierlich, mehr auf Massenwirkung berechnet als von sorgfältiger Behandlung, und im Stile der Ornamente mehr naturalistisch als wahrhaft künstlerisch.

Italien durfte den Ruhm beanspruchen, in Hinsicht auf Credenzen (Dressoirs, Sideboards) im sogenannten Küchen- oder Speisekammerstil alle Concurrenten aus dem Felde geschlagen zu haben. Ferri und Bartolozzi in Siena hatten ein solches Büffet ausgestellt, dessen Betrachtung schon ein Gastmahl aufwog. „Nun habe ich ganz ausgezeichnet dinirt!“ sagte ein britischer Gentleman gerührt, nachdem er mit vor dem Bäuchlein gefalteten Händen lange davorgestanden und sich seufzend zum Fortgehen wandte. In der That war daran alles Wünschenswerthe für einen Gourmand zu sehen: Schweinsköpfe und Hummern, Aale und Butten, Hasen, Schnepfen, Rebhühner, Enten, die kostbarsten Früchte aller Jahreszeiten gemüthlich untereinander, kurz, was nur das Auge zu reizen, den Gaumen

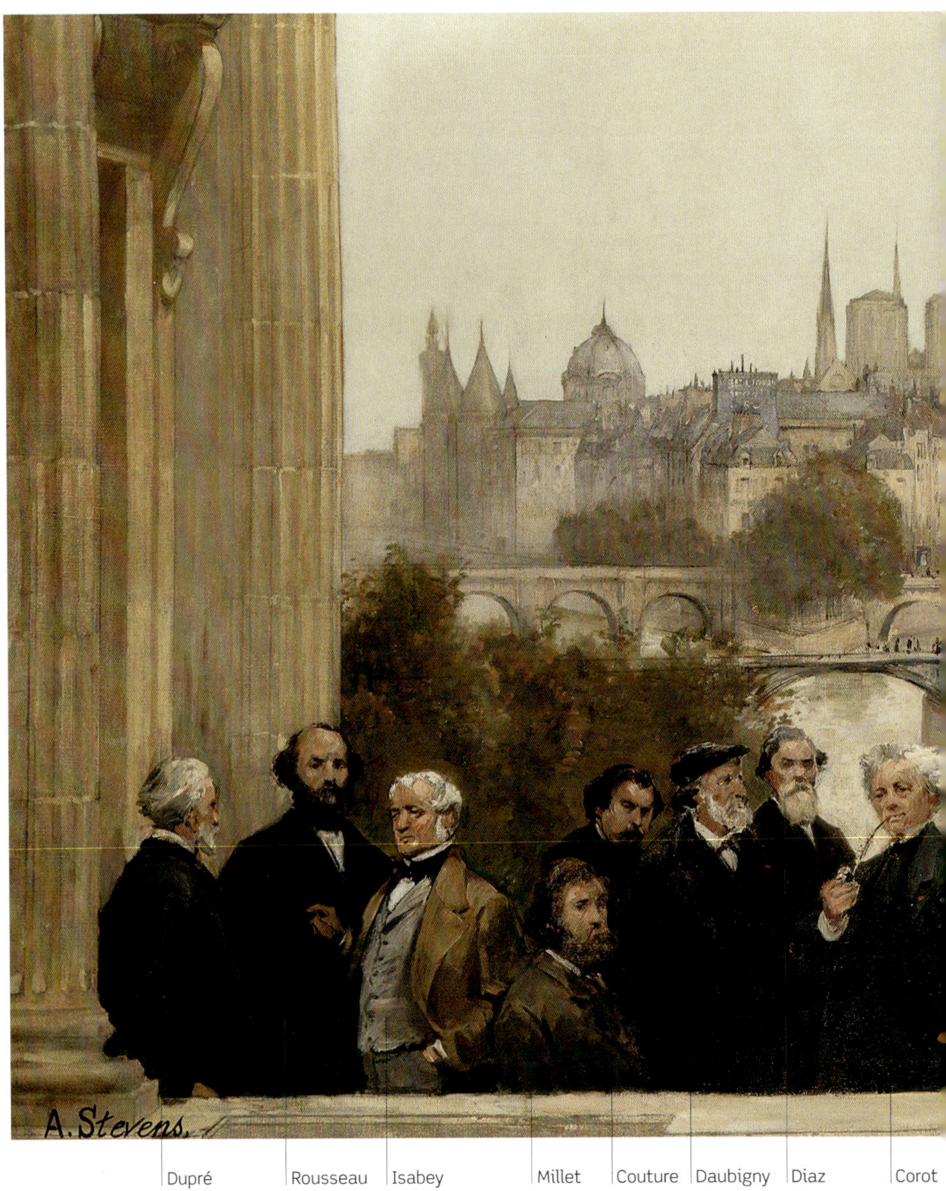

Dupré Rousseau Isabey Millet Couture Daubigny Diaz Corot